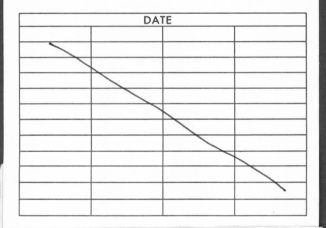

ESSAYS ON MODERN POLITICS AND HISTORY

Written in honor of
HAROLD M. VINACKE

HAROLD MONK VINACKE

ESSAYS

on

MODERN POLITICS
and

HISTORY

Written in honor of
HAROLD M. VINACKE

EDITED BY
Han-Kyo Kim

OHIO UNIVERSITY PRESS
Athens, Ohio

Copyright © 1969 by The University of Cincinnati

SBN 08214-0079-7

Library of Congress Catalog Card Number
LC 75-91958

Published with the help of the Charles Taft Memorial Fund
of the University of Cincinnati.

Manufactured in the United States of America by the Oberlin Printing Company.

TABLE OF CONTENTS

BIOGRAPHICAL RÉSUMÉ OF HAROLD MONK VINACKE ... vii

LIST OF CONTRIBUTORS ... ix

EDITOR'S PREFACE
Han-Kyo Kim ... xi

I. CONSTITUTIONAL DEVELOPMENT IN EAST ASIA
Ardath W. Burks ... 1

II. UNITED STATES INITIAL POSTSURRENDER POLICY FOR JAPAN
John M. Maki ... 30

III. AMERICA'S POSTWAR ROLE IN SOUTHEAST ASIA
John F. Cady ... 57

IV. DUTCH COLONIAL POLICY AND SUKARNOISM
Amry Vandenbosch ... 81

V. INDIA AS AN ASIAN POWER
Paul F. Power ... 107

VI. ARAB-AMERICAN RELATIONS: AN INTERPRETIVE ESSAY
Elie A. Salem ... 136

VII. THE BRITISH LABOUR PARTY IN THE CONTEMPORARY WORLD
Henry R. Winkler ... 156

VIII. THE RADICAL RIGHT IN WEST GERMAN POLITICS AND THE
GERMAN QUESTION
Dieter Dux ... 190

IX. THE JOHNSON STAFF AND NATIONAL SECURITY POLICY
J. C. Heinlein ... 206

X. NATIONAL POLICY MACHINERY AND FOREIGN
POLICY-MAKING IN THE UNITED STATES
Edward R. Padgett ... 226

NOTES ... 243

BIOGRAPHICAL RÉSUMÉ
of
HAROLD MONK VINACKE

Born at Denver, Colo., July 26, 1893
married in 1915; three children

A.B.—Denver, 1914
Ph.D.—Princeton, 1922

Professor of history and political science, Nankai University, China, 1916-17.

From assistant professor to professor of history and government, University of Miami (Ohio), 1918-26.

Professor of political science, University of Cincinnati, 1926-63.

Fellow, Graduate School, Arts and Sciences, University of Cincinnati, 1948-63.

Principal regional specialist and chief Japanese section, Office of War Information. (WW II)

Visiting Expert—Supreme Commander for the Allied Powers, the Far East, 1950.

Consultant—Operations Research Office, 1959-62.

Major Publications (Books):
  Modern Constitutional Development in China, 1920
    (Ph.D. Dissertation, Princeton, 1922)
  Problems of Industrial Development in China, 1926
  History of the Far East in Modern Times, 1928, 6th ed. 1959
  International Organization, 1934
  The United States and the Far East, 1945-1951, 1952
  Far Eastern Politics in the Postwar Period, 1956

(SOURCE
Adapted from *American Men of Science:
The Social and Behavioral Sciences*, 1968)

LIST OF CONTRIBUTORS

(*In Alphabetical Order*)

1. *Ardath W. Burks*: Director of International Programs, Rutgers, the State University, College of Arts and Sciences

2. *John F. Cady*: Professor of History, Ohio University

3. *Dieter Dux*: Professor and Head of Department of Political Science, University of Cincinnati

4. *J. C. Heinlein*: Professor of Political Science, University of Cincinnati

5. *John M. Maki*: Vice-Dean, College of Arts and Sciences, University of Massachusetts

6. *Edward R. Padgett*: Professor of Political Science, University of Cincinnati

7. *Paul F. Power*: Professor of Political Science, University of Cincinnati

8. *Elie A. Salem*: Professor, American University, Beirut, Lebanon

9. *Amry Vanderbosch*: Professor Emeritus of Political Science, University of Kentucky

10. *Henry R. Winkler*: Dean of Faculty, Rutgers, the State University, College of Arts and Sciences

EDITOR'S PREFACE

In the fall of 1966, the Department of Political Science at the University of Cincinnati decided to publish a volume of essays in honor of one of its most distinguished and dedicated former members, Dr. Harold M. Vinacke. The decision was based on the recognition of his long service to the University as a member (later, the head) of the Department of Political Science and of the acknowledged distinction he deserves as a political scientist with special interests in the Far Eastern studies and international relations. After careful deliberation, the general theme of the present volume was chosen; "Modern Politics and History" represents the broad area of concern manifest in Dr. Vinacke's scholarly activities. Articles were solicited from a score of his students, colleagues and friends. Pragmatic and technical considerations limited the number of contributing authors to ten and made inevitable a considerable latitude in the selection of the ten topics.

The gravity and complexity of the international problems facing the United States today are well known. The Vietnam war is perhaps only an immediate, though critical, manifestation of the dangers inherent in a turbulent and fast changing world. In response to the global role the United States has come to play in the crisis ridden world since the 1940s, American social scientists have enlarged, in the last couple of decades, the scope of their inquiries to include areas and peoples that had previously remained largely beyond their scholarly interest or attention. This welcome phenomenon has produced a large number of competent and useful studies. The "knowledge gap," however, has not yet been completely bridged. Indeed, the deeper we delve into the less familiar world, the keener is our awareness of how little we really know. Intellectual challenges confronting us, moreover, are not confined entirely to the "foreign" or non-Western areas and their problems. A genuine need does exist to reexamine and reassess the problems of our own society or of those societies with whom we share common cultural legacies. The contents of this volume reflect these considerations. It is not meant to be a comprehensive treatise on the multifarious problems of the United States and the world. The ten authors—eight political scientists and two historians—wrote freely with minimal editorial restrictions on topics of their own choice and competence. The resulting essays contain more reflection and interpretation than collection of descriptive data; they often are bold with evaluative judgment.

Burks (Chap. I) takes a fresh new look at the constitutional developments in East Asia, thus updating a similar study undertaken by Harold Vinacke nearly a half century ago. Burks, aware of the recent behavioralist trends that tend to ignore the legal or formal political structures, advocates renewal of our interests in constitutional arrangements in which political values, ideology and traditions are manifest. In the postwar Japan, constitutional and other changes first occurred under American supervision in accordance with a state paper prepared by a wartime interdepartmental group (SWNCC). Maki (Chap. II) considers this document, "The United States Initial Post-surrender Policy for Japan," a product of rational and comprehensive planning and extremely beneficial for Japan's subsequent growth and development as a democracy friendly to the United States.

According to Cady (Chap. III), however, the United States displayed neither wisdom nor concern in the post-1945 Southeast Asia. If the initial American policies had been ineffective and desultory, the policies at later times displayed preoccupation with the cold war issues which eventually led America into the unfortunate Vietnam involvement. Vandenbosch (Chap. IV) subjects the Dutch colonial policy in Indonesia to similarly critical scrutiny. The Dutch as colonizers are compared with the British, and the long-range impacts of the colonial rule are hypothesized; the so-called "Sukarnoism" is in part attributed to the Dutch practice of paternalism.

A suggestion that India's foreign relations are undergoing a process of basic reorientation is advanced by Power (Chap. V). A new emphasis on "Asian orientation" and a gradual erosion of the global and nonaligned roles are postulated. An Arab explanation of "Arab mind" is presented by Salem (Chap. VI), who urges better understanding between the Americans and the Arabs; he deplores the alleged existence of ignorance and misinformation on both sides.

An examination of the right-wing NPD in West German politics leads Dux (Chap. VII) to predict an enduring impact of the NPD on the politics of the Federal Republic, especially in the area of foreign affairs. The British Labor Party is selected for examination by Winkler (Chap.

VIII). His hypothesis is that the absence of complete homogeneity and consensus among the members is the source of strength, not weakness, of the Labor party.

Both Heinlein (Chap. IX) and Padgett (Chap. X) are concerned with the foreign policy-making machinery of the United States Government. Heinlein concludes, after examining the roles played by the Presidential staffs in the last few decades—especially the Johnson staff at the time of the Dominican crisis in 1965, that the organizational structure *per se* is not significant. Padgett's main interest, on the other hand, lies in the recent innovations and newer conceptual frameworks for greater rationality in organization of the policy machinery.

If this editor's intention to weave together ten specialists' expertise into a meaningful pattern is too ambitious, he is at least attempting to follow in the footsteps of Dr. Vinacke, whose long scholarly career has displayed this difficult synthesis. As a youth in his twenties he taught history, political science, and English to the newly awakened, if at times demonstratively iconoclastic, young students at Nankai University in China. (He also coached Nankai's athletic team!) This experience, two years after he had graduated from the University of Denver, must have been one factor in the development of his life long interest in Far Eastern affairs. His first book, entitled *Modern Constitutional Development in China* (1920), developed from his doctoral dissertation at Princeton University. His interest in China produced another book six years later, *Problems of Industrial Development in China* (1926). The widely used textbook, *History of the Far East in Modern Times*, first published in 1928, has run into six editions (the most recent edition in 1959); the name Vinacke is almost a part of common vocabularies among the tens of thousand students here and abroad who have since studied this increasingly less esoteric subject. After World War II he wrote two more major works, *The United States and the Far East, 1945-1951* (1952) and *Far Eastern Politics in the Postwar Period* (1956).

Although Dr. Vinacke's scholarly fame as a pioneer and elder statesman of the Far Eastern studies in the United States is generally recognized, it should not eclipse his contributions as a teacher and author in other fields of political science, a career that started over half a century ago. The study of international relations in particular attracted his interest for many years; as early as 1934 he wrote *International Organization*.

Starting with Nankai University (1916-1917), Dr. Vinacke's teaching career took him to Miami University, Ohio (1918-1926), and the University of Cincinnati, where he taught for thirty-seven years (1926-1963). He is currently professor emeritus of political science and a Fellow of the Graduate School at the last named institution. He also has had many visiting professorships at major American universities, including Harvard.

Dr. Vinacke's extra-academic activities include his work during World War II as a principal regional specialist and chief of the Japanese section in the Office of War Information, which took him to the post-liberation Philippines and to Chungking in 1945; as visiting expert to the Supreme Commander for the Allied Powers in Japan in 1950; and as consultant to Operations Research Office, 1959-1963.

As of this writing (August, 1969) Dr. Vinacke is a regular commuter to the library of the University of Cincinnati, a visible testimony to his continuing physical vigor and intellectual vitality. The date of July 26, 1969, marked the seventy-sixth anniversary of his birth. This editor is not alone in wishing him many more happy and productive years.

✿   ✿   ✿   ✿   ✿

Preparation of this volume would have been impossible, needless to say, without the most willing and generous donation of their time and energy by the ten contributing authors. As an editor who had to make imposing demands on them, I am most grateful for their cooperation and patience. Several of them, including Drs. Burks, Dux, Heinlein, and Maki, were also consulted frequently, and their suggestions and moral support were extremely valuable. Special words of appreciation are due to the members of the Charles Phelps Taft Fund Committee, University of Cincinnati, who have approved a most generous financial subsidy for publication of this volume; I am particularly indebted to Professors Cederic Boulter, Alfred Kuhn and Gordon Skinner. For typing and secretarial assistance, the past and the present secretaries of the Department of Political Science, University of Cincinnati, deserve my sincere thanks. For permission to print a biographical résumé of Dr. Vinacke as adapted from *American Men of Science; The Social and Behavioral Sciences*, I am thankful to R. R. Bowker Co.

At the risk of stating the obvious, it must be said that the contents of the articles included in this volume are the responsibilities of the individual authors concerned and that neither the Taft Committee nor the Department of Political Science, University of Cincinnati, is to be held accountable for the views expressed in these articles. It is also necessary to state that these articles were written in 1968. Although efforts have been made by the authors and the editor to update their original writings wherever feasible, technical difficulties have restrained them from making certain changes in the text that the lapse of time may warrant.

H. K.

August, 1969
Cincinnati, Ohio

CHAPTER I

CONSTITUTIONAL DEVELOPMENT IN EAST ASIA

By Ardath W. Burks*

Men come to grasp the idea that they play roles in a community. This is true whether they are acculturated in a "Western" or in a "non-Western" political culture. And perhaps this is a matter of *ideology* as much as it is a question of either *institutions* or of *behavior*.

Popular versions of ideas gain sufficient circulation to be acted upon at strategic moments. In other words, sophisticated political thought gets translated into a kind of shorthand: images, symbols, or slogans have an effect something like that of an ideographic script. They are taken for granted but they are significant, for they do exercise some measure of control over men's actions. Nowhere are these truths more self-evident than in the experience of old China. A Chinese political scientist has written:

> In Western nations the leader obtains office. In China the leader leads; once in power he creates offices for himself and his followers.
>
> Where does power come from if not the office?
>
> Not from law, not from structure, not from title or delegation, but pre-eminently from the hidden Confucian assumptions concerning ideological control.[1]

THE POLITICAL SYSTEM: IDEAS, INSTITUTIONS, BEHAVIOR, VALUES

It was clearly evident in a Confucian society (beneath the old Chinese State), that ideas do not exist in a vacuum. Since ideas interlocked with

---

*Dr. Burks first studied East Asia under Professor Harold M. Vinacke at the University of Cincinnati, where he received his B.A. degree in 1939. He is presently Director of International Programs and Professor of Political Science at Rutgers University.

a system are most likely to impress themselves on men's minds, they are often articulated in the form of institutions. The ideas endow the institutions with purpose; together they generate "an institutional will." Sometimes (for example, in traditional China or in traditional Japan) ideas build a defensive great wall around institutions; at other times (for example, in revolutionary China or in modernizing Japan) ideas provide the rallying-cries for an assault on institutions.

In addition to popular transliterations of ideas, there is also the conscious shaping of concepts into a unified frame of reference. And thus, as we say, *political theory* is born out of political thought. As a grand and abstract intellectual structure, however, a theory of government has a rather narrow appeal. "Typically, its architect is a political philosopher, whose blueprints are seldom widely read."[2]

Implicit in an ideology and especially in a political theory is the assumption that men need some plan, not only of *what is* but also of *what ought to be.* Although it may reveal itself apparently in a set of political institutions, or less apparently in a style of political behavior, a political system is at foundation an articulation of ideas and, above all, an enactment of *values.*

It is precisely on this issue—whether or not political science lets a set of values in the door of the discipline—that an observer encounters some difficulties. When he sets about studying the governing of men in East Asia, he is often deafened by the din of debate and is in danger of hearing very little. Indeed, he may even forget how to listen to really significant political sounds.

"NON-WESTERN" GOVERNANCE

The criticism that the study of so-called "comparative government" has been overly formalistic, descriptive, and legalistic is now familiar to specialists. The description of politics across cultural boundaries has furthermore not been truly comparative, having been more concerned with cataloguing different political institutions than with analyzing comparable political behavior.[3]

To go one step further, the old-fashioned study of comparative government has also been parochial and even dogmatic. It has often made the assumption that our *familiar* ("Western") political systems are normal; *unfamiliar* ("non-Western") systems are strange and exotic, mysterious and inscrutable. Such ideas, themselves historically and culturally determined, tend to confuse a very important *fact* in modern

times—*the impact of the West on East Asia*[4]—with a *myth* of modern
times—*the faith in Westernization.*

In viewing the process of change whereby governments in Asia *seem*
to have adopted Western political institutions, we must indeed exercise
extreme care before concluding that governance in East Asia is becoming uniformly Western. As three specialists phrased it, "many non-
Western countries are often self-conscious about the problem of moving
from a definite past to an idealized future." The nations only *seem* to
have moved toward Western-style constitutions, administrative law,
cabinets, civil service, political parties, manifestoes, propaganda, and
even one-party discipline.[5]

Obviously, change and attitudes toward change in various East Asian
countries have been by no means uniform. There was wide variation in
the cultural and historical conditions under which the impact of the
West was experienced. The rate of change has caused cleavages not
only *between* Western and non-Western nations, but also *among* countries in Asia and even *within* East Asia. The point has been eloquently
documented by Edwin O. Reischauer:

> We always had known that there were vast differences in the speeds
> with which Japan and China began to modernize in the nineteenth cen-
> tury, but we had not fully realized how unsatisfactory were the explana-
> tions of this varying rate of progress.[6]

In other words, the Western impact was perhaps a constant; but then,
how do we explain the variables, the different manners in which China,
Korea, and Japan have responded? Apparently "Westernization" is a
very poor substitute for a more subtle and complex process, "modernization."

This distinction, between Westernization and modernization, does
not imply that either the body of ideas in a modernizing culture or its
value system remains original and pure, or underived and unmixed.
The critical matter is the "mix" of what is traditional, what is in transition, and what is modern. At one point in recent Chinese history, there
was a "self-conscious" movement from "a definite past" (the Confucian
system) to "an idealized future" (a modern, constitutional regime). But
the immediate model adopted by the Chinese in this case was derived
not from the West, but from Japan.

The whole history of Japan is testimony to the ability of the social
system to adopt and to adapt, to derive and to mix, and yet to remain
characteristically Japanese, if not pure. The Japanese process of "bor-
rowing"—as it is so often misstated—began in the seventh century and
followed the brilliant T'ang Exemplar. Later, in the nineteenth century,

Japan adapted Western techniques but modernized in an essentially Japanese style. Much later, even Japanese spoke of the American "democratization" of their society, which has nonetheless remained unique.

To return to the question of values for a moment, *democracy* as a goal and ideal has been an important part of our Western humanist tradition. Soooner or later, it is often assumed, unfamiliar non-Western systems must gravitate toward the familiar, Western, democratic political system. It would almost seem (to paraphrase another dogma) that "internal contradictions" of a despotic regime would eventually and surely work toward the "liberation" of its subjects. The abnormal, undemocratic political system would certainly "wither away"; until this has been accomplished, the system could not be called "modern." The relationship between modern and democratic is, however, a moot and not a settled issue.[7]

Such trenchant criticism has helped observers of "non-Western" politics to escape from the orbit of ethnocentrism. By analyzing unfamiliar political behavior, political scientists themselves have been immeasurably enriched. Generalizations about political culture have been tested in a wider field. Assumptions about how men—even in familiar societies—govern themselves have been challenged. To this extent, what has been called "behavioralism" has contributed much to the study of the governing of men in East Asia.

On the other hand, to the extent that behavioralism has attempted to convert politics into value-free "science," it has tried to exclude the most interesting sector of politics. In fact, it has been said that many behavioralists have been "anti-political" and that they engage in the search for "apolitical politics."[8]

Certainly in East Asia, political traditions have always revolved around values. Governments were regarded as moral or immoral. They could never be conceived as being amoral. Modern constitutional development in this region has reflected these habits.

CONSTITUTIONALISM: WEST AND EAST

One thrust of extreme behavioralism urges us to by-pass structures of government, formal political institutions, and, especially, legal forms. Specifically, *constitutions* are poor guides to political behavior in "late modernizers" (or so it is argued).

In fact, law and legal methods to adjust disputes have traditionally been minor phases of East Asian governance: they received scant notice in the Great Tradition and lay almost totally outside the Little Tradition at the rice roots of village societies.[9] In modern East Asia organic laws, where they were drafted, were imported trappings adopted to deceive men both domestic and alien (it is further argued). Indeed, it may well be that *constitutionalism*, as we know it, does not really exist outside North Atlantic communities.

In our Western experience, clearly constitutionalism has been linked with ideology beneath the political system. On occasion it has provided the ramparts behind which man's individuality might find protection against invasions by political power, including the authority exercised by the organized, formal political community. On other occasions constitutionalism has been heralded by political theorists as social man's most significant achievement. The community defined in organic law has been viewed as an expression of man's better self and as a direct fulfillment of his needs. Thus has constitutionalism related political structure with political behavior and anchored both in political values.

Government by law may be recognized as the foundation of constitutional rule. And law may be something more than edict or statute. It often draws on social experience, the norms drawn from tradition, mores, and customs. Correspondingly, constitutional rule (even in the West) does not require the existence of a formal constitution. It has often signified governance limited by common sense and effected through the consensus of the community; decision in the general rather than in a class interest; law never divorced from men, or so it is hoped.

It is in this sense that one may say with respect to a kind of continuum, the familiar Western political tradition has leaned toward the end of *law as rule*; the unfamiliar East Asian tradition has leaned toward the end of *man as ruler*. It is not, however, altogether that simple a distinction.

CONFUCIAN "CONSTITUTIONALISM"

If social norms are the sum total of man's experience, then to Confucius can be attributed the first definition of Chinese constitutionalism. The Master was a conservative; he sought to conserve Chinese social norms already (five centuries before the Christian era) arrived at by generations of trial and error. Paul Linebarger put it this way: "Confucius articulated the inherent values of the Chinese way in order to arrive at an enduring prescription for the good society."[10] Similarly, if constitutionalism does not presume the existence of a formal constitution; if it signifies governance limited by common sense and, therefore, the consensus of the community; if constitutionalism always implies governance for welfare of the citizens, then one can speak of "constitutionalism" in old China. If, on the other hand, constitutionalism must specify inalienable rights (as well as duties), particularly of the individual (regardless of status); if it must include the right of an ordinary citizen to take issue with the elite (including the wise) so that governance is according to law, then perhaps one cannot speak of "constitutionalism" in old China.

It is best to say that the Confucian system (as compared with modern constitutionalism) was marked by four distinguishing characteristics:

1. The role of the primary regulatory agency was played not by the Government, but by a body of doctrine.
2. This body of doctrine addressed itself to all human relations, public and private, in a comprehensive code of righteous conduct.
3. An officialdom of scholar-statesmen, the celebrated literati, was charged with the dual task of acting as a living example of righteous behavior and of guiding governance along the path of justice and the general welfare.
4. Compliance was presumably insured by making the Confucian doctrine the most important subject of all education; in theory (but not always in practice) it was a case of pure ideological control.[11]

Confucian ideology united institutions and behavior in the widest circle of values, first in the immediate family, neighborhood, village, guild and district. The outer circle, relatively remote from the individual, was the higher authority of the provincial or central Government.

Government might visit punishment on people, but it rarely issued orders. In theory, standards of propriety needed little enforcement because the standards were accepted as having universal validity. Thus they shaped human behavior more effectively than could the impersonal commands of a legal order. One of the earliest Western authorities was cited as follows:

"In the administration of the affairs of the Empire," says Jernigan, "the principle is recognized that laws are the particular institution of the legislator, while customs are the institution of a nation in general, and that nothing tends more to produce a revolution than an attempt to change a custom by a law."[12]

With this background of understanding of the Confucian system, one can then fully appreciate the constitutional development of China, for example, in transition. Fifty years ago, Harold M. Vinacke described China's attempt to find a middle ground "between the old traditional life of the State, and the new conceptions of governmental relationships brought to the East from the West." Professor Vinacke further wrote, "No change, whether in the nature of progression or retrogression, stands by itself, but each links itself naturally with the antecedent and the subsequent condition."[13]

It is also significant that during the period of China's transition, in a final definition of Dr. Sun Yat-sen's position (in his San Min Chu I) the strength of the Confucian tradition as a doctrinal approach of effective Chinese community life was plainly in evidence. Even after thirty years' search for constitutional form and drafting of modern constitutions, the common Chinese people had rights—sometimes protected, sometimes not—but the rights were not those listed in the various constitutions. They were the traditional rights arising from concepts of Chinese social behavior usually enforced through intergroup pressures, not through the Government. Almost as before, the people literally took care of themselves. They did so through institutions dependent on neither law nor constitutions. They existed by the inprescriptible rights of common sense as exemplified in the Confucian tradition. In this sense Dr. Sun (like Confucius) was a social determinist.

With Government nonexistent or at most extremely dilute, it was impossible at first for China to follow the path of Japan, redoing its laws to make a constitutional government.

MODERN CONSTITUTIONAL DEVELOPMENT IN CHINA

In 1905, while China was still under the iron will of the Empress Dowager, Tzu Hsi, a special commission was sent abroad to study foreign constitutional systems. From the time of this group's return (1906) dates the beginning of an almost interminable period of search on the part of the Chinese. Whereas the "Hundred Days" in 1898, under the reign of Emperor Kuang Hsü, had marked an abortive attempt to patch up—without serious alteration—the existing structure; and the uprising of the Boxers, a violent reaction against even these minor changes, the study commissions represented attempts at serious examination of alternatives. As is well known, the efforts were too little and too late.

As a matter of fact, the turn of the century was indeed the beginning of a long search, not simply for constitutional form but also for a whole new way of life. China had entered upon the fateful transition from rebellion to revolution.

It is interesting to note that the first incentive to constitutional change came not from the West, but from Japan. When Chinese asked themselves what was the reason for change in relative position—as between China and Japan—they found one answer ready to hand: *constitutional government*.[14] In the truly-remarkable Meiji Constitution the Chinese identified the source of newfound Japanese power. And specifically, the Empress Dowager thought she saw there a formula for accomplishing two things: the introduction of constitutional reform and, at the same time, the preservation of autocratic power. In her last days, she came to realize that her Imperial Constitution was a rather unimaginative plagiarism of the Japanese Constitution of 1889.

As a matter of fact, enactments of 1908 were far more important than any Chinese was to realize at the time. Aside from the motivations behind them, the promises contained therein were really quite definite and followed three distinct lines: (1) provincial assemblies were to be summoned within a year; (2) governmental changes were to lead to the calling of a national parliament within nine years; and, perhaps most important, (3) fundamental Principles of the Constitution were promulgated. The Principles (August 27, 1908) were of particular interest:

> It should be noted that the nations of the East and the West all have established constitutional governments. Some have done so by pressure from below and some under influence from above. All have constitutions and Parliaments. . . . *The government of China is to be constitutional by Imperial decree. This is an unchangeable principle.* . . . *The principles of the constitution are the great laws which may not be discussed.* Once fixed they may not be lightly altered. . . . *The constitution is designed to conserve the power of the sovereign and protect the officials and the people.*[15]

If political commentary on *what ought to be* is dangerous, then even more hazardous is speculation on *what might have been.* Although the chief motive behind the Principles was maintenance of autocratic government, certainly it can be said that, given half a chance, this first constitution might have offered China as stable and even enlightened a government as was designed under the successor Republic. Professor Vinacke shrewdly commented on the fact (later underlined by Edwin Reischauer) that in Japan the long experience with "centralized feudalism" made it possible to establish constitutional government, leaving the exercise of power in the hands of able samurai. Despite the obvious historical fact of imitation, there is little reason to compare the late Manchu constitutional development with events in Japan after the Meiji Restoration.

Following the fall of China's last dynasty, the Republic was ushered in by the adoption at Nanking of the so-called Provisional Constitution. It was also ominously marked by the inauguration of Yüan Shih-k'ai as President of the Republic. His tragi-comic career could easily be dismissed by the comment that constitutional government was the ornament and not the engine of political power. And yet the experience of China under the semi-monarchical rule of Yüan illustrated several important, if inchoate, constitutional developments.

First, constitutional government was tried for about a year without producing, it is true, the political stability and strength that had been

expected. Second, the attempt on the part of Yüan to turn the clock
back to the time of the Empire ended in dismal failure. Having won a
struggle with the Assembly, it might well have been expected that
Yüan Shih-k'ai would govern as a dictator without reference to constitutional form. It is important to remember that he chose the wiser course
of clothing his absolutism with the forms of Western constitutionalism.
Third, he actually turned back to the Assembly whose first task was to
prepare a revised constitution, promulgated on May 1, 1914.[16]

Whereas previous constitutions had provided for some degree of
cabinet responsibility, Yüan's Constitutional Compact placed administrative power in the hands of the President. Thus under the guise of
constitutional sanction, China reverted for a brief time to a monarchi-
cal—but not an Imperial—form of government. Nevertheless "that national panacea—a constitution—had been preserved."[17] Furthermore,
the Compact was provisional, and one of its sections dealt with procedure for drafting a permanent constitution. That task waited while
China suffered under successive warlords who followed Yüan Shih-k'ai.

That China's first three decades of constitutional development were
totally unproductive, not even the most severe critics would venture to
say. The political education of the people had indeed begun.

CONSTITUTIONALISM AS AN ISSUE UNDER
NATIONALIST REGIMES

Nonetheless, only with the establishment of the National Government
at Nanking did China's constitutional structure and actual government
begin to draw closer together. Thereafter, in the all-too-brief period of
"the fullness of national unity" under Kuomintang (KMT) leadership
in the 1930s prior to the outbreak of war, the Chinese did learn about
the importance of a Chinese state as a legal entity.

> The old imperial society of China was able to dispense with law through
> reliance upon social forces expressing themselves in a large number of
> small but stable units. If these disappear the question arises: How can
> the individual conceive his relationships within Chinese society? Systema-
> tized modern organization requires a legal framework.[18]

As a matter of fact, the Nanking Government was organized under the
KMT in a form unique among modern states. Its distinctive features borrowed a great deal from the thinking of Dr. Sun Yat-sen.

Thereafter, Kuomintang-led governments were marked by a concentration of power in supreme agencies. They operated under a five-fold
division of power and function, through the *yüan*. And Chinese gov-

ernment from that time until this has been characterized by an absence of true parliamentary chambers. On the other hand, the form of government never became simply a camouflage for a military dictatorship (under Generalissimo Chiang K'ai-shek). Certainly one reason was the existence of the Organic Law (in effect, the constitution from 1928 to 1930). Another was the meeting, in 1931, of the National People's Convention, which adopted a Provisional Constitution.[19] Under this law the power of the President was sharply reduced and the Council of State became a more formalized agency of government.

The Provisional Constitution (*Yüeh Fa*), according to doctrine inherited from Dr. Sun, was designed to cover a period (labelled the "stage of political tutelage") between the first stage of revolution (military conquest) and the final destination (constitutional government). Designed for five years' use, it continued in force until 1941. The distinguished constitutional lawyer, Dr. Wang Shih-chieh, defined the system as "party government," signifying control by only one political party (the KMT). Perhaps most important, after China was then plunged into the war years, the effectiveness of the resistance to Japanese aggression depended in part on a successful compromise of the problems of constitutionalism. In the minds of many Chinese, in other words, constitutionalism became a war aim.

On May 5, 1936, the Legislative *Yüan* produced the famous Draft Permanent Constitution (*Hsien-fa Ts'ao-an*), promptly named the "Double Five Draft" after its birthday (5/5/XXV or the 25th year of the Republic). Thereafter it became the center of all Chinese constitutional debate. It stood as the official proposal for a permanent constitution awaiting ratification by the National (Constituent) Congress.

Indeed, the clamor for a constitution continued during the war. Eventually the Generalissimo (more interested in recovering lost territory and reconstruction) yielded to continuing demand. A special constituent assembly was scheduled for convention on November 12, 1940, but large-scale raids on the western capital, Chungking, led to further postponement. Meanwhile, the popularity of the Double Five Draft illustrated a remarkable political fact, that nowhere in China was there outright denial of the need for further constitutional change.

Rather, amidst the chaos and suffering, Chinese debated only the timing of constitutional change. Some argued that a new constitution would lead to the legalization of other parties and would add to wartime discord. The masses were still illiterate, not ready for sophisticated legal structure. Why, then, change constitutions during the struggle for survival? Others replied that, as soon as the Sino-Japanese war broke out, it became evident that more democratic rule was essential for efficient prosecution of the war effort. Legitimization of other parties would contribute to wartime union. The period of tutelage had to come to an end sometime: everyone was ready—the Kuomintang, the Government, and the independents.

Pointed questions were raised by the non-communist Left. Tso Tao-fen, one of the so-called Seven Gentlemen (Ch'i Chuntzu) who led the National Salvationists, wrote:

> If you say that the people do not know what a constitution is, you should enlighten them about the close relationship between themselves and the constitution, not discontinue the constitutional movement.[20]

Even a leader of the Chinese Communist Party (CCP) said, "We want a Constitution, a democratic Constitution—a real democratic Constitution." He added that the CCP was for a democracy, but that the Double Five Draft was "not the constitution of a democracy."[21] On the Right, a Manifesto of the "Sixth Kuomintang Congress" convoked in 1939 at Shanghai by the pro-Japanese puppet, Wang Ching-wei, proclaimed:

> Immediately the war is over, and peace reestablished, the National Assembly (*Kuo Min Ta Hui*) will be convened and the National Constitution (*Hsien Fa*) drafted and promulgated, without suffering any further delay. The period of tutelage is at an end; the period of constitutional government is becoming inaugurated.[22]

The issue of constitutionalism in wartime and immediately post-war China was, in fact, not a simple problem of reactionary ideas versus progressive ideas. The Chinese still faced—despite definite movement toward constitutional government—the question of the limits of democratic toleration during crisis. (Even the most established democracies faced the same dilemma during war.) As early as 1912 China had possessed an excellent, democratic constitution (and many more in the warlord years). Yet the vast majority of Chinese remained illiterate and unprepared to deal with complicated machinery of opinion and elections, spelled out in a constitution. Corruption, wire-pulling, lip-service to form rather than performance of deed—these remained widespread. On the other hand, continuation of sham-democracy would have been no step forward.

To the counsels of caution (within the KMT), advocates of immediately responsive and responsible institutions hammered away at the fact that the Chinese common people were better democrats than their rulers. They threw in the face of the KMT its own professions of democracy, as well as the words of its late Leader, Dr. Sun Yat-sen.

The eventual collapse of the Kuomintang-led National Government (on the mainland) was, of course, compounded of many complicated factors. Certainly two, however, were the twin facts: that the KMT purported above all to be a party-guardian of an ideology; that, in the long run, disparity between constant assertion and reality cast doubt on the ideology itself. Like much of Chinese social legislation, Nationalist organic law lifted China to the level of the rest of the modern world, *de jure.*

> These elevated documents remained elevated; life went on beneath them, and the tragic gap between law and life was so enormous that no one thought of bridging it.[23]

THE SEARCH CONTINUED: CONSTITUTIONS IN POST-WAR CHINA

Once again, in a behavioral mood one might easily dismiss the progress of constitutional development in post-war China. *Legal* guidelines in the form of organic laws have seldom given significant clues to distribution of actual *political* power. And yet the constitutions of this period are of great interest, for other reasons. In the post-war period, there have been two major lines of constitutional development. With the first, the climax (or anti-climax) of constitution-making under Nationalist auspices, treatment can be mercifully brief.

Kuomintang promises to convene a National Assembly to adopt a new constitution and opposition demands for immediate constitutional government might have continued indefinitely, had it not been for the unusual circumstances immediately after the collapse of Japan. Convention of the so-called Political Consultative Conference (PCC), in January, 1946, gave opposition and government alike an impetus to move toward a constitution.

Unfortunately, however, this was not the first nor even the primary task of the Conference. Its principal function, which far overshadowed constitution-making, was to try to arrange for a peaceful solution of major domestic conflict. In other words, the PCC accurately reflected deep divisions in the society; the search was for a whole new way of life, not simply an organic law. Even with regard to a possible constitution, motives varied widely: the opposition looked to this legal symbol as a means of breaking the monopoly of government by one party; the KMT-led Government, as a means of last-ditch defense. Nevertheless, when the PCC adjourned late in January, agreement had been reached on five difficult issues on the agenda. The apparent consensus proved to be deceptive: what seemed to be peace turned out to be only a truce.

On the Draft Constitution (of 1936), the Conference had proposed numerous radical revisions. In brief, the dominant chord of change was the widespread distrust of government by one man, or at least by one party. On the positive side, of interest was the statement of "fundamental national policies," which dealt with the usual matters of national defense, foreign policy, and national economy but also gave voice to ideals of peace, good neighborliness, social reform and a democratic, egalitarian, scientific spirit. (In this sense the proposals were characteristic of many post-war constitutions—including the Constitution of Japan, 1947—in their hope for one world, the United Nations, and the four freedoms.)

Further revisions were the work of Kuomintang delegates and of allied parties, without the consent of the communists and their friends. Indeed, amidst growing signs of a civil war, the Kuomintang decided to convene the old National Assembly and to make of it a constituent conference. Again the communists and many independents abstained. The Constitution adopted by the National Assembly on December 25, 1946, thus reflected mainly the views of the Kuomintang and its close allies. The National Government promulgated the Constitution on January 1, 1947.[24]

Obviously the question, whether the Constitution was in agreement with the prior resolutions of the Political Consultative Conference (which included the communists), is largely irrelevant. Had the constituent National Assembly been a genuinely sovereign body, popularly reelected and representing to some degree the will of the people at large, it would have made little difference whether previous inter-party agreements had been adhered to. As a matter of fact, Kuomintang leaders (elated over short-term successes in the civil war) were confident. Some independents, who attended the Assembly reluctantly, were relieved. Beyond the precincts of the Assembly, however, gloom prevailed. To a vast majority of the Chinese people, adoption of a constitution and organization of a government under it by one dominant party without participation of the opposition signified final extinction of the hopes for a peaceful settlement of the civil war.

A Chinese political scientist who later defected to the mainland regime, Professor Ch'ien Tuan-sheng, singled out one major feature of the Constitution. All-important checks on the powers of the President of the Republic, previously suggested by the inter-party Political Consultative Conference, were not included in the final draft. Otherwise, he concluded,

> . . . The Constitution is a fairly good document, better in draftsmanship,

more democratic in spirit, and more satisfactory in the framework of government that it purports to build up than any other constitution, provisional constitution, or draft constitution, the Republic has had, with the possible exception of the ill-fated Ts-ao K'un Constitution of 1923. Indeed, the two constitutions are in more than one way comparable and kindred documents, similarly created and equally vulnerable.[25]

One thing was certain, added Professor Ch'ien. Whoever in China might attempt to fulfill the promise of the Three Principles of Sun Yat-sen must excel the Kuomintang in several ways. Success would require more understanding of the problems of the people; an efficient regime would not consider itself to be above the people; a successful government would identify itself more with the people. "It must be more truly nationalistic, more truly socialistic, and more truly democratic than a regime which makes mere professions or bad distortions of the Principles."[26] In light of this Chinese academic's choice at the time, it is interesting to speculate on whether he later thought the leaders of the People's Republic of China succeeded where the Republic of China had failed.

In any case, leaders of the Chinese Communist Party took the next steps in producing constitutions, at least for the mainland. As in the case of the organic law for the Republic, the successive constitutional bases for the People's Republic of China should not be lightly dismissed. For one thing, successive drafts clearly reveal the proud boast that "the Chinese people, after more than 100 years of heroic struggle, at last, under the leadership of the Chinese Communist Party, achieved in 1949 the great victory of the people's revolution against imperialism, feudalism, and bureaucratic capitalism." Furthermore, in succeeding versions of organic law one can easily identify the strategy and tactics of the communists: whereas an early document stated that the new republic was established in opposition to "imperialism, feudalism, and bureaucratic capitalism and strives for the independence, democracy, peace, unification, prosperity and strength of China," a later one established as the objective, "the socialist transformation of China."[27] Between the lines, one can visualize the forward movement, the consolidation of Party power during the first five years of the People's Republic, and changes in the organization of government.

At a gigantic rally in Peking on October 1, 1949, Mao Tse-tung proclaimed the birth of a new regime. Simultaneously, three basic documents were formally promulgated, and they provided the legal foundation for the government. These included: (1) the Organic Law of the Chinese People's Political Consultative Conference (the name obviously paralleled those of previous "consultative" bodies); (2) the Common

Program of the CPPCC (the name obviously chosen to reflect common principles of a coalition of a "number" of parties); and (3) the Organic Law of the Central People's Government of the People's Republic of China.[28] The most important of these was the Common Program, which became the first, preliminary, organic law of the communist regime.

Both implicitly and explicitly, the Common Program accurately reflected the development of successive united front experiences on the part of the Party since 1936-37. What was "common program" for all was the "minimum program" for the Party, or a preliminary phase of revolution prior to the advent of "socialism." Moreover, the documents constituted something more than revolutionary rhetoric. They were prescribed as required reading for intensive "study sessions," they made up the "line" for indoctrination, and they became compulsory guides for the entire population. In a country traditionally attuned to ideological conformity, the organic laws were of utmost importance. They did not, of course, even intend to establish constitutionalism in the sense that law would become the bulwark of individual rights. They were, by and large, poor indices to the actual center of gravity of the decision-making process. And they were frankly temporary in nature, suited only to a five-year period of transition.

Five years later, on September 15, 1954, the first National People's Congress was convened in Peking. Over one thousand deputies remained in session until September 28. Their most important task was adoption of the Constitution which formally terminated the transitional period called, after a famous essay by Mao Tse-tung, the "New Democracy" (1949-54). Nonetheless, the new Constitution was supposed to be "based on the Common Program" and a "further development of it." This meant that "New Democracy" was scarcely mentioned and "socialist construction" became the goal of all effort.

China's new constitution was some twenty months in the making, and the very process of drafting was itself most revealing. With a call by the Central People's Government Council for elections to form the first National People's Congress (which would adopt the Constitution) came also appointment of a drafting committee, on January 13, 1953. Obviously the Party retained a firm grasp on the steering mechanism.[29] The committee adopted as "first draft" a document passed along by the Party Central Committee, which in turn had received it from the hands of Mao Tse-tung himself. (Leadership of the Chinese Communist Party (CCP) in drafting thus corresponded closely with that of the Russian Party (CPSU) in drawing up the Soviet Constitution of 1936.)

Beginning in June, 1954, the Government deliberately made a display of "work by over 8,000 people" producing "more than 5,900 suggestions for revision." Thereafter the Government's Council adopted and made public a revised Draft Constitution of the Central People's Republic (*Chung-hua jen-min kung-ho-kuo hsien-fa ts'ao-an*). For the next three months "more than 150,000,000 persons," at the rice-roots level, were officially reported to have taken part in a "second round of discussions." Over one million "proposals" were said to have been transmitted to the drafting committee for consideration. Elections to the National People's Congress took place in July and August. Mao himself opened the Congress, recommending as first order of business adoption of the draft. No one was surprised when, on September 20, 1954, all 1,197 deputies cast their votes in favor of the new Constitution. By Government fiat, Communist China had entered its "constitutional stage."[30]

CHINESE COMMUNIST CONSTITUTIONAL DILEMMAS

It would, of course, be naive to assume that Communist China's "constitutional stage" represents at long last the mainland's entry into constitutionalism, as the system is known in the West. It would be equally naive, however, to overlook the importance of the Constitution[31] in several respects.

First, as to method of adoption: shrewd outside observers were quick to point to the significance of the process. It was a classic example of a modern government's ability to muster support—yes, even popular support—for the regime, what has been called "the engineering of consent." The first round of Party discussions had been carefully used to indoctrinate reliable cadres, who in turn would be responsible for conducting the second round. The latter fulfilled "mass-line" requirements for arousing wide interest in the "transition to socialism."

Second, as to the relation between constitutional "socialism" in the People's Republic of China and in the USSR: expert China-watchers were quick to point to the comparisons and contrasts. Constitutional precedents of the Soviet Union did, it is true, serve as a model in drafting the Chinese organic law. This fact was explicitly acknowledged by Liu Shao-ch'i in an official report: ". . . the Committee for Drafting the Constitution consulted all the constitutions, past and present, of the Soviet Union. . ."[32] There may, indeed, be some connection between that earlier authoritative statement and the later fate of Liu Shao-ch'i, who fell into disgrace during the Cultural Revolution.

Even more authoritative (and predictive) were Chairman Mao's sentiments, aired as early as 1945 in reply to his own rhetorical question:

> Chinese history will determine the Chinese system. A peculiar form—a new democratic state and regime of a union of democratic classes—will be produced which will be entirely necessary and rational to us and different from the Russian system.[33]

Thus Article I of the Chinese Constitution defined the regime as "a people's democratic state led by the working class and based on the alliance of workers and peasants"; whereas Article 1 of the Soviet Constitution defined the Union as "a Socialist state of workers and peasants."

Aside from such subtle niceties, Chinese Communist practice—if not legal theory—did reflect recent Chinese history. The People's Government as it matured from 1949 through the new system of 1954 was, as Mao aptly put it, a "People's Democratic Dictatorship." It was an overlay built on successive united fronts. The Government continued to represent four classes under "leadership" of the CCP, which meant actually that the communists were dominant at the national level. Predominance was assured under the celebrated principle of "democratic centralism."

> The democratic system is to be carried out within the ranks of the people, giving them freedom of speech, assembly and association. The right to vote is given only to the people and not to the reactionaries. These two aspects, namely democracy among the people and dictatorship over the reactionaries, combine to form the people's democratic dictatorship . . . .[34]

A third important characteristic of the Constitution is the manner in which it separates Government and Party under organic law. As Professor H. Arthur Steiner pointed out, the Constitution represents an intriguing combination of classical Chinese allusions, terminology from modern political science, and jargon from Maoism. The "New Democracy" is defined by special formula: "State form [*kuo-t'i*]—dictatorship of all revolutionary classes; government form [*cheng-t'i*]—the system of democratic centralism."[35] Actually, the Chinese Communist Party is mentioned only twice in the Preamble: historically, as the leader of "the Chinese people" in the "people's revolution"; and functionally, as the leader of "a broad people's democratic united front, composed of all democratic classes, democratic parties and groups, and popular organizations." Thus, in constitutional theory the State is multi-party and multi-social and the CCP does not enjoy the monopoly given the CPSU in the 1936 Soviet Constitution (Article 126).

There is, however, another way to look at the system. Chinese Communist doctrine sharply distinguishes the scope and functions of state administration from those of Party power. Party power continues to be exercised through extra-constitutional forms. The CCP jealously guards "direction" of all the nation's social life, including government and administration. In fact, therefore, the Constitution cannot be the supreme law of the land. Although Party members were exhorted to "make themselves an example by observing the Constitutional and all other laws," the Party does not admit that the Constitution restricts its own sphere of action. The Constitution itself is, then, "limited" in that large sectors of Chinese social and public life lie outside its legal boundaries.

Study of the constitutional framework of Communist China therefore must include as well the basic code of the Communist Party of China. The first Party Constitution was adopted in wartime Yenan. Again, whereas the CPSU had been defined (1939) as the "organized vanguard of the working class," the CCP was both that and representative of "the interests of the Chinese nation and the Chinese people." As indicated in its 1945 Constitution, the CCP "accepts critically both the Chinese and foreign historical heritages and opposes the world outlook of idealism or mechanical materialism." In its later Constitution, adopted by the Eighth National Party Congress in Peking in 1956, the CCP could not resist a touch of national pride:

> Marxism-Leninism is not a dogma, but a guide to action . . . . The Party in its activities upholds the principle of integrating the universal truths of Marxism-Leninism with the actual practice of China's revolutionary struggle, and combats all the doctrinaire or empiricist deviations.[36]

The year 1968 saw yet another—the latest—draft of a proposed Constitution for the Chinese Communist Party. Apparently weary and fearful of excesses in the Cultural Revolution, the Party in its Constitution accurately revealed its ambivalence. In other words, the draft of the organic law proved worthy of careful study.[37]

On the one hand, in almost Confucian-style exhortation, the CCP defined itself as "the political party of the proletariat." The "ultimate objective" was set as "the realization of Communism." Chinese Communist pride was once again clearly revealed in the claim that Comrade Mao had "combined the universal truth of Marxism-Leninism with the concrete practice of revolution." He had inherited, defended and developed Marxism-Leninism, "and lifted it to a completely new stage."

On the other hand, a little over a decade after the CCP had boasted that it would never succumb (as Russian Communists did) to a cult of personality, the Party aired a value-laden organic law enshrining Mao Tse-tung and his thought. The CCP, according to the Constitution, has been "consolidated and developed in the midst of big windstorms and heavy seas." It was further predicted, "In this historical phase, classes, class contradictions and class struggle will exist throughout . . ." and such contradictions could be resolved "only by relying on Marxist theory and practice of uninterrupted revolution."

Accurately the Constitution proceeded to define even the specific goals of Chinese Communist foreign policy, as the CCP "fights to overthrow imperialism headed by the United States, modern revisionism headed by the Soviet revisionist renegade clique, and reactionaries of all countries . . . ." And finally, the Constitution saw fit to reveal the Party's strength (or weakness) by specifically naming Mao's heir. "Comrade Lin Piao is Comrade Mao Tse-tung's close comrade-in-arms and successor."

To return to the Constitution of the People's Republic of China, in orthodox doctrine "the law of the people's state is a weapon" and not an end in itself. "State authority and party" can hardly "wither away," however, before "classes, class contradictions and class struggle" are abolished. Therein lies a constitutional dilemma.

Hopefully—even scientifically, according to doctrine—the "realization of Communism" would involve displacement of the Constitution itself. Realistically, what one "class" has constructed—policies "the leadership nucleus" has defined, a successor "advanced elements" have named—these another "class" might remodel, redefine, or disgrace. There is no connotation of permanence. There is no legal bar to the "practice of uninterrupted revolution."

For a time the power of the People's Republic, as heralded by the 1954 Constitution, was supreme. Characteristic communist use of a multi-class united front system avoided further overt expression of class war and substituted a mass response for defense of the *Chinese* People's Republic against domestic "traitors" and foreign "enemies." The CCP formula was available for appropriate use in adjoining Asian countries.

The Chinese Communists were soon to learn, however, that no political system (no matter how authoritarian) may for long neglect its own ideology. Granted, the outside observer must never ignore the possibility that a regime may engage in self-deception. Man's capacity for illusion is limitless. Constitutions may provide the rose-colored glasses with which to view society. There is, however, such a thing as "diminishing ideological returns." What the Kuomintang learned in failure on the mainland, the Chinese Communist Party leaders may yet discover: the danger of disparity between legal assertion and political reality. Too great a gap may cast doubt on the all-important factor of ideology itself.

JAPANESE LEGALISTS

Although Old China did produce a school of Legalists (parallel with the Confucianists), those who emphasized law were never in the mainstream of traditional Chinese life. Rather, as we have seen, the Confucian ethic represented the major current of Chinese thought. In contrast, Old Japan very early drafted *legal* blueprints which set forth Japanese ideals, norms, and even the design for a superstructure of state. In this basic sense, Japan has always been (at least until the appearance of the People's Republic) far more legalistic in its governing process than the Middle Kingdom.

Nonetheless, the earliest Japanese experiment with law-making faithfully reflected Chinese experience. Japan's first written code of ethics was the so-called Constitution of Seventeen Articles, produced in A.D. 604, when Chinese influence on Japan was strong. The first written laws were regulations (in Chinese style) of the Taika Reform, 646, and of the Taihō Code, 702. These formal (and artificial) codes slowly dissolved to a nucleus of indigenous and largely unwritten law after the tenth century.

Just about the time Anglo-Norman law began to take form in an island kingdom on the other side of the world, in 1232 a council of the *Bakufu* ("Tent Government") at Kamakura adopted a set of laws known as the Jōei Code. The chief point of legal interest, as it is under any feudal system, was the regulation of land tenure and rights.

The remote predecessor of feudal regulations, the Taihō Code had been a more systematic (if Chinese-like) set of laws; the Jōei was a more practical summation of a half a century of *Japanese* experience in a young feudal system. The Taika-Taihō had represented the Chinese Empire (Japanese in form), expressed through an elegant, literary aristocracy based in the effete capital, Kyoto; the Jōei marked the florescence of Japanese feudalism expressed through a military-landed nobility based on the countryside. Professor Kōji Terao of Kyoto (formerly Imperial) University explained that the Jōei Code was originally a military house law and rested on military principles (*buke-shugi*), but it also leaned toward legalism (*hōchi-shūgi*). In the centuries which followed there were amendment laws, it is true, but by and large the Jōei remained the legal guideline for feudal governance. The Muromachi Bakufu and the great Tokugawa Bakufu, which ruled Japan from 1600 to 1867, followed it. Not until the Meiji modernizers appeared were the coded successors to the Jōei swept aside.[38]

Indeed, in Japanese feudal experience was a strong sense of legal obligations and rights. These may well have laid down the foundations for the comparatively rapid modernization of the Japanese nation-state (as contrasted, for example, with nineteenth-century China). Japanese scholars have identified an early, rational, and surprisingly modern theory of social organicism as one of the most interesting features of the Tokugawa governing tradition.[39]

After 1867 the privilege of making law returned to the central (Meiji) Government. Japan's first modern, basic codes were constructed parallel to the Meiji Constitution itself. As was the case in China, there was a "self-conscious" movement from a "definite past" (Tokugawa "centralized feudalism") to "an idealized future" (the modern Meiji constitutional regime). Specific law codes did borrow from continental European, especially German, principles. To say, however, that Japan's first modern laws were simply products of an innate trait of imitation would be oversimplification.

MEIJI MODERNIZATION AND CONSTITUTIONALISM

At the time of writing (1969), a century had passed since the profound but relatively quiet revolution in Japan, which ushered in the so-called Meiji Restoration. One hundred years ago, changes in the Japanese way of life came with bewildering speed. The first decisive step was the abolition (in August, 1871) of the old feudal domains (*han*) and their rapid conversion to new prefectures (*ken*). Parallel alterations occurred in the field of education, in the building of a modern peasant-conscript army, and in the establishment of a navy. In 1885, central administration was overhauled and a cabinet was formed, with the famous Itō Hirobumi as the first Premier. Capstone of the modernized structure was the Meiji Constitution, which was drafted in preparation for the first session of the Diet, in 1890.

It is now fashionable in many Japanese circles to criticize severely this constitutional document, as compared with the more democratic Constitution of 1946. In fact, there is some resistance in Japan to celebration of the Meiji centennial. Much of Japanese scholarship comes out on the side of interpretation of the Restoration, and especially of the Meiji Constitution, as a "feudal throwback." Japan's first modern organic law was a monument to "absolutism," a result of an "abortive bourgeois revolution," or at least it contained a large measure of "feudal residue." Some Western studies of the period have reflected this Japanese bias.

The case against the Meiji Constitution, in brief summary, has been formulated as follows: (1) A powerful Meiji oligarchy, led by men like Itō and Yamagata Aritomo, skillfully built bulwarks to withstand the assaults of "public opinion," specifically the demands of the movement for parliamentary government (*jiyū minken undō*). The oligarchy reluctantly granted concessions, among them the promise to write a constitution and establish a parliament. (2) The Meiji Constitution, concomitant laws, and imperial rescripts were masterful maneuvers to establish through legal means certain absolutist and autocratic tendencies inherent in Japanese political behavior. (3) Exploiting a characteristic weakness of Japanese political parties, factionalism, the intrenched oligarchy forced party government into "failure." Historically, the results were frustration of party-cabinet government, the rise of military-led totalitarianism, aggression, war and defeat.

For many reasons it is fortunate that a revisionist history—written by both Westerners and Japanese—has begun to treat the Meiji experiment differently.[40] Just as nineteenth-century Japan in its so-called "crisis of security" stressed the need for a "rich country, strong army" (*fukoku-kyōhei*), the Japanese oligarchy recognized the importance of "civilization and enlightenment" (*bummei kaika*). In other words, the Meiji leadership fixed on both modernization and constitutionalism. One must always link the Restoration *and* the Renovation. A Japanese authority referred to the organic law as follows:

> The Constitution is certainly conservative; but, compared with the Japanese political regime prior to the Restoration, it was definitely a step forward in the direction of democratizing Japan.[41]

In fact, it can be argued that the Meiji constitutional system was a logical outgrowth of Tokugawa "centralized feudalism." For example, Confucianism of the Tokugawa period—as reshaped to suit Japanese conditions—pointed the way toward modernization, by offering the rationale by which the Meiji oligarchy found constitutionalism understandable. The idea of a constitution was not forced on the leadership. In many ways, the political thought of the oligarchs was more "progressive" than that of the opposition. Furthermore, the very idea of a written constitution was an entering wedge. The Meiji oligarchy, by indicating the governmental channels through which the emperor's authority was to be exercised, was itself bound. Itō himself once remarked,

> What are the basic principles on which the constitution is based? The first is the limitation of the powers of the monarch, and the second is the guarantee of the rights of the subjects. Therefore, if in the constitution, only the responsibilities of the subjects, but not their rights, were enumerated, it would be meaningless to have a constitution.[42]

In accepting the principle of constitutional government, the conservative Meiji leadership subscribed to a basic, modern principle of governance: power-sharing. This is quite a different thing from saying, of course, that the oligarchy chose democracy, for none of the major leaders believed in democracy. They did have faith in the Japanese penchant for compromise. They thought they could control the experiment indefinitely, sharing power only in a partial, gradual, and carefully channelled manner. It is a tribute to the power of the political symbol of constitutionalism that they failed.

How else might one explain the remarkable, even promising, development of parties, party leaders, and party-cabinets in the following Taishō period of democracy? Certainly the Meiji Constitution proved to be no bar to vigorous party politics, universal (male) suffrage, the habit of elections, and the oldest parliamentary tradition outside the West.

"DIRECTED MODERNIZATION": THE OCCUPATION (1945-1952)

Paradoxically, the impact of the Allied (but mainly American) Occupation of Japan illustrates similar points. The staying power of legal institutions, once established in Japan, has been remarkable. The possibilities for planned institutional change from the top down and even designed by aliens—at first over-estimated as to effects, then vastly underrated—have provided a fascinating case study for political scientists.

There are still those who like to think that the *true* modernization of Japanese society and political institutions began only after the defeat of Japan in the Pacific War and during the Occupation. More objective observers, with longer historical perspective, have rather adopted the description of the period chosen by the late Professor Kazuo Kawai, "Japan's American Interlude." The term, "interlude," quite properly suggests not only what had gone on in Japan long before the Occupation, but equally important, what has occurred afterward.

In the 1950s (toward the end of the Occupation), even expert observers were gloomy in estimating the life span of the largely alien-inspired political structure of Japan. As Japan approached the time when it would recover the exercise of its own sovereignty, it was fashionable to predict that a reverse course would soon set Japan back into traditional political style. In fact, when one considers the tremendous changes which have occurred in Japan over the past century—the impact of twentieth-century imperialism, aggression, war, defeat, and the Occupation—he cannot help but be astounded at the relative stability of formal, constitutional structure since the peace treaty of 1952.

Most notable are the facts that the Government of Japan, functioning under the terms of an alien-inspired, revolutionary document, has itself led the way to further and far-reaching changes in social, political, and economic life; and that during the two decades since the Constitution went into effect, no government has made an official attempt to revise it. Reflecting on these unexpected developments, Professor Robert E. Ward has commented,

> While it would be excessive to attribute these material successes directly or exclusively to the beneficent effects of the new constitution, it is also improbable that the two phenomena are unrelated . . . . The most remarkable facts about the constitution have been its stability, the degree to which people and government have accepted and adjusted to its spirit and its institutions, and the measure of democracy that it has helped bring to present-day Japan.[43]

It is high time, in other words, that political scientists review the Japanese post-treaty experience with constitutionalism. It is appropriate to consider the advantages and disadvantages of a strategy which frankly adopted the policies of "induced revolution" and consciously or unconsciously capitalized on a unique opportunity for planned political change.

After all, the new Constitution was drafted in record time under largely American authorship. True, this latest organic law for Japan was thus prepared practically in secret by a new oligarchy and then transmitted to the populace, exactly as the Meiji Constitution had been prepared by the few for the many. The new Constitution, however, was among the world's most democratic and progressive. Drawn up in 1946 by officials in the Government Section of the Headquarters, Supreme Commander for the Allied Powers (SCAP), the so-called MacArthur Draft was then translated into Japanese. Even so, in parts it sounded strange in Japanese ears. Product of persuasion, cajolery, and some threat, the draft for all practical purposes became the Constitution of Japan. As such, it was promulgated by the Emperor in the name of the Japanese people and went into effect May 3, 1947.[44]

All the more surprising that this Constitution has yet to be formally amended; that today, despite the fact that there is a politics of revision, most informed predictions allow little chance for wholesale change. There are several reasons for this seeming paradox.

For one thing, the Occupation itself was carried off with a minimum of friction. Both American occupationaires and the occupied Japanese managed difficult roles, leaving a reservoir of good will. The late Premier Yoshida Shigeru, who led Japan during this critical period, wrote:

"Judged by results, it can be frankly admitted that Allied (of course, predominantly American) occupation policy was a success."[45]

The successes of post-treaty Japan cannot, however, be attributed mainly either to the wisdom of the occupationaires or to the admittedly constructive cooperation of the Japanese. To cite former Ambassador Reischauer again, modernization did not begin with the "American interlude" but has proceeded in fits and starts for at least a century.

Nor was it an accident when Allied officials referred, in the Potsdam Proclamation, to "the revival of democracy" in Japan. There had already developed, as has been pointed out, relatively strong traditions of parties, elections, a Diet, and cabinets, which had tried to aggregate interests of the Japanese public. To these traditions were added, during the post-war and post-treaty period, a stake in the "peace constitution," in democratic procedures, and in civil liberties, shared by peasants, professors, women, students, labor union members, and the news media of Japan.

For another thing, the framework of government inherited from the Occupation era was fortunately never so inflexible as to rule out change. Although the Japanese Constitution has not been formally amended, the organic law (like its American counterpart) has permitted informal revision (some examples are cited, below).

On the other hand, the channeling power of law—and the responsibility borne by those who construct such channels—has never been better illustrated than by this experiment. The ironies of history have dictated that conservative governments, which have favored the subsequent American security alliance, have equally leaned toward revision of the Constitution; the opposition, which has opposed the close tie with the United States, has fiercely defended the American-inspired Constitution from any change!

Finally, and this brings us around full circle, beginning about 1948 socio-economic changes within Japan soon made what originally appeared to be an overly idealistic Constitution, a rather more practical organic law. The post-treaty phase of modernization has been marked by further urbanization at a geometric rate of speed, the growth of a new, white-collar, middle class, and almost an obsession with a durable consumer goods boom. The Occupation has been even more dramatically illuminated as an interlude, when what has happened since is taken into account. It was almost as though the Japanese, with American help, had first put up an elaborate but temporary legal scaffolding, within which reconstruction—using largely Japanese materials—resulted in a brand-new social structure.

So far, at least, the Japanese have been able to carry into the present structure a large measure of traditional political behavior with which to protect themselves against the earthquakes of change. But the real test, as between stability and instability, is yet to come. Like other advanced countries, Japan will be able to measure the tensile strength of its post-treaty political institutions only when they are fully subjected to the torque issues of war and peace, gaps between urban and rural ways of life, and desires for individual liberty versus the need for community order.

POLITICS OF CONSTITUTIONAL REVISION IN JAPAN

Despite the relative stability of post-treaty Japanese political institutions, questions about the origins of the Constitution and about the possibility of eventual revision have occupied a significant position in Japan's public life. A brief characterization of the organic law, compared with the Meiji Constitution, will clarify the salient points at issue.[46]

The Meiji Constitution had been granted to the people of Japan by the Emperor. It purported to define the essential nature of the national policy—the *kokutai*—traditionally regarded as located in the "line of emperors unbroken for ages eternal." In the celebrated phrase of the Baron Hozumi Nobushige, it embraced "theocratic, patriarchal constitutionalism." The new Constitution in sharp contrast and in good American phrases began, "We, the Japanese people, acting through our duly elected representatives . . . do proclaim that sovereign power resides with the people and do firmly establish this Constitution." As originally drafted by foreigners, the Preamble was a most explicit and alien doctrine. As had happened before in Japanese history, the legal import was quickly to be Japanized and implemented.

The Meiji system had provided for the execution of laws and ordinances by the Emperor's ministers of state. Beyond doubt the old Constitution favored the executive. The executive was, however, diffuse and complex. The Diet deliberated over laws. The courts were administrative organs operating in the name of the Emperor. Under the new Constitution the Diet, composed entirely of elected representatives, acts as "the highest organ of state power" and is "the law-making organ of the state." Executive power is legally vested in the Cabinet, which is collectively responsible to the Diet. The "whole judicial power" is located in a Supreme Court and inferior courts. In fact, although the Constitution was drafted by Americans, the process of judicial review is the only direct legal import from the United States.

"Rights . . ." in the Meiji Constitution were balanced by ". . . duties of Subjects"; furthermore, rights were subject to public order and could be limited by legislation. The longest section of the new Constitution offers a list of rights which runs well beyond even the American Bill of Rights, and these rights are not limited by legislation.

The most unusual and most controversial feature of the new Constitution—a provision unique in constitutions of the world—is the legal renunciation of war (Article 9). In this article, the Japanese people aspire to international peace and "forever renounce war as a sovereign right of the nation and the threat or use of force as means of settling international disputes." The parallel with the Kellogg-Briand Pact is deliberate. It is said that certain Japanese then left a legal loophole by adding, "In order to accomplish the aim . . ." of the previous paragraph ". . . land, sea and air forces, as well as other war potential will never be maintained."

Turning to the discussion in Japan of origins, effects, and possible changes in the Constitution, it is important first of all to realize that practical politics always guarantees some degree of adjustment. The case of the Japanese Constitution offers no exception. The law has permitted informal revision: covert and then limited rearmament (the official justification lies in the enabling paragraph which, it is argued, permits armed forces for defense); a departure in practice from imported principles of semi-federalism (the movement from local autonomy provided in Chapter 8 to more familiar procedures of a unitary state); and reestablishment to some extent of centralization (of fiscal policy, police control, and education). These were the safety valves which siphoned off some pressure toward outright amendment.

Most often suggested as reasons for change or as specific alterations have been the following: alien authorship in that the Constitution was imposed upon the Japanese people by SCAP; untraditional and unsatisfactory definition of the status of the Emperor and failure to recognize him as the chief of state; the need for more extensive, if limited, armament; and the need for "overall revision of the administrative structure."

The best testimonials to the viability of the Constitution have been the difficulties encountered by a succession of conservative governments bent on revision. They have not been able to alter a single clause, nor have cabinets ever been in a position to sponsor a serious bill of amendment in the Diet. After seven years of study and deliberation, a Commission on the Constitution has endorsed various proposals for constitutional revision. But even the majority of the Commission was fearful that a boycott by the opposition made public support doubtful.

The Government has faced insurmountable obstacles in acting on the recommendations.[47]

In summary, the long-range stability of Japanese political institutions; at the same time, the ability of the Japanese to change and yet remain the same; the genius of this people to meld alien into indigenous and to allow the traditional to co-exist with the modern, these have been some of the clues to Japanese success. Above all, state power and its importance did not have to be learned by the Japanese, as they did by the Chinese, in modern times. As Harold Vinacke put it,

> Japanese traditional conceptions of the nature and purposes of the state and of government were similar to those carried to Japan from the West, while those of China were quite different.[48]

EPILOGUE: THE TWO KOREAS

In this discussion of modern constitutional development in East Asia, the case of Korea (more properly, of the two Koreas) has as usual been neglected and even postponed to the very last, almost as an afterthought. As a matter of fact, experience with the governing of men on the peninsula certainly deserves far more thorough treatment.

One difficulty is, of course, that the people of "the Hermit Kingdom" have been the last to modernize. They are the only ones in the three cultural regions—China, Korea, and Japan—to face the problem of emergence from colonial rule to self-government. Theirs is the briefest experience with constitution-making.

Nevertheless, to the contemporary political scientist the example of Korea ought to represent a case study fascinating enough to generate genuine excitement. The theoretical implications suggested by Korean politics are numerous and intriguing. Indeed, it is a challenge to try to decide what is politically universal in the Korean case, and what is unique.

Even Korean scholars had to have pointed out for them the fact that, in the span of one hundred years, they have made a hazardous journey from a traditional, but unique, East Asian society through colonial rule into two decades of political development as a divided nation. In effect, one traditional Korea and one colony of Japan have been transformed in a relatively short space of time into two Koreas.[49]

The Republic of Korea was born in 1948, following a general election in the South under U.N. supervision. The original Constitution in 1948 has been amended several times, the most significant alteration having been the creation in 1960 of a parliamentary form in place of a presidential form of government. In 1961 this Constitution was suspended by a military junta, and the present Constitution (providing a return to strong presidential form) was approved by national referendum in 1962. So that even in South Korea there has been an interesting variety of constitutional experimentation.

The Democratic People's Republic of Korea was also born in 1948, in theory the result of "nation-wide" general elections but in practice the product of "people's committees," established during the Soviet occupation from 1945 to 1948. Originally the regime leaned to one side, toward the Soviet Union; later, toward the People's Republic of China. Most important, North Korea has increasingly shown a penchant for national individuality (*chuche*). In 1961, Kim Il-sung explained the concept in terms vaguely similar to those used by Chinese Communists, but as applied to Korea. His words were the closest thing to Korean Communist constitutional doctrine:

> By *chuche* we mean that in carrying out our revolution and construction we should creatively apply the general truth of Marxism-Leninism to the specific realities of our country, and precisely and fully take into account our own historical and actual situation, our own capacity and the traditions, requirements and the level of consciousness of our own people.[50]

Indeed, the two Koreas—like the two Chinas and Japan—have illuminated several themes with which we began. The possibility of variations in political structure, relatively independent of changes in other aspects of human behavior, should never be neglected. Political structure, inter-related with ideology, has an overlooked potential for creative, independent impact. Certain goals and overriding values, often idealistically articulated in legal documents, remain important in the process designed for the governing of men. Even within East Asia, where *law* has not always been the very first instrument for ordering the way of life, modern constitutional developments have provided not the *sole* clue (as once claimed) but *one* guide to the varieties and complexities of comparative politics in a cultural region.

UNITED STATES INITIAL POSTSURRENDER POLICY FOR JAPAN

By John M. Maki*

I

It is the purpose of this essay to examine the background and origins, the content and the consequences of "United States Initial Postsurrender Policy for Japan," certainly one of the outstanding papers relating to foreign affairs produced by the United States government in the quarter of a century following the end of the Second World War.[1] It was the foundation in policy of the occupation of Japan, as it can be viewed narrowly as a military operation conducted by a victorious army in the land of a defeated enemy. But it also played a major role in the transformation of relations between the United States and Japan.

It was almost half a century of increasingly bitter rivalry and critical tension between the United States and Japan that brought about the war, made inevitable because the two countries discovered that it was impossible to resolve by peaceful means the conflict in policy and the clash of national interests between them. The war itself resolved in blood the basic issues between the two countries, but "United States Initial Postsurrender Policy for Japan" initiated a new relationship that dramatically transformed rivalry and tension into friendship and alliance.

The brief compass of this policy paper also contained what was regarded at the time as a highly idealistic and therefore most unrealistic

---

*Vice-Dean, College of Arts and Sciences, University of Massachusetts (Amherst), and a former colleague of Dr. Vinacke.

plan for what amounted to a broad reordering of a complex society, a reordering so sweeping that it could be described as revolutionary. Had the Japanese government come forth in 1945 with a "Six-Year Plan" —the effective life of the occupation governed by the policy paper was approximately six years—embodying the goals, means and methods set forth in occupation policy no one would have taken it seriously even though it would have been autonomously formulated to achieve self-selected goals. What added to the apparent unreality of the document was that it had been drafted by a foreign government to be imposed on an alien and defeated nation. Yet the experiment in social engineering came off with amazing ease and success.

To understand the total context out of which this American policy grew it is necessary to examine briefly the manner in which the diplomacies and the foreign policies of the two nations drew them over the brink and into war. The peculiar circumstances surrounding the manner in which the war eventually came to an end helped to mold the content of the policy. Central to an understanding of the nature of the document is an analysis of its content which, obviously today, not so obviously in 1945, also had a great bearing on the eventual and rapid success of the policy. Finally, I shall attempt to account briefly for its success.

II

When the United States and Japan initiated formal diplomatic relations with each other with the signing of the Treaty of Kanagawa on March 31, 1854, the product of three weeks of adroit diplomatic negotiations on both sides (Commodore Perry is always credited with considerable diplomatic skill, but little is heard of the skill of his opposite numbers), the United States was barely three-quarters of a century old as an independent nation, while Japan had behind it more than twelve centuries of recorded history and a still undetermined additional number of centuries of unwritten history as both a people and a nation. But the treaty only marked the beginning of the entry of the older nation into the comity of nations, while the younger one was still only a lively participant in international affairs, not a leading power.

By 1900, less than fifty years later, the two nations had begun to confront each other with growing suspicion and nascent enmity. The fundamental reason was simple: two young modern nation-states, both on the verge of entering the arena of world politics as recognized powers, because of their respective views of their "manifest destinies" and because of their consciousness of their emerging military might became aware that they were developing collision-course policies on an issue of common concern, China.

The "old" young nation-state, Japan, had in the brief span of twenty-five years between 1870 and 1895 passed successfully through the formative stages of political, economic and social modernization, including the creation of what for the times were small, but modern and efficient, national military forces. Japan had passed with flying colors the first major test of its new-found national power and of its new military forces when it fought and won a war against Imperial China in 1894-95. It mattered little that China was on its last legs and in no position to defend itself even against such a newcomer in international politics as Japan. The important thing was that Japan had demonstrated conclusively that it was able to play the basic game of power politics, namely, to fight and win a war and reap the fruits of victory.

By 1900 the "young" young nation-state, the United States, had gone through the formative and creative stages of its own modernization. It sat securely astride its segment of a broad continent. It had developed its characteristic government and political institutions. It had transformed its economy from agrarian-commercial to agrarian-commercial-industrial. It was a contributing participant in the ongoing Industrial Revolution. It, too, had won its war against a decaying imperial state, Spain, in 1898, a war that had given the country a colonial foothold in East Asia, the Philippines, neighbor to Taiwan, the island Japan had won from China three years earlier.

The issue of common concern to the two nations was China, first Imperial and then Republican. Japan not only won a war in 1895, but also established a relationship with China that was to last for half a century. Henceforth Japanese foreign policy was built around the central core of expanding the country's economic, political and military influence in a weak and defenseless China. In parallel the United States consistently opposed Japan in defense of its own interests in China and of China itself, and ultimately stood against the general phenomenon of aggression of which Japan's was only a specific manifestation. And in the middle lay a China unable to administer its internal affairs and to protect itself against the designs of other nations. China's impotence was the result of unplanned and uncontrollable historical developments in the country itself and of its position within a newly developed and developing framework of international politics.

The pattern of Japanese action against China and of American reaction against Japan began with the enunciation of the "Open Door" policy, or equality of foreign commercial opportunity, in the notes of

1899. Japan's victory four years earlier had opened the floodgates to both Japanese and European expansion in a collapsing China. The American advocacy of the Open Door was an attempt to safeguard the treaty-based rights and interests of a nation not participating in the carving of the Chinese melon. Of far greater significance the policy of equality of commercial opportunity remained the cornerstone of American policy toward China down to 1941 and consequently an unresolvable difficulty in Japanese-American relations.

In 1922 at the Washington Conference, called by the United States in an attempt to settle the East Asian issues created by the First World War and left unresolved by the Versailles treaty, the United States and Japan in concert with the other powers apparently arrived at a resolution of the tensions that by 1920 had assumed disturbingly dangerous levels. Japan's twenty-one demands on China in 1915, the disputes and irritations between the two countries in the unhappy Siberian Intervention, an American immigration policy that was both anti-Asian and anti-Japanese, and above all the fact that both nations had arrived as world powers by 1918 had sharpened the rivalry and the conflict of policy that had existed for a quarter of a century. The naval limitation treaty signed at Washington seemed to make it strategically almost impossible for the two countries to wage war against each other, but of even greater significance the Nine Power Pact concerning China apparently removed the main cause of dispute between the two countries. The United States and Japan and six other countries (China itself being the ninth power) pledged themselves "to respect the sovereignty, the independence, and the territorial and administrative integrity of China" and to establish effectually and maintain the "principle of equal opportunity for commerce and industry of all nations throughout the territory of China."

The basic assumption behind the Washington settlement was the simple and realistic one that if the internal problems of China, already critical for seventy-five years at the time of the conference, could be solved by the Chinese themselves then all tensions which had developed for decades between and among the powers, first Western alone and then with the added company of Japan, would disappear. There was nothing wrong with the assumption in 1922; even Japan freely committed itself to abandon the policy of massive intervention in China's affairs that it had been following for more than a quarter of a century.

In spite of its apparent logical and practical soundness the Washington settlement endured as a controlling factor of Asian international politics for less than ten years. Although it remained in existence on paper, as a working political arrangement it went down the drain with dramatic suddenness on September 18, 1931, when Japan's Kwantung Army, the garrison force in the Kwantung Leased Territory in the southern tip of Manchuria, instituted the military operations that resulted in the breaking away of all of Manchuria from Chinese control and the establishment of the puppet government of "Manchoukuo" which ruled territory that was a Japanese colony in every respect save name.

The tragic story of the Manchurian Incident or Crisis has been told and retold. For present purposes it is necessary to state in summary form only that it marked the collapse of the Nine Power Pact, demonstrated the inability of the League of Nations to handle the kind of breakdown of international peace and security it was supposed to deal with, inaugurated the series of events in world politics that led directly into the Second World War, and as the climax of a third of a century of rivalry and tension brought the United States and Japan to a confrontation that was to lead inevitably to war between them.

The sweeping international significance of the Manchurian crisis was matched by the Japanese domestic political developments with which it was coupled. Inside Japan the actions of the Kwantung Army led to a kind of perverted declaration of independence of the Japanese armed forces, particularly the army, from the control of the rest of the Japanese government. From 1931 to 1936 the army developed a dominant and controlling role for itself—carrying along the Navy as well—in government, in politics and within the society itself. From 1936 onward the army, the navy and their civilian supporters in high and low places carried out a foreign policy based increasingly on the instrumentality of military force and created an authoritarian order of government and politics at home. Thus, a Japanese policy based on force had a broad impact on Asia, on Japan's relations with the United States, and on the whole pattern of world politics that was leading inevitably to general war. The tragic course toward the Second World War began in 1931, but the outbreak of general if undeclared war between China and Japan in the summer of 1937 greatly accelerated the coming of the holocaust. It was in September of 1939 that Japan's allies, Nazi Germany and Fascist Italy, fired the first shots in Europe.

In the Manchurian Crisis, as earlier, the United States reacted when Japan moved against China. Early in January, 1932, Henry L. Stimson, then Secretary of State, enunciated what became famous as the Stimson doctrine of non-recognition under which the U.S. refused to recognize any Japanese act which might impair the treaty rights of the U.S. and its citizens in China or violate the Open Door policy. It was this doctrine that remained the central and unchanging element of American policy toward Japan—and China—until the bombs fell on Pearl Harbor.

The decade of crisis in United States-Japanese relations from 1931 to 1941 continued the pattern of Japanese action and American reaction, but with constantly mounting seriousness. Japanese acts after 1937 came to be increasingly directed against Americans and their interests in China. Also Japanese actions and pressures went beyond China, notably into Southeast Asia after the fall of France and the Low Countries in 1940. Japan's alliance with Germany and Italy seemed to grow rapidly into a global menace—military and political—to the United States, its interests, and its ideals (whether real or mythical).

By the spring of 1941 it was perfectly clear that the two governments were set on a collision course; words and policies had collided long since, but now the peril was that of the clash of arms. It was the commitment of both sides to policies that each regarded as sound and correct that was providing an ever-mounting momentum driving both toward war. The secret conversations that began in Washington in April, 1941, were futile because they obviously failed in their objective which was to prevent war. But the conversations were profitable in the sense that they demonstrated beyond challenge that an accommodation of views and policies was truly impossible. Accommodation could have been achieved only if one side or the other had conceded on a matter or matters that by December 7, 1941, had been clearly established as issues on which there could be no compromise. Only a drastic change in the leadership of either country could have possibly brought about a modification of position and policy sufficient to avoid war. The realities of Japan's authoritarian political system and the democratic practices and procedures of the American system operated effectively to bar a sudden and dramatic change in leadership. The only thing that was surprising about the outbreak of war between the United States and Japan was the manner in which the first shot was fired, the attack on Pearl Harbor.

Japan had devised a policy toward China which, it was convinced, served Japan's economic, political and diplomatic interests, the broad interests of China (if China would only understand), and even the interests of world peace. The United States had devised a policy toward China which, of necessity, was also a policy against Japan. China, a generation of policy makers had held, must be permitted to solve its own problems in its own way and must be protected against external interference and exploitation. After 1931 the Japan toward which American policy was directed seemed not only to be vastly accelerating its interference and exploitation, in violation of its treaty commitments entered into at the Washington conference, but also doing it by means of naked military aggression which was tearing down the flimsy framework created after the First World War to guarantee international peace and security. Furthermore, Japan's own government was both militaristic and authoritarian, guilty not only of external aggression, but also of domestic oppression.

The situation was classic: two powers confronting each other, each following a policy that, it was convinced, was both in its own national interest and moral by its own definition, one possessing the power to wage war and the other with an enormous potential for doing so, and neither willing to accept or to tolerate the policy and the actions of the other. The clash of policies had reached its logical climax with war being the only resolution.

The future course of relations between the two countries had to be determined through the arbitrament of arms. Only a truly decisive war could bring about the reconciliation of interests and the possible discovery of a broad commonality of purpose between the two governments and the two peoples. Few discerned even the possibility of such a resolution of the clash of national policy and of national interest in the course of the bitter war between the two countries.

III

This long and circuitous detour into the past has been necessary in order to get into position to address the problem of "United States Initial Postsurrender Policy for Japan." The thrust behind this policy paper originated in the prewar course of relations between the United States and Japan.

To understand "United States Initial Postsurrender Policy for Japan" we must start from two elementary and obvious facts: 1) it was necessarily produced by the war between the United States and Japan which was a major element of the far broader multilateral conflict of the Second World War; and 2) it was, obviously, the United States government that produced it. The first fact has a great deal to do with the manner in which the policy came into being; the second has even more to do with its content.

Shocked as the United States was by the attack on Pearl Harbor, there was never any doubt, governmental or public, that the war would end in anything but a complete victory for the United States. Indeed, it has long been accepted as a truism that the great but unintended consequence of the Pearl Harbor attack was the instant commitment of the nation to exact payment in the form of complete victory. As President Franklin D. Roosevelt declared in his message to Congress on December 8, 1941: "No matter how long it may take us . . . the American people in their righteous might will win through to absolute victory." In more precise strategic terms this determination was based on the assumption that for Japan the course of the war could be described very briefly: invasion, defeat and occupation. Even though Hitler was the principal enemy and his defeat was given first strategic priority, the Japanese enemy was subjected to relentless and constantly mounting military pressure from the late summer of 1942 onward.

It was this determination that led the United States government through the Department of State to begin as early as the spring of 1942 a study of the problems relating to an occupation of Japan more than three years prior to the formal statement of postsurrender policy itself. Note that the study was initiated long before anyone anywhere had any clear idea of when the war might come to an end or under what circumstances. We are indebted to Dr. Hugh Borton, one of the principal actors in the drama, for a general account of the evolution of the surrender policy. He notes, for example, that he and his colleagues were able consistently over many months to consider some fundamental issues: the postwar objectives of the United States in relation to Japan, the political objectives of a military government in the country, and the role and powers of the Emperor after defeat.

As the war progressed, and as the end in both Europe and Asia seemed—correctly—to be approaching, the United States government took an apparently minor but extremely significant step: the creation of the State, War, Navy Coordinating Committee (SWNCC) which was charged with the responsibility of formulating recommendations to the Secretary of State "on questions having both military and political aspects." This was the recognition in formal organizational terms that the total war of 1941-45 was not being fought as a purely military conflict without any overtones and objectives of a political nature. As Professor Borton tells us, it was the Far Eastern sub-committee of SWNCC, formed January 5, 1945, that became responsible for the drawing up of a policy for a postwar Japan. Significantly, the members of this sub-committee were officals in all three Departments who had previously been involved in drafting the preliminary policy papers on Japan.

The sub-committee did not know it, but it had less than eight months following its formation to produce a policy paper of major import. Also its members were in darkness regarding another development that was to hasten the end of the war and, consequently, the conclusion of their labors. That was, of course, the drive to perfect the atomic bombs in time for use against the enemy, barring some completely unforeseeable military or political development.

Behind these two highly disparate events—the bureaucratic act of establishing a committee and the massive process of creating the A-bomb—lay a clear military fact: since the late summer of 1944 the Japanese could no longer hope for a successful conclusion of the war—no matter how they might try to define "successful." Stated even more positively, the defeat of Japan was assured, even though no one could predict either when it might take place or under what circumstances. It was this fundamental military fact that began gradually and slowly to draw three quite different policy problems together at the top levels of the United States government and in impenetrable secrecy: the possibility of bringing the war against Japan to an end prior to an invasion (or, more broadly, by political rather than military means), the use of the A-bomb to knock Japan out of the war, and a postwar policy for a defeated Japan.

The end of the war in Europe on May 8, 1945, meant that the Allies were confronted with only one strategic problem, a vastly difficult, complex and potentially costly operation, the invasion of Japan. But beyond that lay the still invisible issue of the availability and use of the atomic bomb. On June 1, 1945, a special civilian committee recommended to President Truman that the atomic bomb be used against Japan provided that it was ready while the war was still going on. On the basis of the material which is available on the deliberations of the committee—it was called simply the Interim Committee—it is not possible to determine the degree to which their recommendation was influenced by the hope that the use of the bomb would hasten the end of the war. On the other hand, it is clear that its use was thought of in terms of the general military situation, centering on the coming invasion, and so it is reasonable to assume that the possibility of shortening the war was at least discussed seriously even though it may not have been the controlling element.

But Japan's military plight and the imminence of what was considered to be a most costly invasion for both sides thrust forward the possibility of devising an alternative means of ending the hostilities. As Henry L. Stimson, then Secretary of War, stated the problem later:

"The principal, political, social, and military objective of the United States in the summer of 1945 was the prompt and complete surrender of Japan." In the pursuit of that objective he prepared a memorandum for President Truman in consultation with Acting Secretary of State Joseph C. Grew and Secretary of the Navy James Forrestal. This memorandum was transmitted to the President on July 2, 1945. However, according to Professor Borton's firsthand account in his *American Presurrender Planning for Postwar Japan*, the origin of the Stimson document was actually within the Far Eastern subcommittee of SWNCC, where the State Department members had prepared the document which members of Stimson's staff presumably used to draft the memorandum which went over his signature to the President. At any rate, both it and the earlier SWNCC paper were among the documents taken by the American delegation to the Potsdam Conference.

On July 17, 1945, the Potsdam Conference opened with two major items on the agenda: 1) political issues either growing out of the war in Europe or developing subsequent to its end; and 2) agreement on the plans for the prosecution of the war against Japan in the decisive stage which was soon to begin, with the invasion of the island of Kyushu scheduled for early November. Meanwhile, the news of the successful atomic test held at Alamogordo on July 16 was immediately flashed to President Truman, who relayed it to his fellow heads of government. On July 26 the three heads of the principal governments then at war against Japan—Truman for the United States, Churchill for the United Kingdom and Chiang Kai-shek for the Republic of China—with the still secret concurrence of Stalin issued the Potsdam Declaration.

The contents of the Potsdam Declaration can be described simply: 1) a warning to Japan to get out of the war or face "complete destruction of the Japanese armed forces" and "the utter devastation of the Japanese homeland"; and 2) a listing of what the Japanese government and people could expect in the way of military, territorial, political, economic and social changes at the hands of the victorious allies. There was no reference even to the existence of the atomic bomb, let alone a threat to use it against Japan. The essence of the Potsdam Declaration was furnished by the American delegation, but whether the immediate source was the SWNCC paper or the Stimson statement is still unclear. What is clear beyond question is that no other signatory of the Potsdam Declaration either brought about a significant alteration of an American-originated point or contributed directly to the content of the Declaration.

The Potsdam Declaration was not heeded by the Japanese government. The consequence was the series of shattering events that culminated in the final acceptance by the Japanese government of the Allied surrender terms embodied in the Declaration. It has been regarded by the Japanese government, international lawyers and all students of the occupation as the controlling document for the occupation because, quite simply, it embodies what the Japanese government agreed to when it finally surrendered.

For the purposes of this discussion it is of equal importance that the organic relationship between the Potsdam Declaration and the "United States Initial Postsurrender Policy for Japan" be recognized. Because of this relationship the Japanese government in accepting the Declaration bound itself, in effect, to abide by American policy. The relationship, further, meant that the Japanese were never in a position in which they might have argued for rejection or at least nonacceptance of an item of American policy on the grounds that it was not a part of the understanding embodied in the Declaration.

IV

When the surrender documents were formally signed on September 2, 1945, on the deck of the U.S.S. *Missouri*, anchored in Tokyo Bay, the occupation formally began and American postsurrender policy became operative. At this point it seemed obvious that both situation and policy conformed precisely to the classical pattern: a mighty and arrogant victorious occupation army with its heel crushingly on the neck of recently defeated and humiliated people and government which, in their own way, only a few years earlier had been as mighty and as arrogant and apparently as victorious in other lands.

Yet as both immediate and more distant events were to demonstrate conclusively, the pattern just described, though accurate, was only half of a far wider picture. The more visible half was traditional, historical and predictable; the emergent half was innovative (brilliantly so in some respects), perhaps a unique and, in the context of the times, unpredictable event.

The ultimate objectives of the "United States Initial Postsurrender Policy for Japan" statement and the means to achieve those objectives were stated briefly, directly and clearly. The objectives were only two; the means but four. One set of objectives and related means was expected and predictable; the other unexpected and unpredicted.

The first objective was simple: "to insure that Japan will not again become a menace to the United States or to the peace and security of the world." The two means were equally simple. First, Japan's territory

was to be limited to what might loosely be termed its historical boundaries, namely, the four principal islands plus a fringe of closely nearby
and minor islands. The second means consisted of the two "D's": disarmament and demilitarization. The expanded treatment of the means
clearly revealed the classical pattern: (1) wresting away of territory,
all of which (except for those areas under military occupation by the
Japanese to which the government had never laid legal claim) had been
internationally recognized as legally controlled by Japan, though the
basis of the claim varied from a right bestowed by history, through international agreement arrived at through normal diplomatic negotiation, to control gained—and, again, recognized in international law—by
the threat or use of force; (2) elimination of the means—the weapons and
the military units and all supporting activities—by which the Japanese
had waged war; (3) punitive measures against individuals considered to
have been responsible for the policies and actions which had involved
Japan in war against her Asian neighbors, the power that defeated her,
and many other peoples; (4) suppression of institutions "expressive of
the spirit of militarism and aggression"; and finally, with apparently
hopeless naivete, (5) the attack on the spirit (read: cultural, social and
historical beliefs and attitudes) of militarism itself. In brief, this was
the reflex action against a hated and recently defeated enemy.

But the policy statement went farther, listing a number of detailed
steps that were to be a part of the broader means. For example, under
disarmament and demilitarization the following steps were specified:
denial to Japan of "an army, navy, air force, secret police organization, or any civil aviation"; disarming and dissolution of all armed
forces on every level of command; surrender and destruction of all air-
craft, warships, war material and installations; detention of all military and naval officers of high rank, and "leaders of ultra-nationalist
and militarist organizations and other important exponents of militarism and aggression"; removal and exclusion of any "active exponents of militarism and militant nationalism" from public office and
"from any other position of public or substantial private responsibility"; dissolution and prohibition of ultranationalistic or militaristic organizations of all kinds; elimination of anything related to militarism
and ultranationalism from education; the barring of career military
officers and all supporters of militarism and ultranationalism from positions in education; and the destruction of the "existing economic basis
of Japanese military strength."

The detailed program of action outlined above reveals clearly the
care with which the policy planners thought through the processes by

which the general objectives of the occupation could be achieved. Here, as elsewhere, the articulation between broad policy and specific actions was spelled out with the result that when the policy was actually implemented there was a logic and coherence linking policy and action that made the achievement of objectives almost automatic.

It was assumed that disarmament could be accomplished rapidly and effectively because it would be done through the instrumentality of the occupation and because it was essentially a mechanical operation—the final dissolution of Japan's military might, already significantly eroded through the action of war itself. However, it was further assumed that the process of demilitarization would be a slow and gradual one, because it would depend on a basic shift in Japanese attitudes, indeed, in either a destruction of—or a dramatic change in—a system of values deeply embedded in Japanese history and tradition and firmly based on two generations of active indoctrination through mass education and the mass media. But the Japanese people's traumatic experience with war went deeper than anyone assumed, and their rejection of war and all that it stood for was complete and virtually instantaneous with the end of the war. The happy result was that demilitarization was as rapid and as complete as disarmament.

The third "D", democratization, was embodied in the statement of the second principal objective of occupation policy:

> To bring about the eventual establishment of a peaceful and responsible government which will respect the rights of other states and will support the objectives of the United States as reflected in the ideals and principles of the Charter of the United Nations. The United States desires that this government should conform as closely as may be to principles of democratic self-government but it is not the responsibility of the Allied Powers to impose upon Japan any form of government not supported by the freely expressed will of the people.

Here is a clear departure from the traditional pattern of the relation between the conqueror and the conquered. In the first place, this objective explicitly brings out the political foundation of disarmament and demilitarization by stating that the government should eventually be a "peaceful and responsible" one, respectful of the rights of other states, and that it also "should conform as closely as may be to principles of democratic self-government."

It has frequently been stated that this declaration is based on the naive and historically inaccurate assumption that democratic governments are less prone to go to war than non-democratic governments have been. This statement may be true, but it overlooks the ruling consideration in the case of Japan in 1945. For half a century a form of government that by the historical record had been demonstrated to be neither peaceful nor responsible (in the technical political sense) had controlled the people of Japan and had led them to the unhappy state they were in. In logical terms the issue was simple: if a non-peaceful, non-responsible government had taken Japan over the course that it had covered, then the alternative had to be to encourage the emergence of a peaceful and responsible government. Whether or not such a government would respect the rights of other states and would not be a threat to the peace and security of the world could only be determined by the course of the future history.

The second departure from the traditional victor-vanquished pattern was the statement of self-denial to the effect that it was "not the responsibility of the Allied Powers to impose upon Japan any form of government." In addition, there was the supplementary key provision that any new form of government, including that envisaged in the policy itself, should be supported "by the freely expressed will of the people," a fundamental consideration in any democratic political system. Yet the seeming leniency and generosity of these statements immediately raise a serious question.

Logicians of politics can quickly pounce on a contradiction in two elements of occupation policy relating to the political future of Japan. In the first place, it was U.S. policy to eliminate from Japan all traces of militarism and of ultranationalism, including, of course, all of the institutions supportive of them. This removed the status quo from the alternatives on which the Japanese people would be allowed to exercise the democratic freedom of political choice. Therefore, the strict logician could argue, this in itself cut the ground from under the occupation's objective of leading the Japanese in the direction of democratization. However, in the real world of 1945 it was impossible for the United States government to allow the Japanese people the option of continuing to support the kind of militaristic and authoritarian government under which they had suffered so much. Events quickly demonstrated that once they were confronted with a genuine alternative, namely, the kind of democracy envisaged under U.S. policy, the Japanese had no difficulty at all in opting for it. It was the reality of the free political act of choice that eliminated the appearance of logical contradiction.

The basic means by which the goal of democratization was to be achieved was briefly stated in the postsurrender policy statement: "The Japanese people shall be encouraged to develop a desire for individual liberties and respect for fundamental human rights, particularly the freedom of religion, assembly, speech, and the press. They shall also be encouraged to form democratic and representative organizations." Again, the paper entered into detail as to the nature of this basic means. On the negative side, military and civilian leaders, societies, institutions, laws, and government agencies which had created, operated and sustained the former authoritarian system were to be removed from office and positions of influence, abolished, altered, or suspended. Their continued presence would at least have seriously inhibited the development of democracy. Not only as a matter of history had they prevented the development of democratic tendencies, but their continuation was both theoretically and practically incompatible with the achievement of the goal of democratization.

On the positive side a number of steps were to be taken, some without reference to Japanese desires in the matter. Freedom of religious worship was to be proclaimed immediately on the institution of the occupation. The Japanese people were to be given the "opportunity and encouraged to become familiar with the history, institutions, culture, and the accomplishments of the United States and the other democracies." This aim reflected the fact that since about 1930 the Japanese people through government censorship and control of the press had been progressively isolated from the broad stream of international discourse on all levels, whether it might be free access to news no matter how significant or insignificant, or the broad sharing of information and ideas in the sciences, both natural and social, or the dissemination and discussion of political, economic, social and philosophical thought. Looking toward the future, the objective here was to provide the Japanese people with both the information and the attitudes that would enable them to go about contributing to the new democracy envisaged for them.

Democratic political parties were to be encouraged with, of course, the necessary and concomitant rights of assembly and freedom of discussion. Laws, discriminatory on the "ground of race, nationality, creed or political opinion," were to be abrogated. Political prisoners were to be released. The judicial, legal and police systems were to be reformed to the end that they would "protect individual liberties and civil rights."

All of these positive steps in the direction of political democracy were clear reflections of two things: 1) the American concept of what the principal features of a democratic political society should be; and 2) the nature of contemporary democracy, no matter what national society it might be sheltered in. It was the former that was responsible for the presence of these positive items in postsurrender policy; it was the latter on which the hope for a Japanese variation on the theme of democracy was based. For if Japan were to become democratic, it would have to be because universal characteristics of modern democracy would be adaptable to the requirements of Japanese society, not because they also happened to be American.

We have already seen that American policy realistically took into account the fact that disarmament and demilitarization could never be effectively realized if they were held to be operative only in an isolatable segment of Japanese society to which some such phrase as "military activity" could be applied. These two "D's" had to be supported by the third of democracy. This clearly demonstrated the awareness of American policy makers of the multidimensional characteristic of disarmament and demilitarization.

"United States Initial Postsurrender Policy for Japan" paid due respect to the economic dimension of the treatment of the defeated enemy, even though it was not formulated as a third broad objective. However, the relationship between Japan's future economy and the two broad objectives was made abundantly clear.

Naturally, the policy paper dealt with economic disarmament, namely, the prevention or control of all economic activity, ranging from research through production, which might contribute to the maintenance or future development of an aggressively inclined military establishment. This was simply a realistic recognition of the fact that a nation's military power consists not only of its military forces in being but of the total potential capacity of the society to wage war, particularly its overall economic potential.

Yet it is a matter of great significance that what occupation policy envisaged for Japan in the economic sphere was most emphatically not economic strangulation. Although the two basic objectives of the policy said nothing at all about economics, it is of great moment that one of the four principal means for the achievement of those objectives was purely economic. It read simply: "The Japanese people shall be afforded opportunity to develop for themselves an economy which will permit the peacetime requirements of the population to be met." By no stretch of the imagination can this be interpreted to imply the economic strangulation of either the people or the society.

Here a mere outline of the specific points of economic policy aimed toward satisfying the peacetime requirements of the people may be given: encouragement of democratically based organizations in labor, industry and agriculture; favoring of policies permitting a "wide distribution of income and of the ownership of the means of production and trade"; the dissolution of the "large industrial and banking combinations which have exercised control of a great part of Japan's trade and industry" (i.e., the zaibatsu); the eventual resumption of normal trade relations with the rest of the world, which would allow purchase of raw materials and other goods and the export of manufactured products; and a generous reparations policy which provided that no serious drain be placed on a peaceful Japanese economy. The aim of the economic segment of American occupation policy was to be realistic about Japan's future economic requirements, not to pamper the just-defeated enemy. The policy made it perfectly clear that the Japanese were responsible for their own economic plight and therefore bore the burden for getting out of it and for reordering and redirecting their own economy.

Although the policy paper made no explicit statement on the point, it was clearly apparent that the objective of democratization (indeed, any kind of political stability) would be unattainable in a society in which the people were not enabled to achieve a level of economic well-being sufficient to satisfy both the physiological and psychological demands of life.

"United States Initial Postsurrender Policy for Japan" placed no emphasis on social reform or social change, to the point where either was dealt with specifically as an objective, or a means. However, it is perfectly obvious that if disarmament and demilitarization and democratization (including economic, as well as political) were achieved by the means outlined in the policy paper, the overall and inevitable consequence would be a far-reaching reordering of many aspects of Japanese society, including its system of values.

Here it might be well to pause to examine a few of the broad consequences of occupation policy as they were either stated or implied:

1.   A drastic shift in Japanese leadership through the elimination of militarists and their civilian supporters.

2.   A fundamental alteration in an area of the system of values through disarmament and demilitarization.

3.   A broad change in the structure and form of goverment.

4.   A new theoretical basis for both government and politics, actually a shift in political ideology.

5.   A fostering of new political institutions.

6.   The creation of a new relationship between the governing and the governed.

7.   Broad changes in the legal and judicial systems.

8. Drastic changes in the structure of the economy through the elimination of the zaibatsu.

9. The establishment of economic democracy.

10. Alterations in the political and geographical boundaries of the country.

11. Changes in the content of education.

12. A new pattern of relations with the rest of the world.

Even this partial listing of what was both explicit and implicit in occupation policy shows the extent of change that was envisaged for the society of the defeated Japanese enemy. What was very clear was what was in the mind of the victorious United States. What was very unclear was the nature of the possible Japanese reaction to the massive change that had been planned by the victor.

Here it is necessary to go back to the policy paper for a brief examination of the highly important issue of the manner in which the policy was to be implemented. This problem was dealt with in a major section of the paper dealing with the authority vested in both the occupation and in the Japanese government. In the first place, the occupation was to be unambiguously military in the classical style. There was no intent to temper its military, political or psychological impact on the government or the people. It was made equally clear that the United States would play a leading and dominant role in it, while acting in the interests of the nations allied with it in the war against Japan. And the command of the occupation was to be in the hands of a Supreme Commander to be designated by the United States government, which meant unavoidably that he would be a high United States military officer.

But there was a highly significant element: the Japanese government would continue in existence and would be responsible for the administration of the affairs of the country. However, it was made clear beyond question that the Supreme Commander would subject the authority of the Japanese government to his control and that he would "possess all powers necessary to effectuate the surrender terms and to carry out the policies established for the conduct of the occupation and the control of Japan." In brief, the Supreme Commander would be responsible for the administration of American occupation policy.

Nevertheless, it was clearly set forth that the Japanese government was permitted, though under the Supreme Commander's instructions, "to exercise the normal powers of government in matters of domestic administration." It was further provided that the Supreme Commander would exercise his power and authority through the Japanese government, that is to say, the occupation would not directly administer the affairs of the country. At the same time, he was empowered to act directly in the event that "the Emperor or other Japanese authority does not satisfactorily meet the requirements of the Supreme Commander in effectuating the surrender terms."

However, it was made abundantly clear that the continuation of the Japanese government at the pleasure of the occupation did not bring with it support of that government by the occupation. Bluntly, the policy paper stated: "The policy is to use the existing form of Government in Japan, not to support it." The policy went so far as to state that in the event that the Japanese people resorted to force in order to bring about the elimination of "feudal and authoritarian tendencies" the "Supreme Commander should intervene only where necessary to ensure the security of his forces and the attainment of all other objectives of the occupation."

The clarity and precision with which the occupation-Japanese government relationship was defined did much both to establish and to maintain a working arrangement that clearly served the best interests of both parties. On the one hand, the occupation was absolutely sure and confident of its power to direct, guide, persuade and, if necessary, to force the Japanese government to act to the end of converting occupation policy into reality. On the other hand, the continued existence and operation of the Japanese government assured both leaders and people that they had escaped the ultimate humiliation of a military occupation—the complete loss of control over the administration of their own affairs. Though the government was not sovereign and not independent, it still possessed the not inconsiderable degree of autonomy that was expressed in its continued capacity to act—even though within defined limits—on its own behalf and in behalf of its people.

The occupation possessed not only authority but also power—power in all senses, military, political, personal in the form of the Supreme Commander—but it necessarily had to deal with a Japanese entity, one with a will though obviously not a free one. Yet this legal and political relationship was reinforced by a further development that followed with logical necessity from the retention of the Japanese government. From the beginning there was both discussion and negotiation between the occupation and the Japanese government. Even on those occasions where the occupation acted with the greatest apparent degree of arbitrariness, the purge—the barring from public life of militarists and their civilian supporters—and the drafting of the new constitution, the voice of the Japanese government was heard. There was no mistaking the fact that it did not like what it was being forced to do and was doing it only reluctantly; but this was both psychologically and politically a situation far different from the completely arbitrary exercise of power in which the weaker partner has no alternative but dumbly to accept the dictate of the powerful. We may note that it was the Japanese position that prevailed in respect to the purge, which to all intents and purposes came to an end five years after its institution. In addition, the Japanese government was able to introduce certain modifications in detail, at least, in the draft constitution. More significant is the fact that what is frequently termed in Japan the "occupation-imposed constitution" was fully accepted by the Japanese, if acceptance of a constitution is to be measured by the absence of amendment.

Here it is necessary to return briefly to the 1895-1945 span of American-Japanese relations. It is clear that the intent of American postwar policy toward Japan was aimed at breaking the historical mold of their relations. A disarmed Japan would not only cease to be a threat to the peace and security of the United States; it could no longer think realistically of itself as a rival of the United States in terms of national power. A demilitarized Japan would no longer think and act in terms of the utilization of military power to achieve self-determined objectives in its foreign policy. A democratic Japan would hopefully find more in common with a democratic United States and would be more inclined to act responsibly in its relations with all other nations, responsibly in the sense that it would remain within any general framework of international peace and security that might be established.

China's civil war that took place within the years spanned by the occupation removed that country as a source of American-Japanese friction—but that is another story.

V

To conclude this rambling essay this writer must address himself, however briefly, to the obvious and central question: why did American policy, as embodied in "United States Initial Postsurrender Policy for Japan," turn out to be so highly successful? It was successful for the simple reason that the objectives of the policy were achieved.

It seems that the listing of the main elements of the answer is so simple as to verge on a redundant statement of the obvious. First, the U.S. had a clear view of its ultimate objective toward the Japanese enemy. Within days of Pearl Harbor it was both stated and understood that the United States was committed to inflicting a crushing defeat on Japan, so crushing as to eliminate that nation as a threat to the

security of the U.S. that it had been for half a century. It was this gener-
alized aim that was converted easily, almost automatically, into the
two more specifically stated objectives of the double D's, demilitarization and disarmament, and the basic political goal of democratization.

Another circumstance of great utility was the fact that the policy
planners had almost exactly three years to work on various aspects
of what eventually turned out to be a policy for a defeated enemy.
Here the benefit was not simply the gift of calendar time, but the opportunity to evolve policy, to reflect upon its content and its implications, and finally to sharpen it to fit a situation in the world of actual
military and political events: ending the war by means short of an actual invasion and the handling of a freshly surrendered enemy.

There is also the obvious fact that the policy was initiated and developed by a singularly able group of men. Only men of great intellectual power, political realism, deep insight into the problems of society,
and a practical awareness of economic realities could have produced
such a basically sound policy. Another vital ingredient in their makeup
was a firm awareness of the dictates of their country's national interest,
tempered—and this is rare indeed—with an equal awareness of the
eventual role that the defeated enemy was to play in world affairs, to
say nothing of its ability to absorb the drastic and dramatic changes
that were being planned for it. Unfortunately, we know too few of the
names of the participants in the drama. Stimson, Grew and Borton have
been mentioned here. But behind and around them were others whose
names should long since have been made a part of the public record.

In addition, there were two other considerations relating to the actual policy. First, there was its comprehensiveness; and then its firm
realism. It was comprehensive in two senses: first, the problem of the
occupation was dealt with as a whole; military, political, economic,
social and diplomatic facets of the transformation of Japan were not
only recognized but also dealt with as the interrelated phenomena
they actually were. Another aspect of comprehensiveness is the demonstrated fact that there was nothing omitted from the basic policy that
would have served to impede the development of the overall plan. To
put the point directly: implementation of the occupation policy never
had to come to a halt while policy makers tried to hammer out a means
to deal with a fundamental issue omitted from the basic policy.

The realism of the policy is simply the fact that the policy statements on paper were converted into real actions, real situations, and
real operations. For example, disarmament has been criticized as be-

ing a most unrealistic objective of the occupation. But what the critics tend to overlook is that disarmament was a logically and politically necessary element of policy; that, as emphasized earlier, it was carried out rapidly and efficiently; and that it was a policy that was supported by the American government and people, the Japanese people, and all the governments associated with the United States during the war. What made it unrealistic was the rapid development by 1950 of a world situation and of a situation—both military and political—in the vicinity of Japan that dictated a substantial modification of the policy as firmly and as logically as the war had dictated the adoption of disarmament as a necessary and realistic policy goal.

Finally, to repeat, the policy was enormously successful simply because it was implemented, or again converted into a concrete and observable situation, inside Japan. Disarmament, demilitarization and democracy were achieved and by the means that were set forth on paper in the late summer of 1945. But this statement immediately raises another question: why was it possible to effectuate implementation so easily and rapidly?

The answer to this question comes from an answer to two subsidiary questions: Why was the United States government able to act as effectively as it did in the process of implementation? Why did Japan and its people respond so positively to a policy devised by a foreign government and forced on it by that government, a recent enemy?

From the American side, the single factor that contributed most to the success of occupation policy is that the United States had effective control over the target of its policy, namely, Japan. This guaranteed that what the United States deemed desirable for Japan—and consequently necessary for the achievement of the American objectives toward Japan—was going to be converted into reality. As I have already pointed out, there were elements in U.S. policy that Japanese, individually and collectively, either positively disliked (i.e., the purge) or thought were unsuitable for Japan (i.e., the emphasis on individual rights and freedoms), but they were unable to prevent by either active or passive resistance implementation of American policy.

The relations between nations being what they are and the nature of foreign policy being what it is, what the United States enjoyed in Japan during the 1945-1951 period was the optimum situation for the successful achievement of a foreign policy goal: first, a policy that was "good," that is, one that the U.S. government itself deemed to be designed to achieve desirable ends, and second, a situation in which the U.S. was able to apply maximum pressure to achieve acceptance of the policy by the government and the society toward which it was directed.

The sources of American power in this situation are very clear. The first was military victory itself. It was clearcut and unambiguous because vastly superior and irresistible military might had been applied to the Japanese government in such a manner that it was forced to accept the terms of surrender set forth by the victor. There was, in other words, no manner in which, militarily, politically or psychologically, the leaders of Japan could maneuver in order to escape the full pressure of the victorious government. In more concrete terms, the second source of American power was the provision, fully accepted by the Japanese government, that the authority of the occupation inside Japan was supreme. This went beyond the victor-vanquished relationship established by the military decision and created a political and legal relationship of ruling-ruled which established an interplay that was both effective as far as the implementation of occupation policy was concerned and mutually beneficial in the sense that it yielded advantages to both sides.

To understand the full significance of the American possession of control over the target of its foreign policy in this situation one has only to glance briefly at the unhappy fate of American policy toward China during the same years that the success of occupation policy was being unfolded. Any objective analysis of American policy toward China, as enunciated by President Truman in December, 1945, must end with the conclusion that it was both wise and practical, if one starts from the basic premise that it was to the advantage of both the United States government and the Nationalist government of China to avoid a civil war inside that unhappy country. What guaranteed the failure of U.S. policy toward China was that the U.S. government had no way to influence effectively, let alone control, the Chinese situation. American policy, if it could have been implemented, would have prevented the Chinese civil war, for it presented the only alternative to a military resolution of the domestic political situation, namely, a political solution. It was fated to fail simply because neither side in China could be either forced or persuaded to follow a peaceful political road to stable government and political unity.

As important as the factor of control was to the success of American occupation policy, there was a more fundamental consideration that lay at the basis, not only of the successful implementation of American policy, but also of control itself. This consideration was simple: from the time that the shooting stopped in August, 1945, it served the inter-

ests of the Japanese government and the Japanese people to work positively to achieve the goal of an occupation policy which by every realistic measure available was being imposed upon them.

To summarize the brief but imposing list of advantages that the
Japanese derived from the occupation and its policy:

1.   The end of the war meant the end of the "agony and suffering of
the Japanese people," as President Truman expressed it. However, in a
real sense, it saved Japanese society from greater disaster. As the Japanese knew—at least the intelligent Japanese—and as any sophisticated observer could see once he set foot on Japanese soil, the whole
structure of Japanese society was under enormous stress in 1945. Economically, there was vast physical destruction, unsettling inflation,
growing shortages of food, and widespread unemployment, in short, a
situation in which both individuals and the economy could barely live
and operate on a day-to-day basis. Sociologically, millions of Japanese
had been sent overseas; family life had been disrupted by both military and industrial mobilization and the destruction of cities; urban
society itself had been sadly disrupted; the impact of economic difficulties on the orderly processes of social life was beginning to be felt.
Politically no one, and especially Japan's leaders, could be sure what
would happen in the event of further economic and sociological dislo-
cation and disruption, but as some said after the war, the thought of violent revolution had begun to haunt at least a few.

In minimal terms, the sustaining of a situation of non-war even under a military occupation could only represent a net gain to Japanese
society. The best means to continue a state of non-war was to cooperate with the occupation.

2.   The political advantages to Japan, both those stated and inherent
in occupation policy and those that could reasonably be expected to
flow from occupation implementation of its own policies, were both obvious and considerable.

By the end of the war the leadership of Japan was both bankrupt and
discredited in the eyes of all, save its own. Perhaps even in its own eyes
it had reached the end of the line, because it was clear beyond challenge that it had failed to achieve its self-determined goals of foreign
policy by aggressive means, and the destruction, devastation and death
on the homefront demonstrated beyond cavil its inability to defend its
own country by military means. Occupation policy directed against the
militarists and their ultranationalistic civilian supporters was not a
policy to eliminate from public life patriotic and loyal Japanese, but a
group of thoroughly discredited leaders.

On the positive side, the occupation decision to retain a Japanese government in operation could mean not only that new Japanese leaders would have to come forward to replace the old, but that thousands of lesser Japanese could continue to enjoy some authority, no matter how restricted by the occupation, and some slight measure of prestige, to receive vitally necessary income, no matter how insufficient it might be to cover the cost of daily existence. Beyond this, it was perfectly clear that the occupation envisaged new institutions in which new forms of power could be wielded in new ways by new leaders.

Another political decision with important psychological and sociological overtones for the Japanese was that to preserve the Emperor, both as an individual and as an institution. The Emperor was not only the locus of sovereignty in the Japanese state and therefore the source of legitimacy for government; he had also been the mystical object of the loyalty and allegiance of the people. In 1945, a minority of the Japanese probably would have welcomed his elimination; many would have been shocked and horrified; and some would have been indifferent in the face of the numbing effects of the war and of the critical pressure of trying to live from day to day. But it is interesting to speculate as to whether an abrupt and possibly bloody elimination of the Emperor would have been taken in stride as simply another in the whole series of dramatic and shattering events of the last half of 1945 or whether it would have called forth a spasmodic and violent reaction to all that was happening to the Japanese collectively and individually.

Another political advantage, alluded to earlier, is that the democracy envisaged appeared to an indeterminate number of Japanese as a reasonable alternative to the authoritarianism of the right they had been living under and to the authoritarianism of the left being forwarded by a minority at the time.

3.   Economically, the end of the war meant at the very least that the people would no longer have to bear the burden of war taxes, of long hours in field and factory, and of a shortage of food and consumers' goods. They would be able to turn to peacetime economic activities, not only of their own volition, but also they would be forced to do so by occupation policy. No matter how vague the key economic phrase in occupation policy might be, "an economy which will permit the peacetime requirements of the population to be met," it clearly did not mean the economic enslavement of the country and its people. The implications of the democratization of economic institutions and of the wide distribution of income and the ownership of the means of

production and trade were almost equally vague, but they portended something better for the future.

The specific implementation of policy soon demonstrated that there were to be concrete economic gains: the favoring of labor unions, the land reform program, and the dissolution of the zaibatsu firms. In addition, the occupation very soon after it began instituted a program for the supply of minimum amounts of food, clothing and medical supplies in the form of relief.

Thus from the beginning the Japanese could expect tangible gains from the implementation of occupation policy. It is no wonder that they found it a matter of profit to work with and under the kind of occupation provided for in American policy.

In summary, then, a fundamental reason for the success of American occupation policy as based on "U.S. Initial Postsurrender Policy for Japan" was simply that very rapidly both the occupation and Japan discovered that they had a mutuality of interest to be served by the rapid and effective implementation of a policy that turned out not simply to serve the purposes of the victor.

There is a final criterion for judging the contribution of "U.S. Initial Postsurrender Policy for Japan" to post-1945 American foreign policy, namely, its consequences for the general pattern of American-Japanese relations. It will be recalled that the policy statement set forth the negative goal of dealing with Japan so that it would never again be a threat to the peace and security of the United States, thus ending the pattern of relationships that had endured for about half a century. This goal was achieved, the war itself having provided the necessary ingredients for the change.

Though the policy paper did not state as either an objective or as a means the creation of a close alliance between the U.S. and Japan, it has certainly been attained as a consequence of occupation policy. The dramatic shift in the nature of U.S.-Japanese relations is a complex story which cannot be explained solely in terms of American occupation policy, but this writer believes his account to have demonstrated that the policy did set in motion a series of broad developments that served to bring the two nations close in friendship and cooperation. Whatever the problems that may erode good relations between the two countries, and certainly some such as the security issue must be taken with great seriousness by both sides, the fact remains that for almost a quarter of a century relations between the U.S. and Japan have been as close and as friendly as they were tense and unfriendly in the preceding twenty-five years. Here the general contribution of "U.S.

Initial Postsurrender Policy for Japan" must be gratefully acknowledged.

This writer has thought intermittently for some years about the possible relevance of this outstanding policy paper to the broader issue of the formulation of equally effective American foreign policy on other even more significant and critical problems. Reluctantly, he has concluded that it cannot serve as an exemplar for American policy planners. The total body of circumstances, even as sketchily outlined in this essay, constituted a problem different from any the United States had previously encountered. Nor is it likely that she will be faced with a similar problem in the future. When it becomes possible to write the definitive history of "United States Initial Postsurrender Policy for Japan," the final judgment will surely be that it was one of the great state papers of American foreign policy, even though the situation it dealt with was unique. We should honor the achievement for itself without searching for a wider relevance.

CHAPTER III

AMERICA'S POSTWAR ROLE IN SOUTHEAST ASIA

By John F. Cady*

INTRODUCTION

This chapter is in the nature of an interpretive essay covering postwar developments in Southeast Asia with which the writer has had long continued and fairly intimate contact.† Because much of his interpretation is based on personal involvements and is not therefore amenable to exact scholarly documentation, the customary footnotes will be kept to a minimum. The essay represents a point of view arising from long acquaintance with postwar Southeast Asia, and its validity will have to stand or fall on its own intrinsic merits.

POLICY BY DEFAULT

The increasingly heavy involvement of the United States in the affairs of postwar Southeast Asia since 1953 has developed in large measure not from deliberate choice but from the logic of events attend-

---

*John F. Cady, an alumnus of the University of Cincinnati and the recipient of one of its Taft Fellowships in History in 1923, is Professor of History at Ohio University.

†The writer of this article taught at the University of Rangoon from 1935 to 1938, served as Burma analyst in the wartime Office of Strategic Services and as State Department desk officer and intelligence specialist relating to the area from 1945 to 1949. Since leaving the Department for Ohio University, he has enjoyed at various times extended leaves as Visiting Professor at Cornell, as Guggenheim Fellow in both Rangoon and London, and as Rockefeller Foundation assignee to Thammasat University at Bangkok for research in Southeast Asian history.

ing a continuing revolutionary situation. Although the defeat of Japan's imperialistic designs was essentially the work of MacArthur's Pacific Command, (Burma's liberation alone was accomplished by British-Indian-African forces), Washington in 1945 decided rather abruptly to entrust the acceptance of the Japanese surrender throughout most of Southeast Asia to Lord Mountbatten's Supreme Allied Southeast Asia Command. The exceptions were the American occupation of the Philippines and liberated New Guinea, the American-sponsored sending of Chinese forces to occupy North Vietnam for purposes of evacuating Japanese forces, and Australia's assignment to East Indonesia. Washington's general disinclination to accept heavy responsibilities in postwar Southeast Asia was attributable in large part to the inescapable and staggering burdens to be borne by American forces in occupied Japan and liberated China and Korea.

In the one country of Southeast Asia where the United States accepted postwar responsibility, the Philippines, Washington's previously determined policy was to grant full independence. This goal was accomplished on July 4, 1946. Problems of decolonization throughout the rest of the region were left primarily to the British, the Dutch, and the French, who perforce had to accept responsibility for making their own accommodations with emerging nationalist movements. The primary American postwar objective in Eastern Asia was to demilitarize Japan and to develop Nationalist China as a bulwark against possible subsequent Soviet Communist aggression in Eastern Asia.

Washington's postwar hesitance to get involved in Southeast Asia was further strengthened by the overwhelming priority which it accorded to considerations of European policy. Much was indeed at stake in Europe, where Russian troops in 1945-1946 occupied six Eastern European countries, and Communist conspiracies also threatened both Greece and Turkey. Apart from America's sole possession of the nuclear deterrent during the early postwar years, there was little to prevent the still mobilized Soviet armies from marching westward to the Atlantic. If the faltering capitalist economies of Western European countries should collapse, as Moscow hoped, thus according increasing political predominance to Communist Party organizations within the several states of the area, a Soviet empire far surpassing Hitler's Germany in cohesion and extent could conceivably emerge in Europe. Senior Foreign Service officers of the State Department who were obliged to deal directly with French, Dutch, and British embassy officials in Washington over matters relating to the Soviet-Communist threat, were generally unresponsive to policy proposals based on the assumed importance for American long term interests in the political developments taking place within Southeast Asia. For this neglect of Southeast Asian affairs the United States was destined to pay a heavy toll.

Kremlin officials themselves were in substantial agreement with the State Department's attribution of priority to Europe. Moscow, for example, did not actively encourage overt Communist revolution in Southeast Asia until early 1948. The anti-French struggle of the nationalist-Communist Viet Minh, in progress in Indochina after December, 1946, received little encouragement and no aid from the U.S.S.R. prior to 1948 due to Moscow's concern not to embarrass the French Communist Party politically. It was the spectacular economic recovery of Western Europe, starting in late 1947, which prompted the Soviet's invocation of the Leninist principle that imperialism was simply the projection of domestic capitalism, and that the latter could be made to collapse if colonial props were removed. In early 1948, the moderate P. C. Joshi was replaced as Secretary of the Indian Communist Party, and overt Communist rebellions were initiated in Burma, Malaya, Java, and the Philippines. The coincidence was more than casual, although local factors also impinged.[1] The Kremlin's assessment of the revolutionary possibilities inherent in the anti-colonial nationalism of Southeast Asia was essentially doctrinaire and on the whole poorly informed.

Despite some awareness of the increasingly sensitive situation in Southeast Asia, the State Department was slow to develop any articulate and realistic policy covering the area. For approximately a full year, 1945-46, the Department's views were completely deadlocked so that acquiescence in French and Dutch sovereignty won out by default. Only by 1948-49, when Communist-sponsored rebellions developed, did Southeast Asian affairs begin to receive serious attention in their own right. Unfortunately, by this time general considerations relating to the developing cold-war dichotomy and to China's move toward Communist domination took precedence over intrinsic political realities within the countries concerned. From official Washington's point of view, the Southeast Asia problem thereafter was to be interpreted almost entirely within the context of the overriding need to thwart the spread of world Communist influence.

In only one country of Southeast Asia, namely Thailand, was the State Department's postwar Southeast Asian policy division able to exercise considerable freedom of decision. Here there were no senior European desk officers to interfere, since Thailand alone in the area had never been subjected to colonial rule. Furthermore, the Free Thai movement nurtured by Ambassador Seni Promoj in Washington and by Pridi Phanomyong's civilian political faction in Bangkok had gone far to eliminate, from Washington's point of view, the stigma of Thailand's anti-Allied declarations of war in alliance with Japan. Washington concurred in Allied demands requiring Bangkok to surrender border territories acquired under Japan's auspices from Cambodia, Laos, Malaya, and Burma, but Secretary of State Acheson interposed at London to modify the British proposal to treat Siam as an enemy country.[2] Thus a foundation was laid for United States-Thailand friendship and cooperation.

THE PHILIPPINES

As previously indicated, the only problem of postwar Southeast Asia which claimed immediate and detailed attention from the American government related to the implementation of the promised independence for the Republic of the Philippines. Acting President Sergio Osmeña returned to the reconquered islands as early as October, 1944, and resumed formal control over civil administration by February, 1945. Nation-wide elections held in the spring of 1946 elevated Manuel Roxas to the Commonwealth Presidency. He acceded to the Presidency of the new republic on July 4, 1946, when America's President Truman, by proclamation, formally withdrew American sovereignty and recognized the independence of the Republic.

Subsequent negotiations were conducted on a friendly but realistic basis, reflecting the continuing dependence of the Philippines on American cooperation in such areas as rehabilitation, security concerns, and trading relations, and the agreements reached were open to subsequent reconsideration. The military agreement of March 14, 1947, accorded to the United States for 99 years the "right to use and retain" sixteen designated Islands bases, including Clark Field and Subic Bay, and emergency access to seven other defense installations.[3] Mutual consent was required before any third power could acquire any similar rights. An American military aid program was initiated shortly thereafter. The essential security requirements of the new Republic, which called for unimpeded U.S. access to such bases, served to bridge over the inevitable differences and misunderstandings regarding their administration, which developed in subsequent years. In 1950 and later in 1954, Washington reaffirmed unequivocally its commitment to defend the Philippines.[4]

In the area of trade, the Bell Trade Act passed by the American

Congress in April, 1946, established tariff schedules for various classes of Philippines imports, increasing annually over a twenty-eight year period. The value of the Philippine peso was pegged at US$0.50, and the two were made freely convertible. Implementation of the terms of the Bell Trade Act was made contingent on the much-argued acceptance of an amendment to the Islands' Constitution granting to American firms parity status with Filipinos in developing the Islands' natural resources and public utilities. The amendment was approved by the Manila Congress in September, 1946, and ratified by plebiscite in the following spring, but not without arousing considerable public protest. In 1954, a supplementary trading agreement extended free trade with the U.S. for eighteen months beyond the original expiration date of July 4, 1954, pending renegotiation of aspects of the original settlement. Tariff and quota provisions were eventually revised in favor of Philippine trading interests. These revisions became operative in 1956 after receiving approval by appropriate legislative action from the two Congresses.

America's program of economic aid covering compensation for wartime property damage amounted to some two billion dollars in reparations. Unfortunately, this and other forms of aid were badly administered. By 1950, the Islands' faltering economy became so precarious that President Truman's Economic Survey Mission undertook, with Manila's embarrassed consent, to make appropriate recommendations. The resulting report released in October, 1950, made the approval of further grants and loans, amounting to a quarter billion dollars annually for five years, contingent on Manila's carrying out under American supervision basic economic, land, and fiscal reforms.[5] In 1952, the American government responded favorably to Manila's request to assist in obtaining a reparations treaty with Japan, which was later concluded in 1956.

American relations with the Philippines differed markedly from Washington's involvement elsewhere in postwar Southeast Asia mainly because full responsibility for launching the Island Republic was assumed, conflicting interests were directly negotiated, and relations were developed in realistic fashion and in an atmosphere of mutual concession.

AMERICAN POLICY AND BURMA'S INDEPENDENCE

At no time during the postwar period did the American Government become actively interested in the progressive liquidation of British colonial holdings in Southeast Asia. As of early 1946, Burmese nationalists, including Communist elements of the Anti-Fascist Peoples Freedom League, were not sure that the country's independence could actually be achieved without interposition by either the United States or the Soviet Union. But the subsequent decision of Prime Minister Attlee's Labour Party Government to concede independence to India destroyed the essential basis of Britain's century-long dominance in Southeast Asia. It was in May, 1946, that Attlee rejected the antinationalist counsel of Governor Sir Reginald Dorman-Smith and eventually, in August, replaced him with Sir Hubert Rance, a protégé of Lord Mountbatten. The British Prime Minister conceded at the London Conference in early 1947 the nationalist requirements presented to him by the Burmese mission headed by Thakin Aung San.[6] Burma was thus spared the agonies of a bitterly contested independence struggle. The price for Burma was cancellation of Britain's postwar plans for economic rehabilitation.

The two groups who were most unhappy with London's conciliatory policy, but for different reasons, were the Karen nationalists, who distrusted majority Burman rule, and the Communists. The latter were denied opportunity to exploit the anticipated freedom struggle to accomplish their intended modulation in the direction of Soviet-patterned control. Burma's realisation of independence on January 4, 1948, happened to coincide roughly with Moscow's decision to initiate the previously mentioned series of "people's independence struggles" throughout Southeast Asia. Burma's Communists initiated their rebellion in March, 1948, to be joined in May by a disgruntled veterans' group and, in 1949, by dissident Karen nationalists. During the ensuing two years of civil strife, Premier Nu's government was accorded military assistance from Britain and Colombo Plan countries, so that it managed to survive the uncoordinated attacks of rebel elements. The United States all the while regarded Burma as Britain's exclusive responsibility, although Washington was gratified that independence was achieved—and peacefully.

Difficulties developed between Washington and Rangoon in the early 1950's over America's response to a Burmese request to assist in preparing economic development plans. The technically-competent planning mission provided at Washington's expense was not very realistic. It failed to take into account the manifold deficiencies of Rangoon's government in areas of statistical data, administrative competence, and lack of the business experience essential for operating the projected economic programs. Too little attention was given to expanding the vigorous agricultural base needed to produce the requisite foreign exchange.[7] The collapse of world rice prices in 1955 following the end of the Korean War brought the over-ambitious industrialization development program to a complete standstill. American economic assistance thus proved unproductive as well as minimal in extent.

Meanwhile the initial refusal of Washington authorities to accept responsibility for curbing the operations of Kuomintang intruders into Burma's Shan States bordering China had aroused resentment at Rangoon. The refugee Chinese were found to be in receipt of American arms sent by planes from Taipei. Issues connected with the cold war thus took precedence over good relations with Burma. In 1953, Rangoon abruptly repudiated any further American aid. Later American efforts to assist in road construction running northward from Rangoon were discredited, partly on suspicion that the project was associated with ulterior American designs against Red China. Burmese-American relations were thus reduced to minimal dimensions by 1957. Thereafter Rangoon assumed a consistently neutralist stance in the cold war dichotomy and undertook to avoid giving offense to Peking by refusing further acceptance of American aid. This led to the eventual expulsion of all American Foundation help, discontinuance of Fulbright grants, and the expulsion of the century-and-a-half-old American missionary presence.

MALAYA AND SINGAPORE

Washington played no role in Britain's granting of independence to the Malaya Federation in 1956. This action on London's part followed Britain's successful coping with the difficult Communist Emergency rebellion started in 1948 by dissident Chinese. Singapore was eventually brought into the Malaysian Federation in 1963. Britain's North Borneo colonies of Sarawak and Sabah were also included, partly as a means of expediting British withdrawal and avoiding a Chinese population plurality over indigenous Malays. The marriage of convenience between Malaysia and Singapore was wrecked two years later, when Lee Kuan Yew demanded freedom for political activity throughout the Federation and equal opportunities for Singapore's non-Malay citizens to employment within the Malaysian bureaucracy as a whole. Lee insisted that Malaysia must be Malaysian; but Kuala Lumpur refused.

Contemporaneous with the Malaya-Singapore friction was the Indonesian Confrontation over the Federation's absorption of the North Borneo territories. Because the China-oriented Communist Party of

Indonesia (PKI) enjoyed encouragement from Sukarno, the crisis involved broad international implications. The threat subsided following the abortive anti-army coup of September 30, 1965, which disrupted Sukarno's pro-Communist alignment. The eventual ending of the confrontation crisis in 1966 was followed by the British government's announcement that it would have to withdraw from its security commitments in Southeast Asia by 1974, a date later moved forward to 1971. These developments suggested possibly increased dimensions for America's future responsibilities within Southeast Asia.

INDONESIA

Although the United States played a more active role in postwar Indonesia than in the British-held colonies, America's presence here also was on the whole desultory and ineffective. During the immediate postwar period, Secretary of State James Byrnes refused to accede promptly to Dutch requests for the immediate transfer to Java of Dutch Marines who had been trained during the course of the war in the Chesapeake Bay area, and also for ships to repatriate debilitated Dutch survivors of the Railway of Death ordeal in Thailand and Burma. Javanese nationalists, mistakenly anticipating the arrival of American forces to disarm the Japanese army, plastered approaches to Djakarta's harbor with quotations from America's Declaration of Independence. The actual British-commanded Allied occupation forces were so limited in number that they had to make temporary use of Japanese troops for policing Java pending the arrival of Dutch forces after October 1, 1945. Meanwhile, Indonesian nationalists had established *de facto* control over parts of Java and Sumatra. On the most important question of Indonesia's future independence, Washington came to no positive decision, thus conceding continuing Dutch sovereignty. The official State Department position nevertheless emphasized Dutch responsibility for working out some accomodation to nationalist demands. Both the returning Dutch and their Indonesian nationalist opponents were angered by America's allegedly equivocal role.

The widespread furor aroused by the first Dutch police action in Java, staged in July, 1947, brought the issue of Indonesian independence before the United Nations. The United Nations' Good Offices Committee which was sent to Java to assist in drafting the abortive Renville Settlement of January, 1948, had the United States representative Frank Graham as its chairman. Following the second Dutch police action of December, 1948, the revamped United Nations Commission for Indonesia was again headed by an American, Merle Cochran. He displeased both Dutch and Indonesians. The effectiveness of his mediatorial role was dubious at best. Washington's subsequent attempt to take substantial credit for the eventual realization of Indonesian independence was based in some measure on Merle Cochran's exaggerated assessment of his personal role.

The United States' refusal to provide Dutch troops with all the arms requested by The Hague failed to curb Dutch intransigence. It was actually Pandit Nehru's convening of the highly volatile Conference of Asian, African, and South Pacific countries at New Delhi in January, 1949, which changed U.S. policy and also forced the Dutch eventually to abandon their colonial struggle.[8] Some fast footwork by Ambassador Loy Henderson at New Delhi prevented any effective pro-Communist exploitation of the occasion, but the Indonesian nationalists felt they had little cause to thank America for any long-term concern for their political liberation.

From this unpromising start of American rapport with the new Indonesian state, relations failed to improve materially despite repeated grants of United States economic assistance, albeit in diminishing amounts. Indonesia's halting efforts to develop a Parliamentary system (elections were held in 1955 and regionally in 1957) gave way to President Sukarno's "guided democracy" by 1958. Sukarno's inability to cope with economic problems and his efforts to generate political cohesion within his island empire by keeping revolutionary fervor ablaze contributed in time to his decline. Alleged secret C.I.A. assistance to rebel army elements in the Padang area of Sumatra and in the Celebes poisoned American relations further. Sukarno's demand for the Dutch cession of West Irian, a crisis magnified far out of proportion to its intrinsic importance, coupled with American abstention in the United Nations vote, eventually played into Russian hands. Indonesia acquired sophisticated Soviet military equipment in substantial quantities. Washington's eventual pressure on the Dutch to cede West Irian to Indonesia came too late to mend relations with Djakarta.

Surkarno's subsequent withdrawal from the United Nations in connection with his confrontation of Malaysia resulted in his sponsorship of a rival world coalition called the Newly Emerging States. This contributed to his eventual political alliance with the China-oriented Indonesian Communist Party (PKI) to the virtual exclusion of other civilian political groups. Even so, the Indonesian army was squarely opposed to the prospect of Communist political control. Western offers to assist Indonesia's recovery from imminent economic collapse, advanced in 1964, were rejected in favor of another of Sukarno's frantic nationalistic ventures in the confrontation of the emerging Malaysian Union previously mentioned. Washington demonstrated commendable patience with Indonesia under the circumstances but did little else to salvage the seemingly dismal situation.

AMERICA'S VIETNAM INVOLVEMENT

The most thoroughgoing example of increasing American involvement in postwar Southeast Asian affairs occurred in the former French territories of Indochina. American relations with Vietnam nationalists were poisoned from the outset by the fact that Washington elected not to challenge the restoration of French sovereignty after World War II. At the outset this decision was prompted by an overriding concern to avoid embarrassing American interests in Europe. The policy was later strengthened by the fact that the leadership of the nationalist liberation movement in Vietnam fell progressively under the control of Ho Chi Minh's Communist following. Ho nevertheless emerged as Vietnam's George Washington, its dedicated hero. During the immediate postwar period, 1945-1946, British occupation forces in Southern Indochina facilitated the restoration of titular French control. Ho Chi Minh's *de facto* control of the north, on the other hand, was contested for a time by occupying Nationalist Chinese troops, who sponsored a rival nationalist organization.

So ominous did Ho regard the prospect of continued Chinese intervention in Tonkin that in March of 1945 he decided to agree to a French return to Hanoi as a means of expediting Allied negotiations for Chinese troop withdrawal. French promises, given to Ho at the time, pledging Vietnam's new status of political "freedom within the French Union" were later vitiated by Governor d'Argenlieu's abrupt action of late May, 1946, withdrawing the investment-rich Cochin-China area from the proposed Vietnam state. As head of the Vietnamese negotiating delegation invited to journey to France for negotiations in June, 1946, Ho Chi Minh was acknowledged by Paris as leader of the nationalist movement. During the course of the abortive negotiations held at Fontainebleau (June to September) and even after the inevitable outbreak of open rebellion occurred in December, 1946, Ho continued to be treated by Paris as the *bona fide* nationalist spokesman. The final French efforts at peace negotiations, conducted in the jungle by Professor Paul Mus in March, 1947, were with Ho Chi Minh.

The ensuing anti-French independence rebellion commanded widespread Vietnamese support both in the north and in the south. The French-commanded Vietnamese army by contrast left most of the anti-nationalist fighting to Foreign Legion mercenaries. Ho and General Vo Nguyen Giap maintained the struggle for several years with virtually no aid or encouragement from Moscow and very little from China, even following Mao Tse-tung's triumph in 1949. The Korean war intervened from 1950 to 1953.

The eventual American reinterpretation of the Vietnamese independence struggle as basically an example of Communist subversion was encouraged by the tactics adopted belatedly by the French. As early as September, 1947, Paris invited ex-Emperor Bao Dai, (who had previously abdicated in August, 1945) to return to Hué as a non-Communist symbol of Vietnamese nationhood. Appeals for American aid made thereafter by harassed French forces were invariably couched in anti-Communist terms. Forgotten by 1948 was the initial French insistence that Vietnam involved no legitimate American concern. Washington authorities decided to second the French invitation to Bao Dai by assuring the ex-Emperor, on the side, that American aid to the Vietnamese nation would be more readily forthcoming if some indigenous rallying standard could be raised to dilute the nationalist appeal of the anti-colonial but pro-Communist Viet Minh. Tentative agreement for Bao Dai's return to Hué was reached in June, 1948, but Paris' generous paper concessions of self-rule were not fully implemented until March, 1949. Bao Dai then insisted as a final demand, in April, 1949, that Governor d'Argenlieu's decision of May, 1946, withdrawing Cochin-China from inclusion within the new state be reversed. Paris did not ratify the final agreement until early 1950.

United States and British *de jure* recognition in 1950 of Bao Dai's patently artificial regime carried more political than legal significance. For several years thereafter, American financing of the supposedly sovereign Hué government was possible only on terms set by the French, to whom all American aid was actually delivered. Meanwhile non-rebellious Vietnamese elements discovered that office-holding under the Bao Dai government was limited strictly to persons demonstrating complete loyalty to French control. Convinced nationalists thus had virtually no choice but to give their allegiance to Ho Chi Minh. Thus did the United States come to share the unpopularity and distrust exhibited toward the French not only by nationalists in Vietnam, but throughout much of Southeast Asia.

The hopelessness of the Bao Dai gamble was reflected in President Eisenhower's subsequent admission that the ex-emperor could not have commanded more than twenty percent support in any election contest with Ho Chi Minh.[9] As early as the spring of 1953, some fourteen months prior to the military debacle of Dien-bien-phu, the State Department was becoming actively interested in lining up Ngo Dinh Diem as an anti-French but non-Communist nationalist replacement for France-sponsored Bao Dai. Not until April, 1954, did Paris concede "independent and sovereign" status to Vietnam, qualified only by Hué's voluntary association with the French Union. Diem was formally installed by U.S. nomination as Bao Dai's titular Prime Minister in June, 1954. Meanwhile French spokesmen at the simultaneous Geneva Conference directed all negotiations, to the complete exclusion of Hué. Paris accepted responsibility for implementing the agreed military evacuation and preparation for the promised nationwide elections of 1956.

What initial popularity Diem enjoyed during the first two years of his nine-year rule stemmed mainly from his maneuvering of the retirement of Bao Dai in October, 1955, following a carefully-staged ninety-eight percent plebiscite victory, and his acceleration of French military withdrawal by April, 1956. The French thereby kept their Geneva promise to withdraw militarily but defaulted in their pledge to implement the nationwide elections scheduled for the summer of 1956. Since the Geneva settlement expressly declared that the seventeenth parallel truce partition line did not constitute an international boundary, thus denying separate sovereign status to either fragment, the American-sponsored Diem regime enjoyed no more impressive legal status than had the emperor's predecessor puppet government. The case for unification of the nation as contemplated in the compromise Geneva Declaration was based on compelling practical as well as political considerations, which persisted long beyond the passing of the election deadline of July, 1956. Political experience and military leadership plus industrial resources lay in the north, while surplus food and plantation export commodities (rubber, tea, and tobacco) were available only in the south. The Saigon regime of Diem meanwhile flatly refused to restore economic cooperation with the north. Diem survived all rivals after 1956, mainly by reason of lavish American financial assistance, which provided a revenue base unavailable to his political opponents.

UNITED STATES SPONSORSHIP OF SOUTH VIETNAM

Behind the increasing American concern for South Vietnam in 1954-56 was the cumulative experience of the previous decade. The period had witnessed the Communist-inspired insurrections in Burma, Malaya, Indonesia, and the Philippines, the costly anti-Communist struggle in Korea, plus Red China's insistence that Americans evacuate Taiwan and the offshore islands. The viewpoint also reflected postwar difficulties encountered in Iran, Greece, Berlin, and Western Europe generally. Anti-Communism developed into a compelling political issue in successive American election contests. America's "loss" of China to Communism in 1949 claimed its scapegoats and victims not only within the Institute of Pacific Relations but within the State Department itself during the disturbing McCarthy-Dulles era.

The superficial map image arising from China's allegedly falling victim to the world Communist conspiracy suggested that the food-surplus countries of continental Southeast Asia were surely the next intended victims. Since the charismatic figure of Communist Ho Chi-Minh would admittedly dominate any nationwide Vietnamese elections, free or otherwise, the world Communist menace came to focus increasingly on Indochina by 1954. The emergence of the nationalist but anti-Communist Ngo Dinh Diem was therefore a veritable godsend for Washington's anti-Communist crusaders. His survival was so crucially important as a cold war issue that questions of legality and political morality simply ceased to be relevant and binding. Diem just had to succeed, for no alternative to him was available.

For some two-and-a-half years (until early 1957) it appeared that the miracle performance which the sacred cause of freedom merited would actually come off. Diem curbed a hostile army clique and emasculated militarily the Cao Dai and Hoa Hao sects in the Mekong delta. Few South Vietnamese shed tears over the hurried departure of Bao Dai or the French colonial rulers. The 900,000 refugees from North Vietnam, a majority of them Catholic peasants, were resettled in sparsely-occupied areas, aided by financial assistance from America. Catholic partisans were named to important posts in the government, extending from the President's advisors down to the village level, where traditionally locally-chosen officials were replaced. Because in mid-1956 Hanoi was in serious trouble with food shortages and peasant resistance to ambitious plans for communization of land, and because the issue of national unification was not as urgently desired in the food-surplus south as it was in the north, Diem's defiant refusal to prepare for the promised elections seemed to be politically, if not legally, vindicated. No one in Washington wished to repudiate the political miracle thought to be happening at Saigon. On the occasion of Diem's visit to the United States in May, 1957, he was accorded a hero's reception not only by Catholic admirers, but by both the President and the Congress as well.[10]

Some evidence of official American reserve was exhibited even during these encouraging years. Out of deference to the Geneva Declaration's withholding legal recognition to an admittedly *de facto* arrangement, Vietnam, Laos, and Cambodia were not made parties to the SEATO treaty of February, 1955, but were covered only as so-called protocol states. Washington's first direct promise of American assistance to Diem's regime was also accompanied by President Eisenhower's fatherly admonition that receipt of such aid should be accompanied by the implementation of needed land reforms.[11] The joint communique of May 11, 1957, issued at the time of Diem's American visit, also paid lip service to the cause of the eventual "peaceful reunification" of Vietnam. There was no evidence that such discreet expressions of informed State Department concern had, at the time, any appreciable effect on the arrogant assertion of arbitrary power on which the Diem regime was well launched by 1957.

The North Vietnamese view of developments in the south from 1954 to 1957 differed markedly from that entertained in Washington. The Viet Minh victory over the French colonial forces had been complete in 1954, and Hanoi had accepted the Geneva compromise settlement only when pressed to do so by both Moscow and Peking. Ho's following was also aware that Tonkin's economy needed time to recover from the exhaustion of the long-continued war. Ho was confident, as were all other observers, that he would triumph politically in the 1956 elections which were promised in the Geneva agreements. Even after the eventual repudiation of the election agreement, Hanoi preferred down to 1960 to try to achieve the necessary unification of Vietnam by political rather than military means.

Hanoi's first serious quarrel with Diem developed over the latter's flat refusal in 1955-56 to undertake joint preparations for eventual unification and for immediate resumption of normal communications and economic relations. Cochin-China's surplus rice was badly needed at the time in near-starving Tonkin. It was on this occasion that Khrushchev arranged during his Burma visit in early 1956 to purchase some 150,000 tons of deteriorating and otherwise unsalable Burmese rice and to send it directly to Hanoi.[12] The food crisis in the north led in time to overt peasant resistance against excessive regimentation measures imposed by the government.

Following Diem's definitive rejection of the elections pledge in mid-1956, on the grounds that free elections were impossible, came his inauguration of systematic suppression of all elements of political opposition. Victims were both civilian and military, Communist and anti-Communist, but the principal target was the previously anti-French Viet Minh leadership in the South. Diem also favored landlords over peasants, North Vietnamese over South Vietnamese, Catholics over Buddhists, lowlanders over *montagnards*. He restricted candidates for successive elections to persons amenable to the authority of his regime. Diem's three brothers, one of them a Catholic bishop, played prominent roles in policy making, in police control at Saigon, and in the administration of the Annam littoral. By the end of the decade, opposition to Diem was mounting in the countryside, as well as within the Buddhist majority in the cities and in the armed forces.

The National Liberation Front, which began counter operations against Saigon's authority in late 1957, was at the outset not drawn from top Viet Minh leaders of the south, most of whom were already jailed. The Front was composed at the start of South Vietnamese, and it enlisted an expanding following among peasants resentful to Saigon's repression.[13] The peasants as a whole objected only mildly to the Front's tactics of selective murder of local officials who had been appointed by Saigon, of local landlords and money lenders, and even of schoolteachers and other personnel suspected of being government informers. By 1960 the Front was exercising control over more than half the South Vietnamese countryside. This much was accomplished in the face of equally ruthless governmental repression and with little encouragement or military help from Hanoi authorities. Professors Devillers and Kahin have cited numerous complaints advanced by the Front, extending as late as 1960, to the effect that Hanoi had deserted the nationalist cause.[14] The Front was never as doctrinaire as was the northern Communist leadership; it tended to be pro-Buddhist in its sympathies and was less concerned than was Hanoi with accomplishing immediate national unification. Not until after some eighteen elder statesmen in the South suffered imprisonment for their respectfully staged protest against the tyranny of the Diem regime in the spring of 1960 did Hanoi finally and explicitly identify itself with the National Liberation Front.[15] The union was effected in September 1960, and open collaboration started only after the first abortive army coup against the Presidential palace took place in November.

From late 1960 to the assassination of President Diem and his brother in November, 1963, the trend was downhill all the way for the American-supported Saigon regime. Part of the mounting non-Communist opposition to Diem was based on concern that his growing unpopularity was clearly playing into the hands of the pro-Communist Viet Cong Liberation Front. Reasons for the debacle of the assumed miracle of the middle 1950's can be identified. One was peasant resistance to the ambitious but ill-conceived "strategic hamlet" resettlement program, which undertook to remove villages from easy liaison with the Viet Cong.[16] Another was the avarice and ruthlessness of brother Ngo Dihn Nhu's secret police, especially as applied against the Buddhists. A third had to do with the spirit of mutiny within the armed forces. More conveniently plausible as an explanation from Washington's point of view was the allegation of Communist "aggression from the north," with the Viet Cong acting as the spearhead of the world Communist conspiracy.

The unavoidable collapse of the Saigon regime was attributable to its almost universal rejection. The situation following Diem's assassination in November, 1963, became ominous because the divergent successor factions which emerged failed to attract any unified popular support and found it almost impossible to reach agreement among themselves. Thus the village-based Viet Cong Liberation Front managed to fill a political vacuum and began to emerge in 1964 as probably the strongest single political entity in South Vietnam.

Since it was inconceivable from Washington's point of view that any sensible people would ever voluntarily opt in favor of Communist dictatorship, the seriousness of the deteriorating South Vietnamese situation was not realized until almost too late. In February, 1964, when American "advisory" military assistance was first increased to some 20,000 men, Washington insisted that the bulk of the fighting must be done by the South Vietnamese army but withdrew earlier prophesies that United States forces would be able to leave Vietnam during 1965.[17] A succession of somersaults occurred within the ruling elite at Saigon during 1964, producing a situation of near political collapse. Only massive U.S. reinforcements and escalation of the air war in early 1965 prevented a military and political debacle. Viet Minh infiltration from the North had increased meanwhile, but few if any organized North Vietnamese military units were operating in the South in 1965. Political stability was finally achieved at Saigon only in June, 1966, when a military government was installed representing, in a rough way, all of the major non-Communist factions. Nine members of the new ten-man *junta* had fought with the French.

The official American contention was that Communist aggression against a friendly suppliant government must not be permitted to succeed lest all of Southeast Asia be overrun by China. This interpretation begged a great many questions. The World Communist conspiracy which had loomed ominously in 1949 had lost its original significance following the development of the open rift between China and Russia in the early 1960s. By 1965, the two rivals could agree on virtually no world issue except that neither could permit Ho Chi Minh's regime to be destroyed by the American intervention. The Hanoi government was still strongly opposed to any kind of Chinese interference in its affairs but managed to obtain maximum aid from both Communist giants. Growing confusion within China on account of the Red Guard madness of 1966-67 provided additional grounds for discounting any immediate threat of Red Chinese invasion of Southeast Asia. Moscow obviously desired no general war to grow out of the Vietnam affair, although the USSR was obviously prepared to resist any attempted disruption by America of Soviet seaborne assistance to Hanoi.

Meanwhile Washington's oft repeated commitment to halt "Communist aggression from the north" was being made largely to itself and to an American-sustained and unpopular government at Saigon, whose members earlier had fought with the French colonialists. Prominently at stake on the American side was also the future of a politically-motivated President and the pride of the air force, which refused to concede that its massive bombing operations in both North and South Vietnam were not able to force the surrender of the Liberation Front and Hanoi. Apparently something more compelling than a Hitler-like thirst for aggression and regularity of daily Communist devotions kept the beleaguered Viet Cong guerrillas in the field.

THE LAOS PROBLEM

American efforts following the Geneva Conference of 1954 to generate within the emerging Laotian coalition regime some resistance to an assumed Communist threat quickly ran into difficulties. Nominated by Washington for the leading anti-Communist role was the pro-French Prince Boun Oum of Southern Champassak province, assisted by his youthful but reactionary protégé, General Phoumi Nosavan. The titular Laotian ruler at Luang Prabang in the north, King Sisavang Vong, was also provided with American aid to develop his Royal Laotian army. Authority at the Laotian administrative capital at Vientiane was shared in 1956 by two princely half-brothers, both of them *persona non grata* to the King, the neutralist Souvanna Phouma and Souphanouvong, leader of the Viet-Minh influenced *Pathet Lao* (Lao Country) faction. The general ineffectiveness of the American aid program to Laos derived in large measure from the absence of any sense of nationalist cohesion. The demonstrated lack of fighting spirit within the expanding Laotian army was matched by civilian demoralization accompanying the thriving black market operation at Vientiane in consumer goods provided through dollar-financed import licenses.[18] These and other factors added to the progressive deterioration of the narrowly-based coalition regime.

The first gesture of overt American interference occurred in 1958. In an effort to halt the corrupt juggling by members of the ruling clique of the value of import-licensed goods back and forth between dollars and the over-valued *kip*, a swindle which was dissipating over half of the aid funds, American authorities demanded that a more realistic rate of exchange be substituted. Devaluation of the *kip* was forced in mid-1958 only by Washington's outright suspension for four months of all aid contributions. The principal political result was the displacement of Prince Souvanna Phouma by Premier Sananikone in June, 1958, and the eventual drifting of the Pathet Lao faction included in the 1956 coalition government into guerrilla resistance by late 1958. The specter of rising Communist insurrection brought a hurried restoration of American assistance, so that corruption quickly resumed on an expanding scale. A year later in December, 1959, the faltering Sananikone regime was displaced by one headed by the American-nominated General Phoumi Nosavan of Champassak, cousin of Thailand's Marshal Sarit. He promptly imprisoned all the Pathet Lao leadership remaining in Vientiane and then in April, 1960, staged a rigged election from which his opponents were carefully excluded.

This game of musical chairs continued throughout the remainder of 1960. In August, Captain Kong Lê, a paratrooper, left alone in Vientiane at the time of the new King's coronation, seized control of the capital. He demanded an end of civil strife and the cessation of American interference in Laos. Prince Souvanna Phouma then returned to join Kong Lê briefly and initiated a vain attempt to negotiate another agreement with the dissident Pathet Lao faction, whose leaders had meanwhile escaped from jail. The United States countered by again suspending aid to Vientiane and by supporting a second attack on Vientiane by the troops of Phoumi Nosavan in December, 1960. This move drove Souvanna Phouma into exile in Cambodia and Kong Lê into open alliance with the Pathet Lao forces. The response of the Soviet government was to accord to the Kong Lê-Pathet Lao alliance substantial arms assistance via the Hanoi air lift. The new situation raised the stark prospect of a major cold war confrontation in an area where neither the U.S. nor the U.S.S.R. had any vital interest at stake. Meanwhile, the unprincipled price manipulation of available gold stocks by General Phoumi Nosavan undermined his presumed military effectiveness. Eventually, China also became involved in the active encouragement of Viet Minh intervention in the confused Laotian tangle.

Finally, in 1961-1962, the United States with Soviet cooperation undertook to neutralize the dangerous situation. Souvanna Phouma was restored as Premier for the third time, backed locally at the outset only by the forces of Captain Kong Lê, now defected from the Pathet Lao. The Cuba crisis of 1962 exerted a sobering effect on the Soviet attitude toward the rebellion. Peking, on the other hand, undertook to upset the prospective power *detente* over Laos by encouraging more active Viet Minh intervention. The ensuing crisis resulted in the sending of substantial American forces up to the Thai-Laotian border area late in 1962. Souvanna Phouma's neutralist regime managed to survive, partly because hill tribesmen occupying the watershed areas between Laos and Tonkin were encouraged by drops of rice and arms to resist the operation of Pathet Lao forces. As of 1963, more than half of the imports of Laos were still provided by American funds. American A.I.D. fund contributions in 1967 were over fifty million dollars plus several times that much in military aid.[19]

The manifold problems of the essentially artificial Laotian state proved incapable of solution by assorted sanctions relating to cold war tension. Their attempted application seemed, in fact, to aggravate the problems of a very confused situation. No conceivable American controntation with the Soviet Union or with Red China would ever be contested in the backward hill country of Laos.

CAMBODIAN-AMERICAN RELATIONS

Cambodia's role in postwar American policy in Southeast Asia since 1954 has been conditioned by Prince Norodom Sihanouk's almost pathological concern to obtain international guarantees for the survival of his highly vulnerable state. The effort began at the Geneva Conference of 1954, when the Cambodian delegate took an adamant stand in demanding unqualified acceptance of his country's independence, including freedom to take all measures necessary to maintain its national security. Sihanouk from the outset hoped that the United States might be prepared to underwrite Cambodia's independence in the discouraging situation which seemed to promise the early absorption by the victorious Viet Minh of South Vietnam as well as Laos. But Washington in 1954 was wary of the dubious advantage to be gained from contracting any bilateral alliance with a virtually defenseless Cambodia. The United States could have responded affirmatively, in any case, only in violation of pledges made by the negotiating powers at Geneva that the several decolonialized French Indochina territories should not attract foreign military bases. Cambodia was, accordingly, not included as a regular member of the SEATO alliance. America after 1955 did grant limited assistance, up to twelve million dollars annually, to help develop a Cambodian army, and also accorded three times that amount in economic aid. Anyone who viewed, as the writer did in 1956, the state of comic indiscipline prevailing within the emerging Cambodian army can appreciate Washington's discounting that country's role in any defense of the free world.

Prince Sihanouk's modulation in the direction of a policy of neutrality began as early as 1954, largely in imitation of India's Pandit Nehru. The trend was attributable in part to domestic political considerations. Allegations from opposition elements that Sihanouk had sold out to America could best be refuted by assuming a neutralist stance. At the Bandung Conference in early 1955, he capitalized on the absence of any formal U.S. military presence in Cambodia and the country's exclusion from SEATO to obtain pledges respecting its territorial integrity and independence from both Chou En-lai and North Vietnam's Pham Van Dong.

Diplomatic relations between Washington and Phnom Penh deteriorated further after 1958, when substantial American military equipment began to be delivered to neighboring South Vietnam, Thailand, and Laos. Cambodia complained of border harassment on all three frontiers and demanded that America take effective measures to curb the allegedly aggressive tendencies demonstrated by its assumed puppet regimes. The general situation seemed to worsen after 1960, culminating in the neutralization of Laos in 1962 and the collapse of the Diem regime in 1963. Prince Sihanouk finally decided to set a new course in anticipation of the eventual withdrawal of America and the victory of pro-Communist elements in Vietnam and Laos. Marshal Sarit in Bangkok was also hinting as early as 1957, and following the neutralization of Laos in 1962, that Thailand also might have to seek an accommodation with Red China. Prince Sihanouk's frenetic efforts after 1962 to obtain international guarantees via special conferences, exchange of "official letters" by world powers as suggested by President Kennedy, or through the United Nations, all ran aground against America's necessity to heed the negative views of Saigon and Bangkok authorities and in view of the danger of exposing America's whole South Vietnam commitment to partisan Communist and neutralist attack. Only France among the Western powers acceded to Phnom Penh's proposals, whereas the entire Communist bloc accepted them, having nothing to lose thereby. Even after

Sihanouk's announced decision to seek Communist accomodation, America persisted in efforts to retrieve the situation. The final break came over Cambodia's unproved accusation that the United States was collaborating with Cambodia's enemies in advocating Sihanouk's overthrow.[20] American assistance was accordingly ended in November, 1963, and subsequent efforts by Phnom Penh to revive the rejected conference proposal and to obtain United Nations consideration of Cambodia's complaints proved abortive. Diplomatic relations with the U.S. were completely severed in 1964. Cambodia's postwar problems like those of Laos could not be comprehended, much less solved, within the context of the cold war dichotomy.

VIEW OF ASIAN PEOPLES TOWARD AMERICA'S INVOLVEMENT

The Asian governments most sympathetic to America's military role in Southeast Asia were Thailand, Taiwan, and South Korea. Bangkok saw in the American presence in South Vietnam the means of thwarting the ambitions of China-supported Vietnamese enemies who had from time to time shared traditional Thai suzerainty over both Laos and Cambodia. Dissident subversive operations (*à la* Viet Cong) at the village level in the northeastern provinces of Thailand increased substantially in 1966-1967, especially following Bangkok's consenting to American use of its territory for bombing bases against North Vietnam. Behind this potential Viet Minh subversive threat lay the huge mass of China's population, whose expatriates, although apolitical, largely dominated Thailand's economy. In lieu of requested SEATO military aid, Bangkok secured bilateral pledges of American military support in case of attack. Meanwhile, Thailand kept its frontline participation in the Vietnamese fighting at minimal levels, while Bangkok's governing elite profited from a variety of American economic and military aid projects. Behind Thailand's reserved posture was an occasionally revealed popular hostility to the increasing American presence and a revival of traditional care to avoid any risk of incurring colonial status. The governing circles, on the other hand, feared that America's anti-Communist commitment, so greatly to their advantage, might not continue indefinitely.

Chiang Kai-shek of Taiwan and Vice-President Ky of Saigon would presumably both like to see America's anti-Communist struggle in Vietnam expand to include mainland China. Such a hope was encouraged at Taipei by the mainland Red Guard agitation of 1966-67 which threatened to engulf China proper in rebellion and prospective civil war. Taipei was nevertheless fully aware that the United States was not prepared to sponsor Chiang's grandiose plans for reconquest of China or to encourage Taiwanese forces to participate in the defense of South Vietnam. The latter move would have offended all Vietnamese peoples, north and south, and would probably have precipitated overt Red Chinese intervention. Meanwhile South Korea sought to enhance its political and military prestige by sending some 48,000 able fighting men to South Vietnam, with America paying the costs.

The Philippine government, like Thailand until late 1967, sent only a token force to South Vietnam in an unenthusiastic gesture of military solidarity with the United States. A Filipino medical mission sent to Laos was also American financed. Meanwhile, Manila's failure to implement its agrarian reform laws, long since approved by the Philippine Congress, and the ever-growing exhibition of bureaucratic corruption provided grounds for a possible revival of Hukbalahap pro-Communist disaffection in central Luzon. The Filipinos, at the same time, tended to resent being taken for granted by an America whose interests in Asia extended far beyond those of the Island Republic and who allegedly frequently treated fence-sitters more generously than loyal Filipino friends.

Alongside these Asian supporters of American policy in Southeast Asia were other states in the area which entertained strong reservations concerning the Vietnam war. The Tokyo government accepted America's necessary presence along the Asian periphery, even though Tokyo would very much like to recover sovereign control of the Ryukyus. But the Japanese people reportedly would not accept indefinitely American escalation of military operations in North Vietnam involving, as it did, the obvious danger of precipitating a general Asian war. Burma opposed the pro-American stance assumed by Thailand as being inevitably provocative of hostility on the part of China. Like Sihanouk, the Burmese assumed that China would remain in East Asia long after the Americans had gone. Finding, presumably, that good relations with Peking called for severance of all American connections, which Rangoon had reason to distrust in any case, General Ne Win's military government, after 1962, cut virtually all aid ties and cultural contacts with the West and sought in Maoist style to fashion a "Burmese Road to Socialism" on an essentially military-peasant base. This China-accommodation tactic ran aground in mid-1967, when the Red Guard furor was transmitted to Rangoon. It was not immediately clear what change the rift with Peking might entail in Burma's attitude toward America. Actually, little changed.

Malaysia and Singapore were too preoccupied by the threat of the Indonesian confrontation until early 1966 to consider supporting the American policy in South Vietnam. Even after 1966, neither party was willing to make any explicit commitments. At the same time, both were far from happy over the announced withdrawal of British security forces from Malaysia by 1971. British withdrawal would leave America as virtually the sole great power recourse against any future Chinese threat.

Post-Sukarno Indonesia would have to qualify at least temporarily the assertion of its pretention of primacy in Malay-inhabited regions of Southeast Asia, because of urgent need for non-Communist economic aid, but it would have difficulty reconciling such residual ambitions with an indefinite American military presence. The spirit of confrontation could not be assumed to be entirely dead. For the moment, however, the island empire since 1967 was so completely alienated from Sukarno's erstwhile friend, Communist China, that a moderately cooperative course with its neighbours was the only feasible one to pursue. Indonesia accordingly restored diplomatic relations with Singapore and Malaysia and rejoined the United Nations. Australian participation in the Vietnam war, although minor in extent, was genuinely effective.

The Association of Southeast Asian Nations (ASEAN) was formed in 1967 as an instrument of cultural and economic cooperation, including five states of the area, Indonesia, the Philippines, Malaysia, Thailand and Singapore. The Association might in time be able to assume limited political and military responsibilities. Any hope of including India and Pakistan in an effective regional security arrangement was ruled out because of their mutual hostility and their general opposition to the American conduct of the Vietnam War. Pakistan's obsessive desire to annex Kashmir made it willing to court the friendship of Red China, while India, on its part, was still struggling after 1962 with chronic food deficits which could only be met by massive grain shipments from the United States.

Red China's profound hostility to the American military presence in Southeast Asia was part of a more extended confrontation extending from Korea, Japan, Okinawa, and Taiwan, to the Philippines, Guam, South Vietnam,and lastly Thailand. The role of the United States as Peking's favorite enemy centered primarily in its support and protection of Chiang Kai-shek's so-called "bandit" regime in Taiwan. The massive buildup of American air power in Vietnam and Thailand from 1965 to 1967 served therefore to intensify the fear of American encirclement by China's leaders. One might better understand China's concern by considering how the American people would respond if faced with six or seven Cuban-type missile bases located offshore extending from Newfoundland to Mexico, coupled with a massive Communist intervention in a civil war currently raging below the Rio Grande boundary.

Hanoi's equally profound distrust of America's postwar role in Southeast Asia was based on accumulated experience. It began with Washington's agreement to temporary Chinese occupation of northern Indochina in 1945-1946, followed by subsequent American support of French sovereignty and colonial reconquest. It included Washington's support of the hopeless Bao Dai experiment, followed by the Ngo Dinh Diem regime and the succession of unrepresentative juntas presiding since 1963 at Saigon. The North Vietnamese were not alone among Southeast Asians in their skepticism regarding the allegedly temporary character of the costly American port facilities and air bases constructed in both South Vietnam and Thailand. Nationalist Vietnamese argued that a new colonialism based on puppet rule at Saigon was in the making—an accusation which contributed to solidifying Vietnamese resistance to America's military presence. One need not concede that all such fears were well grounded to appreciate the logic of Hanoi's refusal to accept as valid Washington's repeated affirmations of its dedication to Vietnam's political freedom, to resistance to aggression, and to peace.

Political necessity will probably counsel the continuation in some form of the American military presence in Southeast Asia for an indefinite period. There is no other Western power capable of keeping the peace, able to contribute to economic rehabilitation, and willing to prevent possible Chinese domination of the area. It is, nevertheless, equally clear that the central problem will involve the definition and realization of essential national interests and aspirations. Most of these carry little ideological identification with the outdated issue of America's "sacred" cold war crusade against a Communist world conspiracy. The continuing need, once the Vietnamese conflict is ended, will be for a steady and persistent effort on the part of America and other friendly nations to support through international agencies the basic aspirations of all Southeast Asian countries for dignity, security, and the opportunity for economic development. As part of America's eventual recognition of the fact that artillery and bombing forays have failed to solve basic economic and political problems in Vietnam must come the acceptance of moral responsibility for rebuilding the shattered nation, resettling the destitute refugees in the south, and restoring the destroyed transportation and industrial base of the north. Hopelessly compromised leadership at Saigon could be admitted as refugees to the United States. It is Washington's long-term response to such a constructive commitment that will test American *bona fides*.

❖   ❖   ❖   ❖   ❖

CHAPTER IV

DUTCH COLONIAL POLICY AND SUKARNOISM

By Amry Vandenbosch*

"The evil that men do lives after them; the good is oft interred with their bones." William Shakespeare, Marc Antony in *Julius Caesar*, Act III, Scene 2.

Western imperialism, that amazing phenomenon of modern history, has about come to an end. It is not surprising that in many cases its passing has been attended by convulsions. Colonial rule had become so deeply imbedded in the life of vast areas and become so important a factor in the world's political structure that the rapid dissolution of colonial empires could not take place without profound disturbances. Colonialism generally did not promote an easy transition to self-government. If the alien ruler yields his responsibility too easily and rapidly, the result may be chaos; if he resists a strong nationalist movement too long, violence will erupt. Pressure and resistance in the situation was practically inevitable. Also, world politics as it developed in the modern period stimulated rather than discouraged the acquisition and retention of overseas territories. Governments were fearful of doing anything which might weaken their relative economic and military strength, though in retrospect it is easy to see that the idea that colonies were a source of economic strength was very much an illusion.

The colonial problem was complicated by at least two factors, as is well illustrated in the case of the Dutch and especially in the East Indies. The Dutch essentially were a democratic people with a long republican tradition. Those who had liberal views on colonial policy could think of transferring sovereignty in the dependency only to a democratic

*Professor-Emeritus of Political Science, former Director of the Patterson School of Diplomacy and International Commerce (1958-1965) at the University of Kentucky, and a former colleague of Dr. Vinacke.

government, but the basic conditions necessary for such a government were absent in the Netherlands Indies.[1] Nor was there a native ruler to whom the government of all the Indies could be turned over. There was none with enough prestige and authority to command the allegiance of the various ethnic groups of this large insular empire to whom the reins of government could be transferred, even if there had been many Netherlanders inclined toward this solution.

DUTCH POLICIES AND NATION-BUILDING

Modern government to be effective requires a nation to sustain it. This is especially true of democratic governments, for election compaigns and the legislative process can be very divisive. Where there is no nation there can be no national government. This is true by definition and in fact. This is obvious in many of the new states of Africa which have difficulty in holding together. The newly independent peoples ardently desire higher levels of living, but modernization requires discipline and sacrifice, for which a strong national sentiment is necessary. Lack of unity in Indonesia accounts in large part for the turbulence of the first two decades of its national life. There was little unity when the Dutch arrived and too little when they left to support an effective modern government. Indonesia is composed of thousands of islands spread over a vast area; its population is divided among scores of ethnic groups, with many distinct languages. Even a carefully planned policy to promote integration, pursued with skill and determination, might not have succeeded, but unfortunately many features of Dutch policy tended to retard rather than promote the unification of the peoples of Indonesia.

In so far as there was an Indonesian nation at the time of the Japanese invasion in 1942 it was largely the result of Dutch administration over the Indies. When Indonesians speak of the meager achievements of the Dutch in advancing their welfare and building a nation in three centuries of rule, they fail to take into consideration all of the relevant facts of the history of Dutch administration.[2] While the Dutch fairly early staked out their claims to the territory that is now Indonesia, they restricted their activities and effective administration to Java, the Spice Islands and some outposts on the larger islands. Indeed, the Dutch deliberately followed a policy of "abstention" or "non-penetration" in a large part of the colonial empire until about 1900. There were "Little Netherlanders" who argued that their country's colonial task was too much for it and advocated giving up a large part of its territory in the East. It was not until about the turn of the century, when the international situation permitted no delay in the matter, that the Netherlands began to penetrate every corner of the archipelago with its administration. The process involved some costly colonial wars. The conquest of Acheh, which was a bitter, protracted affair, drained the Indies government of so much energy and money that it delayed the intensification of administration outside of Java. West New Guinea had to wait until the 1920's, and then only a few administrative posts were established at strategic points.

The concentration of Dutch activities and administration on Java and the neglect of the outer islands has helped to produce a serious maldistribution of Indonesia's population and a consequent grave political problem. The very term "outer islands" is an indication of the Java-centered thinking of the Dutch. In 1815 the population of Java and its appendages was not much larger than that of the outer islands, but by 1930 it was twice as large. The large, dense agricultural population mass on Java is not due solely to the Dutch administration. Nature has made this tropical island one of the most productive areas in the world. But, by putting an end to incessant wars, by bringing modern hygiene, developing irrigation, and introducing better seeds and methods of cultivation, Dutch rule made it possible for larger numbers to live in this limited area. The introduction of the highly productive sugar industry also enabled Java to support a large, essentially agricultural population. With two-thirds of the population of the country on one island and its appendages, which embrace less than a fourteenth of the area of Indonesia, the peoples of the outer islands naturally fear a Java-centered, Java-dominated government. If Indonesia were a solid land mass, such regional concentration of population would create a political problem; the fact that Indonesia is composed of islands spread over a vast area accentuates a political problem which will not be easily solved.[3]

The development of a prosperous modern economy in Sumatra and other outer territories—a development in which the indigenous small holder also shared to some extent—contributed considerably to a growing difference in political, economic and racial outlook between the people of Java and those of the other islands. The fact that the Dutch administration varied so greatly in duration and intensity in various parts of the Indies is one reason why the country was so poorly integrated and lacked unity in 1949. Indirect rule also retarded the process of nation-building. About seven percent of the area of Java and a little over half of the outer islands or territories, as the Dutch called them, were governed indirectly, that is through native rulers. Only about a fifth of the population was found in the native principalities. The largest—one of the four native states in Java—had a population of less than three million when Indonesia became independent, while the smallest had jurisdiction over only a few hundred people. Under the pressure of intense colonization and the demands for better administration the actual amount of autonomy had to be reduced steadily, so that towards the end of the Dutch administration indirect rule was in reality a form of decentralization rather than of self-government. But whether it was more one than the other, it served to retard the unification of the country.

The same was true of the policy of nonassimilation and the closely related policy of differentiation in accordance with need—both cardinal features of Dutch rule in the Indies. In contrast with the Americans and the French, the Dutch were not cultural assimilationists. They were not strong cultural nationalists at home. Their weakness was probably the reverse, that they too easily adopted foreign ideas and ways. The complaint was made at times that there was little Dutch national culture. For a considerable period French was the language of the upper classes. There are explanations for this. A small nation of wide traders, situated at the crossroads of Western Europe, was bound to be somewhat cosmopolitan in character since a relatively large part of the population was in contact with foreigners and exposed to alien cultures. Foreigners were attracted to the Netherlands, and it was long a haven for exiles from many lands. Whatever the reason, the Dutch manifested little desire to make over the Indonesians after their own image.

Indonesian nationalists were prone to ascribe this nonassimilationist attitude to a determination on the part of the Dutch to keep Indonesia backward. The introduction of Western learning, science and ideas would strengthen Indonesian nationalism and lead to demands for political independence. On the other hand, nationalists were averse to assimilationist policies because they were considered destructive of an Indonesian identity. The two attitudes may seem inconsistent but are readily understandable. Nationalists in non-Western countries faced the dilemma of wanting to adopt the tools of the West but not its values. Is this possible? The struggle to resolve this difficulty remains a cause of unrest in many developing countries.

In addition to indirect rule, the Dutch policy of recognizing native societies, their institutions and customs was most actively followed with respect to native customary law and local government and administration. No attempt was made to place all the population groups, or even all of the Indonesians, under the same law. Each element of the population had its own legal system, and to a large extent each had its separate judicial administration. Some twenty native customary law areas were recognized, thus making for a multiplicity of law.[4]

The Eurasians were legally assimilated by the Dutch, but they really constituted a separate community in Indies society. Their position was often difficult, caught as they were between the upper (Western) and the lower (Indonesian) millstones. The plight of the Eurasian after Indonesian independence was hardly enviable. Migration to the Netherlands did not appeal to many, and they did not feel at home in Indonesia where they were doomed to submergence in the masses. Concern for the Eurasians was an important factor in the Dutch decision to retain West New Guinea as a potential home for this group, which had been very loyal to the Dutch. As a settlement area for Eurasians it was a failure, while the determination to hold on to the territory embittered relations between Indonesia and the Netherlands and drove moderate Indonesians to the support of Sukarno's anti-Dutch fury.

A long struggle preceded the adoption of the policy. On the surface the easiest solution would have been "European law for all." The advocates of unification on a Western basis frequently quoted the statement made by Macauley in the debates on Indian law reform, "Uniformity when you can have it, diversity when you must have it; but in all cases certainty." The world was moving toward judicial integration, whereas the advocates of adat law wished the Indies to move in the opposite direction. It was also argued that adat law was incapable of meeting the legal needs born of rapidly changing social conditions and increasing intercourse between the various juridical groups.

The advocates of the retention of customary law won. They contended that adat law was the law living in society and that it would be unjust to impose an alien law on a people whose social conditions, mores and social development were quite different from those of the Dutch. Adat law could also develop, it was argued, but it should develop along its own lines. The result was that there was no single law for the peoples of the Indies, and the lines separating the various population groups hardened rather than softened. This clearly did not operate in the direction of building a nation; it retarded the economic and social development and integration of the country. Not only was it a matter of observing customary law, but also of preserving the communal adat communities. The ardent advocates of customary law seemed to want to keep the Indies an anthropological museum. They seemed to be totally unaware of the rapid changes that were taking place in Indies society. They could not, of course, have foreseen the social upheaval which was to come.

In adopting the policy of protecting customary law and social institu-

tions the Dutch were dealing with a difficult problem of underdeveloped
societies. Modernization was necessary to provide the production for
higher levels of living and the public income to support welfare policies,
but modernization tends to disintegrate traditional society. In this matter the policies of the British in Burma and those of the Dutch in the
Indies were quite different. As put by J. S. Furnivall, a member of the
civil service in India and Burma who made a very basic and thorough
comparative study[5] of the two colonial policies, the basic principles of
the British policy in Burma were the rule of law and economic freedom,
while the Dutch imposed restraints on economic forces "by strengthening personal authority and by conserving the influence of custom." In
Burma there were, he said, five notorious evils: "the failure of western
self-governing institutions; the growth of debt and agrarian distress;
the multiplication of litigation and crime; the rise of disaffection and unrest among the Buddhist clergy; and widespread corruption in the judicial and administrative services." He was convinced that all these evils
were caused by the disintegration of social life by "the working of anti-
social economic forces" which the law was unable to control. In all these
matters the Indies presented "a notable contrast." While critical of other
aspects of Dutch policy, he urged the British to incorporate in their policy "the principle of controlling economic forces in the interests of social welfare" and he recommended the adoption of certain devices of
Dutch administrative machinery in order that "this principle might be
applied to cure the ills of modern Burma, and to lay the basis of a new
and constructive policy."

Was this analysis by the wise student and able practitioner correct?
The traumatic experiences of both peoples—the Japanese invasion and
occupation and the violence which followed—were such shattering experiences that no judgment can be made on the question of whether the
Indies society could have adjusted to modernization without severe
shock if there had been no war. Did the Dutch protective policies merely
delay the inevitable shocks which must come with entrance into history?

The Dutch policy of differentiation in accordance with need was especially marked in education and led to a bewildering multiplicity of
schools. There were folk schools and standard schools, "continuation"
and "link" schools, Dutch-Indonesian and Dutch-Chinese schools, to say
nothing of the various types of vocational schools. Secondary and higher
education was Western with Dutch as the medium of instruction, but
in the elementary schools Malay or the local vernacular was employed.
Education was not used to promote a unified, national society.

The structure of the representative institutions also tended to accentuate rather than soften the divisive tendencies of Indies society by the introduction of communal and proportional representation. The members of the local and provincial councils and the Volksraad, as the central legislative body was called, were chosen by separate electorates representing the three main racial groups, namely the indigenous peoples, the Europeans and the nonindigenous Asiatics. There was little statesmanship exhibited in introducing proportional representation from an old, settled, relatively homogeneous society like that of the Netherlands to a plural, heterogeneous society like that of the Indies. It encouraged ideological groups, however small, to seek political power and thus tended to produce the hardening of ideological lines. Political fragmentation and an uncompromising spirit were its natural fruits.

NATIVE WELFARE AND WESTERN CAPITAL

When the Dutch became concerned about their responsibilities for the welfare of the Indonesians they were confronted with another dilemma. Schools, libraries, public health, good roads and the like cost money. Modern social institutions can only be provided and supported by a modern economy. The system of state exploitation, which had for a while enabled a stream of gold to flow to the Netherlands treasury, was doing very poorly. Its profits were withering away. At the same time the rising Dutch middle class were demanding ever more insistently that private capital be permitted to develop the Indies. Much was expected from encouraging private capital to invest in the dependency. It would, it was claimed, develop the colony more rapidly, provide a flourishing market for Dutch goods, stimulate the flow of profits to the Netherlands and improve the welfare of the Indonesians. Capital did begin to flow into the Indies in an increasing volume, but while it did some marvelous things, its achievements were not all on the credit side.

Dutch capital seeking profitable investment in the Indies encountered two problems. Large agricultural enterprises offered the greatest promise, but the Agrarian Law of 1870 prohibited the alienation of land to non-Indonesians. Use of the necessary land was made possible by long term concessions of public lands and the renting of private lands. However, there was little public land left in Java due to the pressure of a rapidly growing population, and the renting of land was surrounded by numerous regulations to safeguard the interests of the peasants. There was this handicap in operating in Java, but the sugar industry for a long time managed to thrive there in spite of it—aided, no doubt, by the abundant supply of cheap labor. In the outer islands the situation was the reverse of that in Java. There were vast areas available for concessions for private exploitation, but an adequate labor supply was lacking. This problem was solved by the labor contract with penal sanctions, with recruitment of coolies in Java and China. But the immigration of large numbers of Chinese created a grave social problem which became especially acute after Indonesian independence.

Dutch and other Western capital did flow into the Indies in increasing volume, but the results were not all that had been promised for it. It did increase the public revenues. In the 1920's, their most flourishing period, Western enterprises contributed forty percent of the government revenues. Europeans paid over half of the income tax alone. The East Coast of Sumatra, which had developed into a very prosperous center of Western agricultural industry, yielded the central treasury a surplus of 50,000,000 florins, which was about equal to the amount spent on education by the central government. It was also successful in stimulating an increasing stream of profits to the Netherlands. But this produced other effects scarcely beneficial for the Indonesians. The Western entrepreneurs, their representatives and beneficiaries became an influential force opposed to social legislation and the extension of self-government. Many Netherlanders at home became convinced that the Dutch economy was highly dependent on the retention of the Indies as a dependency. This was not conducive to a more liberal Indies policy.

Nor was it so evident that the presence of the Western capitalist enterprises promoted native welfare. While they increased the social income, they tended to block the development of an independent farmer class and offered Indonesians few opportunities of advancement in the industry. In the sugar districts of Java the native landowner became a laborer on his own land and in the factories. On the other islands, where the great Western agricultural enterprises were located, only the soil had a purely native character. For the rest, everything was imported: capital, the managers and the assistants were all Western, the laborers were from Java and China. There were no gradations in this economic structure which would have enabled the native to climb to higher levels. Between the native small holders and the highly, technically-organized Western industry there was nothing. The Indonesian, for the most part, found it practically impossible to forge ahead in the presence of these powerful economic units. Also, there were complaints from the Javanese peasants that government officials, Indonesian as well as Dutch, did not protect them in their rights against the sugar industry. The native peasant, so ran the frequent complaint, did not get a fair deal in such matters as water division and land rent.

The development of the great industries—rubber, tobacco, tin, oil, bauxite, copra—in the outer islands and the heavy pressure of population in Java created an economic imbalance which became politically disturbing after independence. The outer islands came to earn more than three-fourths of Indonesia's foreign exchange receipts. The introduction of a multiple exchange rate system which discriminated aganst exporters led to serious administrative, fiscal and political problems. To escape the exchange controls which reduced the profitability of exporting through legal channels, smuggling and other irregularities became rampant, resulting in heavy losses to the central treasury. This situation stirred up the latent desire of the outer islanders for regional autonomy. They wanted to retain a greater portion of the foreign exchange which they earned and to keep for local development a larger percentage of the taxes they paid. If not carefully handled, this could easily lead to a "free from Java" movement. It was an important factor in the 1957-58 rebellion.

The Dutch were not unaware of these dangers, and in the last decade or two of their rule they sought to bring about a greater economic integration of the country. Transportation between the islands was improved and the industrialization of Java was promoted. Inter-island trade was increasing, chiefly between Java and the outer islands, but the process of integration had not proceeded far at the time of the Japanese invasion.[6] One writer has characterized colonial Indonesia as "a bureaucratic wonderland: a cluster of interacting but basically separate linguistic and cultural universes, linked by the miracle of modern bureaucratic and technical organization."[7] This is an apt if exaggerated characterization.

The Netherlands Indies was a paradise for civil servants. Candidates for the Interior Administration (*Binnenlandsche Bestuur*) were carefully selected and then sent to Leiden University or Utrecht (in later years) and given five years of training, at government expense, in law and Indological studies, including two Indonesian languages. Scientifically trained and their curiosity aroused, these young men at once became keen students of Indonesian life. Until the last few years they could work free from political pressures; it was a bureaucrat's heaven. The standards of administration in the Indies were very high.

But here again the best was the enemy of the good. The Dutch insistence upon efficiency and tidiness made them loath to bring Indonesians into the service, since they were convinced that administrative standards would suffer unless this were done gradually. The civil service personnel before the war represented a pyramid with Europeans (almost exclusively) at the top, Eurasians and Indonesians (far more Eurasians than Indonesians) in the middle, and Indonesians at the base. Not only had very few Indonesians been given superior positions by the time of the Japanese invasion, but also the Indonesian and Dutch corps were kept separate. The process of "deguardianization" involved the withdrawal of the Dutch from succeeding levels of administration until they should finally be completely withdrawn. The semi-hereditary regents were important officials, but they were generally regarded by the nationalists as loyal to the Dutch. With independence the "cooperators" were either removed or under suspicion while the "non-cooperators" who got on the government payroll after independence were generally untrained, inexperienced and political. Thus in Indonesia there was no body of trained, experienced native public administrators to furnish such a steel framework of government as was so highly effective in holding the Indian government together in difficult times. For a government determined to set up a welfare state this was a serious handicap.

There was a similar problem with respect to the armed forces. The Netherlands Indies Army was a body of professional soldiers recruited chiefly from the Dutchified Ambonese and Minahassans with many Eurasians among the officers. Since they were loyal to the Dutch they were not very welcome in the forces of the Republic. The Republican Army was swollen by patriots, and when the government sought to professionalize the army and reduce its size such a political storm arose that the reorganization could not be effected.

FAIRNESS IN JUDGMENT

One must be careful in applying present day ideas and standards to policies and measures of half a century and more ago.[8] The climate has changed radically. Social thinking and social movements have accelerated tremendously in the last three or four decades. There is a tendency to condemn colonial powers for not doing in their dependencies what Western countries were not yet doing at home. In some respects Dutch policy might be considered advanced. Many social anthropologists would probably approve the policy of preserving adat law and communities. In the matter of trade the Netherlands maintained the open door in the Indies in sharp contrast with the assimilated and preferential tariff policies of the French in Indochina and the United States in the Philippines. There was a strange contradiction in both American and Dutch policies in this respect, but in opposite directions. American policy was directed toward preparing the Philippines for early political independence but its commercial policy (of one hundred percent trade preferences between the United States and the dependency) made for steadily greater economic dependence of the Philippines on the United

States. The Dutch policy of the open door made for the economic independence of the Indies, but the Dutch had only a faint or halfhearted interest in preparing their dependency for political independence.

The Dutch also adopted the mixed form of public and private exploitation of natural resources with the object of obtaining the advantages of private initiative and efficiency and conserving the public interest in its natural heritage, a device increasingly adopted by developing countries. Much of the mining of tin and the extracting and refining of oil was brought under this form of exploitation. Corporations were set up in which the government and the private companies owned equal amounts of stock. Nor was the Indies government afraid of "socialism." Under the conditions prevailing in the colonial society, the government felt justified in engaging extensively in business enterprises. In addition to such traditional public services as postal services and savings, telegraph and telephone services and harbor works, the government owned and operated railroads, bus lines, gold, silver and coal mines, teak lumbering, and also operated large cinchona, rubber, tea and gutta percha plantations. A large percentage of the government's income derived from these sources. Here mention should also be made of the Dutch policy of prohibiting the alienation of the land and natural resources to non-indigenous persons. There was no large-scale ownership of land or other resources by Westerners. The Dutch had not developed an integrated economy, but they did leave Indonesians the land and the natural resources without alien encumbrances.

The Dutch were content to go slowly in preparing the Indonesians for self-government. Caution and thoroughness are leading traits of their national character. Mistakes had to be avoided; Indonesians should not be educated more rapidly and in larger numbers than the slowly changing society could abosorb. Imbalance could create serious social problems. Indonesians should not be given positions in the intermediate and higher ranks of the government service so rapidly as to lower the high standards of administration set by the Dutch civil service—standards which had to be maintained to prevent social disaster and to stimulate economic development. The Dutch proceeded as if they had unlimited time. World War II, and especially the Japanese invasion, brought their orderly plans to a cataclysmic end. How much time the Dutch would have had if the war had not intervened no one can say, but probably not very much. In any case, the pressure of the Indonesian nationalist movement had already reached a point of such accelerating intensity that the days of effective Dutch administration were about over. Would the Dutch and the Indonesians have reached some accommodation which would have made continued fruitful cooperation between the two countries possible? If so, the course of Netherlands-Indonesian relations and of early Indonesian national history would have been quite different. How differently would the decolonization process have taken place if there had been no war? One can argue plausibly that the Dutch and the Indonesians would have come to a gradual accommodation without resort to organized violence, and with equal logic that the Dutch would not have yielded rapidly enough to prevent protracted hostilities. What would have happened would have depended a great deal on the course of the decolonization movement generally.

In examining the relation between Dutch colonial policy and post-independence developments it must not be forgotten that the Dutch were not the last to exercise alien rule in Indonesia. The three and a half years of Japanese occupation and administration had profound effects on Indonesian society. The Japanese conquest had so shattered Dutch prestige and authority that the Dutch rule could never be restored in anything like the old form, if at all. The Japanese systematically undermined the Dutch position and whipped up anti-Dutch, anti-Western sentiment. Under the Dutch policy of neutralism with respect to religion, Islamism had penetrated widely and deeply in Indonesian society. The Japanese aided the Muslim teachers in the villages to strengthen their position at the expense of the adat officials who had cooperated with the Dutch. Until the last few weeks of the occupation the secular nationalists were ignored, and while the prestige of reformist and moderate Muslims was depressed, that of the Muslim extremists was raised. The Japanese, on the other hand, used Islamism for their own ends. Also, the Japanese created a whole new class of military leaders. The convulsions of the Japanese invasion and occupation and of the political revolution greatly changed Indonesia's temper and brought changes in its society. The horrible Japanese interlude contributed to the conditions which made for Sukarnoism.[9] The effect of Japanese policy was to sharpen the conflict between the elite groups in their struggle for power. The divergent and irreconcilable aims of these groups rendered the Indonesian government impotent and led to the abandonment of parliamentary democracy. The Japanese left two time bombs in Indonesia: a mass paramilitarized nationalism and a heightened tension between militant theocratic and moderate Muslims.

NO BASIC COLONIAL PHILOSOPHY

Did the Dutch have a fundamental colonial philosophy? Professor G. H. Bousquet, a French student of Dutch colonial policy, concluded that the Dutch had no colonial ideal and no conception of their task in the colonies.[10] To the French with their pronounced views of cultural and political assimilation, the Dutch attitudes seemed colorless and incomprehensible.[11] C. Snouck Hurgronje, the great Dutch scholar of Islamism and Indonesian society, did advocate a policy somewhat akin to that of the French. He contended that the alliance with the adat chiefs was an inadequate basis for a policy, for a modern society could not be built on adat and adat rulers. Indonesians had lost whatever of distinctively indigenous political and cultural life they had possessed and it could not be revived. Islamism had only slightly penetrated Indonesian life by 1900, but it was advancing. Snouck Hurgronje advocated the rapid westernization of Indonesia by a policy of "association" of the Indonesian elite with Dutch culture. Western education would alienate young Indonesians from Islam and traditional Indonesian life. Only a policy of association offered any hope of a prolonged role for the Dutch in the eastern archipelago.

It is obvious that there was a basic inconsistency in the thinking of most Netherlanders and in the government's colonial policy. The ideal behind their policy was the ultimate association of Dutch and Indonesians in a European-Asiatic state. The policy advocated by Snouck Hurgronje was more in line with this ideal than nonassimilation and the protection and strengthening of adat and adat institutions. This policy served to retard both the unification of the Indonesian peoples and their receptiveness to Dutch culture. But it is doubtful whether the rapid westernization of Indonesia would have had the effect Snouck Hurgronje expected of it. It would very probably have accelerated the development of a secular, anti-Western nationalism.

Snouck Hurgronje was mistaken in several respects. He underestimated the vitality of Islam and he was wrong in assuming that religion and politics in Islam could be separated easily. He did not foresee the awakening of Islam. The Japanese shared with the Muslim the view that religious and political community coincide; their propaganda strengthened the ideal of an Islamic state embracing all of Indonesia. The Darul Islam movement, adopting terrorism as its method of setting up a theocratic state, was a natural product of the Japanese policy.

A semiofficial philosophic justification for colonialism was made by A. D. A. de Kat Angelino, an official in the Netherlands Indies government, only a decade before the Japanese invasion brought an end to Dutch rule in the East.[12] He saw the function of colonial government as a phase of the world problem of the reconciliation of East and West, which could only be solved by a synthesis of the cultures—a synthesis

which could best be achieved under the colonial relationship. Unless
this meeting of the Occident and the Orient took place under wise leadership and careful protection, human culture would be impoverished
rather than enriched. Eastern society might disintegrate and the peace
of the world be endangered. The chief function of colonial administration, then, was the protection of native society. The idea of a continued
Dutch-Indonesian political association underlay the argument.

Each generation judges the past in the light of its own interests and
ideals. About the only function and justification of colonialism the present generation can admit is preparation of the people in a given territory for nationhood. This may or may not be fair, but if this is to be the
basis of judgment Dutch policies as a whole were ill conceived. Unfortunately, the Dutch compounded their mistakes by resisting the Indonesian nationalist demands with violence and by insisting upon
terms of settlement which were highly unpopular with the Indonesian
leaders—terms which the latter probably accepted as a matter of tactics
but with no intention of carrying out. The Dutch resort to violence to
reestablish their authority had embittered relations between the two
peoples; the insistence upon the formation of a Netherlands-Indonesian
union and the withholding of West New Guinea from the territory of the
new Indonesian state further poisoned the atmosphere.

The Dutch were pathetically eager to maintain some kind of association with their erstwhile dependency, probably because they feared
that without the Indies their position and role in the international community would be sadly diminished. The Netherlands was small and
crowded; the Indies large and populous. The Dutch had invested heavily in the Indies and were convinced that their economic welfare was
highly dependent on the colony. Fortunately, events have shown that
this dependence was greatly exaggerated. Undoubtedly, Dutch membership in the European Common Market helped absorb the shock.
But more than these considerations, over the centuries untold connections
had developed between the Dutch and the Indies. Many Dutch fami-
lies regarded the Indies as much their home as the Netherlands. Severance of the close ties with the Indies involved a psychological lacera-
tion. But every attempt by the Dutch to maintain some association with
Indonesia was regarded by the Indonesian nationalists as evidence of
Dutch unwillingness fully to recognize their national freedom. This increased their determination to effect a complete severance and assert
their independence. The Dutch were unwise to insist on a union and at
the same time to demand the retention of West New Guinea. For the
union to be successful much good will was required on the part of

both parties, but the effort to hold on to West New Guinea made for extreme ill will.

It is quite natural to assume that if the Dutch had yielded more graciously and completely Dutch-Indonesian relations would have been good and mutually profitable, but this may be erroneous. The presence of so much Dutch capital and of so many Netherlanders in business and in managerial posts, plus the intensity of Dutch rule, made the Indonesian nationalists extremely sensitive about their independence of action. Their ego suffered in the presence of their former rulers, and they easily concluded that Indonesia had not truly acquired its independence so long as the Dutch continued to play so important a role in the life of their country. It is difficult to believe that there would not have been trouble between the two peoples.

The attempt to hold West New Guinea boded no good either for the future of Dutch-Indonesian relations or the democratic development of Indonesia. It played into the hands of extremists. It gave substance to the frenzied harangues of Sukarno to his people to carry on the unfinished revolution. The new state was drawn away from constructive national endeavor to demagoguery and to wasteful national ventures.

TRANSITION TO INDEPENDENCE

One of the more unfortunate aspects of colonialism was that it provided no easy shift from dependence to national freedom. Unless real pressure were put on the colonial government by the nationalists, the metropolitan country would find it difficult to believe that the latter really wanted independence or that the people were ready for it. On the other hand, if the nationalists were forced into a role of opposition to practically all the policies and measures of the colonial government not because they were bad but solely because they were sponsored by the alien ruler, constructive cooperation was at an end and with it effective government. This produced at least two bad effects for the future independent government. Since there was no likelihood that they would suddenly become responsible for carrying on the government, the national leaders developed an irresponsible, negative attitude toward serious problems of government and administration, and in order to get mass support for the nationalist independence movement, they aroused expectations for an independent government, headed by these leaders, which could never be fulfilled. This was the case in many newly independent states but it was especially true in Indonesia where the undisputed national leader was a person gifted with charismatic leadership and an extraordinary demagogic ability but with no understanding of economics and with no feeling for the importance of efficient administration for national development. Whether the course of events in Indonesia would have been greatly different if another type of personality had been the national leader is another of the unanswered "ifs" of history.[13]

INDONESIAN INDEPENDENCE AND THE RAPID
DECLINE OF CONSTITUTIONAL GOVERNMENT

Indonesian political leaders complained bitterly about the heritage they received from the Dutch, but they did little to change the institutions and practices which they took over from them. Under pressure from the outer islands, a federal constitution was agreed upon by the Indonesians just before the transfer of sovereignty, but no real effort was made to put it into operation. Within nine months, and without a national referendum, it was replaced by a fundamental law setting up a unitary system of government. The federal constitution was stigmatized as Dutch fabricated and imposed (through the federalists of the outer islands) to deprive the leaders of the Republic of the full fruits of their revolutionary victory. So Indonesia went back to a unitary system, which was what they had under the Dutch, and in less than a decade a rebellion broke out against "Javanese centralism." This is not to suggest that if only the federal system had been retained there would have been no rebellion; that would have depended upon the policies pursued. But the adoption of the unitary constitution was a clear invitation to trouble. The irregular manner in which the shift was made boded no good for the development of constitutional government. Moreover, after nine years of Japanese occupation and Dutch-Indonesian hostilities, economic rehabilitation and development had become extremely urgent. As a result of the constitutional struggle, a precious year was wasted and matters were allowed to drift and deteriorate.

Indonesia began with a parliamentary system modelled after that at The Hague, of which a marked feature was the multiplicity of parties. As in the Netherlands, political divisions were along religious as well as economic and social lines. The numerous parties made for political instability. The only governments possible were coalitions which were formed with difficulty but easily fell apart. Since elections could not be held for some time, the membership of the provisional parliament was distributed among a score of parties on the basis of assumed popular support. With the deferment of elections the authority of parliament and the rapidly succeeding ministries so declined that the territorial military commanders successfully defied the Ali cabinet and brought it down.

It was expected that the national elections held in 1955 would clarify and stabilize the political situation, but they did not. On the contrary, after the national poll had been taken the political deterioration went on at an accelerated pace. One reason for this was probably that the divisions in the provisional parliament, which had been thought to be superficial, were now seen to represent basic conflicts. Thanks in no small measure to proportional representation, twenty-eight parties and individuals won seats, eight more than in the provisional parliament. Instead of reducing the conflicts to manageable proportions, the elections had accentuated them. As a result of the operation of the system of proportional representation used, Java actually received a larger percentage of the membership of the new parliament than its proportion of the total population of the country. This undoubtedly heightened the fears of the outer islands of a Java-dominated government.

Indonesians expected a rapid improvement in economic conditions after independence. With the Dutch "imperialists" no longer in control and with Indonesians in charge of the government, great changes should quickly take place. Instead, the economy deteriorated. They lived in the hope that the national elections would bring political stability and government able to take the measures necessary to promote rapid economic development. The nationalist leaders had convinced the masses that the country was rich in natural resources, and that its people were poor because of the alien rulers. Now that the alien rulers were out and the Indonesians were masters in their own house, surely conditions would rapidly change for the better. But it did not take many months of the first government after the elections to convince many that political stability had not been achieved and that all hope that the new government would seriously grapple with economic problems was vain. Confidence in the political process declined precipitately.

This is not the place to trace in detail the course of events during the decade following the resignation of the second Ali cabinet in March 1957. The years from 1957 to 1965, the year of the abortive Communist coup, may be described as the period of Sukarno's "Guided Democracy." The deeply troubled government successfully met a formidable rebellion and managed to get the Dutch out of West New Guinea and to incorporate the territory into the national domain. These were no mean achievements, but Sukarno's position was precarious. He maintained himself in power by balancing the army and the Communist party against each other. When the Communists tried to take over on the night of September 30, 1965, the army came back so powerfully as to destroy the Communist party as a strong political force for some time. Cautiously but firmly, General Suharto managed to strip Sukarno of his prestige and power. Sukarno's guided democracy thus came to an inglorious end, replaced temporarily at least by a democracy guided by the army. Would the army be able to make a real beginning of solving Indonesia's economic problems, hold the country together and restore democracy?

On the economic side the story of Indonesia under Sukarno is one of steady deterioration. In spite of considerable foreign aid and Japanese reparations, the country had been reduced to near bankruptcy by 1965. Deep-seated political tensions had made impossible a serious attack on the country's economic problems and tended to aggravate them, while the deteriorating economic conditions heightened the political tensions. In view of all the severe blows which it had to endure, it is surprising that the economic life of the country did not grind to a complete stop. The multiple exchange rate system, which discriminated against the export industries of the outer islands and favored the importers of Java, caused discontent and led to large-scale smuggling—and was an important factor in the outbreak of the rebellion in 1957-58. The cost of putting down the uprising was a heavy drain on the treasury. The anti-Chinese and anti-Dutch measures were damaging to the economy, as these two groups played an important role in the economic life of the country. The takeover of the Dutch enterprises produced, among other things, a paralysis in inter-island shipping. The "confrontation" with the Dutch and later with Malaysia was very costly.

Indonesia needed badly to augment its capital assets; instead it depleted them as can be seen from a few statistics. Production in practically all areas declined. One of the notable exceptions was the oil industry, which remained under foreign control until 1965. Exports in value declined by half from 1959 to 1964. The cost of living index shot up over 6500 percent from 1953 to early 1965. The money supply increased nearly a thousand times from 1955 to 1966; the value of the rupiah on the black market declined from 1800 to $US 1 in June, 1964, to 10,000 to $US 1 a year later. Except for a few of the early years, government expenditures far exceeded total public revenues. In 1964 expenditures totalled 680 billion rupiahs; revenues came to 283 billion rupiahs.

SUKARNOISM

Sukarno early developed a hypnotic power over the masses with the spoken word. Words intoxicated him. He read widely in revolutionary literature and social theory and was under a compulsion to philosophize in all his utterances. As early as 1945 he laid down the Pantja Sila, the five basic principles of the Indonesian state. These five principles, which he states as constituting "the philosophy, the innermost idea, the soul, the deepest desire upon which to build the structure of an Indonesian Merdeka [freedom]," were nationalism, internationalism, democracy, social justice, and belief in God. Sukarno proclaimed these principles, very probably, because he felt that the Indonesians needed an ideology as a cohesive force to hold them together and develop an identity, but these principles have little distinctiveness. They are so vague and broad that almost anybody can accept them. In numerous speeches Sukarno elaborated on them and tried to give them more specific meaning.

As his difficulties as political leader of his country mounted, his views changed and moved steadily more to the left. Never in close touch with reality, he moved further away from it as his country's troubles and his own deepened. His addresses, especially his annual Independence Day orations, carried florid, mystical titles such as "Attuned to the Cosmos," "The Realization of the Message of the Peoples' Suffering," "The Year of Living Dangerously," and "Rediscovery of our Revolution." As the failure of Indonesian parliamentary government became more and more obvious, Sukarno turned against what he contemptuously called "free-fight liberalism, majocracy" and "50 percent plus one democracy" and advocated an Indonesian or Asian democracy, a "democracy with leadership" or simply "guided democracy." In his 1959 Independence Day speech which was given a month after he had by decree dissolved the constitutional assembly, abolished the 1950 constitution and proclaimed the return to the 1945 constitution which bore the title "The Rediscovery of our Revolution," he ascribed Indonesia's ills to the sacrifice of the spirit of revolution in order to survive. "Through the Dutch, via the Round Table Conference, we were made to dilute our revolutionary spirit; in Indonesia itself we had to compromise with groups which were non-revolutionary: Dutchified groups, reformist groups, conservative groups, contra-revolutionary groups, chameleon and cockroach [spy for the Dutch] groups. Until at last, in sacrificing this revolutionary spirit, we went away and left the 1945 constitution as an instrument of struggle. Indonesia had deviated from the Spirit, from the Principles and from the Objective of the Revolution."

As his own position became more precarious and conditions in the country worsened, he found emotional outlet in revolution, perpetual revolution, revolution as an end in itself. This was all the Great Leader of the Revolution had to offer his countrymen. In his 1960 Independence Day speech he extolled revolution in a frenzied peroration:

I tell you frankly, I belong to the group of people who are bound in spiritual longing by the romanticism of revolution. I am inspired by it. I am completely absorbed by it. I am crazed, I am obsessed by the romanticism of revolution. . . . That is why I who have been given the top-most leadership in the struggle of the Indonesian nation, never tire of appealing and exhorting: solve our problems in a revolutionary way, make the revolutionary spirit surge on, see to it that the fire of our revolution does not die, or grow dim, not even for a single moment. Come then, keep fanning the flames of the leaping fire of revolution! Brothers and sisters, let us become logs to feed the flames of revolution.

Sukarno never had kind words to waste on capitalism, but as time went on his language took on an increasingly Marxist character. All the ills of the world were charged to capitalism; paradise was to be ushered in with socialism. "The dangers of the A-bomb and the H-bomb—all born of the capitalistic system—should be wiped out," he declared in April 1958. "The new era will be marked by socialism and the brotherhood of man and the fall of capitalism and imperialism which is an historical certainty. Those who cannot understand or oppose the trend of the times will be destroyed."

How seriously is this talk to be taken as ideology? One student of Indonesian society dismisses it as a "smokescreen for failure, a diversion to stave off despair, a mask to conceal reality rather than a portrait to reveal it."[14] Another characterizes it as "a cloak for a power struggle, a façade built out of myths and slogans to shield a system of autocratic personalized rule."[15] Still another student of Indonesian life and politics, however, is much impressed with the ideas which he categorizes as totalitarian democracy.[16] To say that Sukarno's pronounced views are entitled to be recognized as an ideology is not saying much. Radical leaders seek to rationalize and justify their movements by asserting that they are based on universal values, have universal validity and represent a "whole way of life." Even the Afrikaner Nationalist leaders claim this for their policy of apartheid. This is not surprising. An ideology cannot serve to legitimitize a policy or a program unless it can pretend to universal validity. More important than consistency or pretension is whether the ideas correspond to the facts of life and the world —and how the world reacts to them.[17]

One need not be a victim of the verbal magic of a Sukarno to recognize the importance of a national ideology for a young nation in an old and complex world, just as some kind of a life and world view is necessary for an individual. Nkrumah, Nu and Sukarno are examples of the more articulate leaders of new nations who were strongly ideologically minded. All three came to the same political end. Sukarno

seems to have convinced himself as well as many of his fellow countrymen that slogans had a mystical quality and an effectiveness in themselves. They had only to be uttered to produce results. It is important
to remember that Sukarno used ideology as a weapon against his political enemies. All who did not share his ideology were not loyal Indonesians.

While Sukarno himself has gone into political eclipse, Sukarnoism
undoubtedly is still a force, just as Peronism continues as an evil force
in Argentine politics long after the erstwhile leader's departure from
the political scene. Sukarno left Indonesia's economy in shambles; recovery will be a slow painful process which no magic words can lighten.
It would be strange if during these years of toil and sacrifice the minds
of many Indonesians did not turn back in nostalgia to the exciting
days of Sukarno.

It would be absurd to suggest that "guided democracy" received
its inspiration from Dutch rule, but it takes no great stretch of the
imagination to see a relationship between it and the personal character
of Dutch colonial administration. Netherlands officials relied heavily on
personal influence, "gentle pressure," in achieving their administrative goals and in controlling the people. There were frequent complaints
that the people were treated as children who would never grow up. It
was said that "a villager cannot scratch his head unless a district officer
gives him permission and an expert shows him how to do it." J. S. Furnivall, a remarkably keen student of colonial policy and administration,
in a comparative study of Dutch and British colonial policy, concluded
that the caricature which depicted the Dutch system as a *baboe*, a
nursemaid, and the British as a *babu*, a clerk, "does emphasize a difference in vital principle."[18]

Sukarno frequently expressed the wish to be remembered as the
tongue, the mouthpiece of the Indonesian people. It is not a caricature
of Sukarno's attitude toward the Indonesian people to depict it as that of
a *baboe*. He had quick, easy answers not only to the problems of Indonesia but also to the riddles of life and the universe. His Independence
Day addresses have been characterized as "Messages on the State of the
Universe."

In view of the bitterness with which the Indonesians criticized the
political institutions of colonial days, it is surprising how little they
changed the system when they became independent. Where they did
depart from the colonial pattern they unfortunately returned to it. Under the Dutch the government was highly centralized. Many Netherlanders recognized the desirability of decentralizing administratively

and politically, and in fact took the first steps in this direction. For a very brief period Indonesia had a federal system of government; it was abandoned without a fair trial. The "exorbitant" powers of the governor general were often sharply attacked by both Netherlanders and Indonesians; Sukarno as president assumed powers which by comparison made the governor general look like a feeble constitutional monarch. Nationalist leaders were dissatisfied with the limited powers of the Volksraad; they pressed hard for making the government fully responsible to parliament. Yet after independence the role of the representative body declined steadily, and finally precipitately—declined until it was nothing more than the tool of the president. The obviously bad features of the Dutch colonial system, such as proportional representation and the concomitant multiplicity of parties, were not abandoned but retained, and others capable of constructive development were corrupted. The practice of "gentle pressure" to goad the people into a more rapid pace of social and economic development degenerated into "guided democracy" or simply dictatorship. The extensive government participation in business enterprises and the mixed economy became outright dispossession of ownership and economic chaos.

That he welded the peoples of Indonesia into one nation is Sukarno's proud boast. "In twenty years," he declared to newsmen, "I have made this country of 7,000 islands, from Sabang to Merauke, stretching wider than the United States, composed of people of different heritage, speaking different tongues, with varying demands and needs, into one language. They think and do—as an Indonesian."[19] This claim is widely accepted. One observer adds that he gave the Indonesians "some of those intangibles precious to peoples emerging from foreign rule—a sense of national identity and importance, racial pride, the end of inequality and second-class citizenship."[20]

He is sometimes credited with giving his people a national language. Some see in the creation of the Indonesian language a remarkable achievement of the nationalist movement and an essential for the unification of the Indonesians and the modernization of Indonesian life. They seem to forget that Malay was one of the two official languages of the Netherlands Indies and that Indonesian is essentially an expansion of that language. Some go further and engage in linguistic mysticism. One sees it as an "enterprise for the mastery of a gigantic cultural crisis, and a partly subconscious *project* for the assumption of 'modernity' within the modalities of an autonomous and autochthonous social-political tradition."[21] He further states that "The new Indonesian has had to develop into a means of communication which can not only express Indonesian nationalism, but Indonesian aspirations, Indonesian traditions and international 'realities' within the limits of a single vocabulary." He speaks of it as a "colossal cultural effort." It may be observed that nationalism frequently seeks a language of its own. An interesting parallel with the development of Indonesian is that of Afrikaans in South Africa. But surely Dutch and English are capable of expressing most ideas, even the peculiar ones of Afrikaners!

That the Indonesians were experiencing an acute cultural crisis is no doubt true, but that it could be resolved by the hasty, artificial creation of a new language, or the rapid expansion of one already widely in use, is difficult to see. The cultural crisis was not created by the language situation, and no amount of tinkering with the media of communication could cure it. But from the point of view of the unification of Indonesian society, the fact that no language, whether Malay, Javanese or Dutch, had a wide currency was a distinct handicap.

SUKARNOISM IN ECLIPSE

Undoubtedly, Sukarno did accomplish something like welding the country into one nation, but there remains the question of how deep and enduring is the national sentiment which he evoked or stimulated. But if this is his achievement, it also marks his failure, for he did it at the expense of economic development, and even worse, for the economy in 1965 had deteriorated to the point of disaster.

In this connection it may be profitable to note the experience of the Dutch in attempting to promote the welfare of the people in their Eastern dependency. A coalition of Christian parties came to power in the Netherlands in 1901. Its leader, Dr. Abraham Kuyper, had long denounced the policy of exploitation and had pleaded for a policy based on moral duty. His government initiated what became known as the "ethical policy." But the Dutch soon discovered that promoting Indonesian welfare was no easy matter. The Indonesian peasant was slow to adopt new methods and resisted change. This led to an intensified paternalism on the part of the Dutch civil service. The Dutch also discovered that welfare policies were costly, and that the native economy could not support them. When the depression of the 1930's crippled the Western industries in the country, the sources of financial support dried up and the welfare program dwindled away. After independence Indonesia received much foreign economic aid, but to no avail. Foreign paternalism is no longer possible; any conditions attached to aid are resented. Twice Sukarno told the American ambassador, and that in public, that the United States "could go to hell" with its foreign aid. The Suharto regime is humbler and more willing to receive advice as well as aid from the outside. However, the basic problem is no easier today than the Dutch found it over a half century ago.

General Suharto's government is working heroically to repair the damage and to stimulate economic development. Will his regime be granted enough time to perform this difficult and prolonged task? The general elections promised for 1968 have already been postponed—an indication that Suharto and his advisers fear what might happen if their program were submitted to the judgment of the people within the next few years. The horrible bloodletting which followed the abortive coup has certainly not made for tolerance and a compromising spirit.

In October, 1967, General Suharto consolidated his own position by reshuffling his cabinet. An election now would probably produce political chaos from which anything might emerge, but much hostility and discontent can build up in a long period of military rule. Hence, if Sukarno prevented the breakup of his country by his flamboyant nationalism he may have prepared the soil for a succession of dictatorships and revolutions.

There remains the exceedingly difficult problem of the relationship of Java to the outer islands. Often this is put in terms of the Javanese who constitute only one, but by far the largest, of the three chief ethnic groups inhabiting the island and its appendage, Madura, and the non-Javanese peoples of the archipelago. The more important issue is the differing, sometimes conflicting, interests between Java and the other larger but less populous islands. About 1900 the Dutch became aware that the welfare of Java, already low, was declining. They turned to a scheme of colonizing the Javanese in the outer islands as a means of relieving the population pressure in Java. The scheme was costly and at its peak succeeded in transplanting only 50,000 a year. This was too small a number to have a perceptible effect. Moreover, unless the new settlements were set up to encourage large-scale cultivation, transmigration merely spread the unfavorable condition obtaining in Java to the outer islands.

There are basic differences in religious, political and economic outlook between the people of Java and those of the outer islands. This was reflected in the vote in the first and only parliamentary elections of 1955. Three-fourths of the vote for the Communist party, which was surprisingly strong in the national poll, were cast in East and Central Java. By contrast, the Masjumi, the moderate Muslim party, received nearly as many votes in the outer islands as in Java. In this connection it must be remembered that two-thirds of the total population live in Java and only a third in the more spacious outer islands. A careful and able student of Indonesian politics has concluded that the explanation of the extremism of Indonesian politics, and especially its anti-Dutch fury, is to be found in the fact that effective political power was in the hands of the Javanese who are economically dependent on the peoples of the outer islands. Because of their precarious economic position they are reluctant "to permit the devolution of political power from themselves to the other peoples." They legitimitized the retention of political power by an extremely anti-Dutch attitude.[22] The argument implies that a more conciliatory policy on the part of the Dutch, especially with respect to West New Guinea, would have taken the wind out of the sails of the extremists and aided the moderates, but the question may be asked whether the Javanese political leaders would have yielded so easily, and whether they would not then have resorted to other measures—such as action against Portuguese Timor or pressure on east New Guinea—just as they later turned on Malaysia as a means of legitimitizing the retention of power. However that may be, there is no doubt about the existence of a grave, unsolved problem.

There is another aspect to the problem. Malaysia is no more unified than is Indonesia. The sudden expulsion of Singapore from the federation gave clear evidence of that. The Malays cannot make up their mind whether the overwhelming Chinese island of Singapore constitutes a greater threat to their interests inside or outside of the federation. With Singapore inside, Chinese and other non-Malays constitute fully half of the population and, in time, would become a formidable political power; conceivably, under certain conditions, they might win control of the government. The Chinese of Malaya have displayed strong leftist tendencies. Singapore needs an economic hinterland; if rejected by the federation, a leftist government might turn to Communist China for help. About the only sure way of controlling the Chinese and Singapore would be the union of Malaysia with Indonesia. The Malays of Malaysia, however, would not be eager to form a union which included Java because of its poverty and its tremendous population. They would be lost in this kind of a union. On the other hand, the peoples of Sumatra, Kalimantan and Sulawesi have looked with envy at the stability and prosperity of Malaya. Union with Malaysia, with Singapore as the great commercial center, could become very attractive to the Malays of Sumatra and Kalimantan. This would lose little of its attraction if it involved getting rid of the burden of Java. At the time of the rebellion, Sukarno and his followers seemed convinced that Malaysia was seeking to break up the Indonesian republic. Dr. Sudjarwo, the Indonesian representative before the Security Council in 1964, declared "From Singapore we suffered and continue to suffer economic subversion and manipulation, and both Singapore and Malaya . . . have provided not only a shelter but an active base for secessionist rebels against the Republic since 1958."

The lines drawn by British and Dutch colonialism on the map of Southeast Asia had little reference to ethnic, geographic or economic reality. They may not withstand the pressures of the forces operating in the area.

CHAPTER V

INDIA AS AN ASIAN POWER

*Paul F. Power**

Frequently, India's policy-makers have cast their country as a leader of the nonaligned, ex-colonial states of Afro-Asia. Occasionally, they have considered their nation a global actor. The adopted roles have prevailed through the shocks of discord with China and Pakistan, the loss of Jawaharlal Nehru and war in Southeast Asia. A rearmed India has learned to live with its China problem, and toward Pakistan a rigid confidence has replaced the pre-1965 mixture of uncertainty and emotionalism. Leadership attuned to the Nehru tradition has emerged. Vietnam has been left to the major states to decide. Yet foreign policy orientation may change despite adjustments. For the shocks have adversely influenced New Delhi's position in the nonaligned community and world affairs. The setbacks have brought into greater prominence earlier self-criticism about economic development, national integration and public order, a process drawing national thinking in from the horizons. While decisive evidence is not available, as India enters the 1970s it is provisionally in a time of transition in foreign affairs.

A leading candidate for a new departure is an Asian option to compete with the country's global and nonaligned roles. An Asian orientation for Indian foreign policy would draw from cultural, intellectual and political sources of India's past and contemporary history. There are three major origins—the meaning of Asia to Indian modernists and nationalists before freedom, the policies free India has followed toward China and other Asian nations, and India's view of Russia, America and the United Nations in Asian affairs.

---

*Professor of Political Science, University of Cincinnati, and an associate of Dr. Vinacke.

I

An awareness of India's close relationship to a continent emerging from beneath Western controls to assert its rightful place in world affairs was a major current in the Indian Renaissance school of the last century. The awareness stemmed from the rediscovery of the past achievements of Indian civilization and of Asia before Western intrusions. Cultural nationalists stressed Indian traditions and values, yet their study also taught them about India's ties with Persia and Central Asia and the outward movement of Hinduism and Buddhism. Although few were adherents, many Indian intellectuals prized Buddhism as a link with other Asian lands. Some tended to consider India the best of Asia, as did the Arya Samajists and Bal Gangadhar Tilak. The pioneer of the Indian Renaissance, Ram Mohan Roy, and his followers, Ranade, Gokhale and the Tagores, inclined toward continentalism without denying their cultural nationalism. Thus Rabindranath Tagore expounded an "Asian morality" superior to "Western materialism" that he feared Asians had emulated. Although Indian Renaissance leaders differed on the relative weight to be given to Pan-Asianism, their school helped to support the position, elaborated after Indian freedom by C. H. Alexandrowicz at the University of Madras, that European imperialism had been an interlude and that the new Asian states were returning to world affairs on a legally equal basis which the Western law of nations had denied to them.

Nearly all leaders of Indian thought and politics who lived to react to the wars and revolutions in Asia during the first two decades of this century received additional support for their belief in the resurgence of Asia from the victory of Japan over Russia, the Young Turk uprising in 1908, and the Chinese Revolution of 1911. Later, appeals to Asian peoples came from Soviet Russian interests in Asia, voiced in the Baku Congress of the Peoples of the East in 1920, and from Japanese sources dedicated to expanding Japan's influence in Asia at the expense of the West and China. Whatever the source, as Sisir Gupta and Werner Levi have shown in their writings, the spirit of continentalism among Indians and other Asians did not penetrate below to the masses. Pan-Asianism was an ideology of a few. Moreover, national revolutions eventually triumphed in Asian politics, not one or more kinds of Pan-Asianism.

Because of their leading places in modern Indian history, Mohandas K. Gandhi, and especially Jawaharlal Nehru, deserve particular mention. Although retrospective and modernizing nationalists influenced Gandhi, he emphasized ideas many of them did not stress. Recognizing the peasant as the central fact of India and by implication of Asia, Gandhi turned the attention of the Indian National Congress and some

Asians and Western observers not only to the problems but also to the representativeness of village life. Indicative of his outlook, in April, 1947, at the closing session of the Asian Relations Conference in New Delhi, he told the delegates that village India was the heart of the country, not the great cities.[1] Gandhi's focus on the peasant, dating back at least to the close of World War I, predated Marxist attention in Asia to the same social type. Another theme he projected, as had Swami Vivekananda and Rabindranath Tagore, dealt with the beneficial influence of Asia in world affairs. At the same meeting he spoke of Asia's "message of love" for the nuclear West which had become corrupted by doctrines of force. Characteristically, he advised Asians not to react in kind to Occidental wrongs against them. Gandhi's call for personal and national self-respect and his insistence on the redeeming nonviolence of *satyagraha* in all struggles for reform added still other elements to traditions available to Asian states.

In contrast to Gandhi, Nehru developed a more comprehensive outlook on India in world affairs. In his international thought, European influences exceed those from the East. The European stamp came especially from Nehru's direct exposure and favorable response to anti-imperialist and antifascist developments in European affairs during the 1920s and 1930s. Although these experiences did not make Nehru an intellectual expatriate, they gave his Indian nationalism a cosmopolitan quality not found in Gandhi's thinking. Marxism supplied an important link between Nehru's European concerns and his view of Asia. In addition to learning about the relation of capitalism and imperialism, he found in Marxism the need to tie the struggle for self-determination to revolutionary social and economic changes. To Nehru's mind, however, the variety of Asian conditions was not thereby reduced to the simplicities of Marxian teachings about exploitation, class struggle and war. Although he deplored some Asian ideas and institutions, especially metaphysical justification of caste, he did not use Marxism to deny the integrity and contributions of Asia which he felt the West had abused after Vasco Da Gama.

One theme appears often in Nehru's view of Asia before he took formal charge of Indian foreign policy in 1947—that Asia, long mortgaged to Western diplomacy and imperialism, is qualified to play a leading role in world affairs. In a typical mode, he said in Lahore in 1930 that it was wrong to believe that Europe had always controlled international relations. He reminded his listeners that not only had Asia, and India in particular, achieved much in thought, but also in action. India, he said, had broken the military power of Alexander. He hastened to add that he did not wish the legions of any nation or continent to overrun the world. Nehru's efforts to restore the self-esteem of Indians served his objectives of removing Western power from non-Western areas and achieving social reconstruction. On the threshold of freedom, he felt less need to stress Asia's past greatness. He told delegates to the 1947 Asian Relations Conference to look out into the world and contribute to the reduction of conflict and poverty on the basis of equality and mutuality.

On intra-Asian political relations, before freedom Nehru advocated a vague association of Asian nations. This thought had received support from the Agha Khan in 1918, C. R. Das in 1922, and Mohammad Ali the following year. A Congress resolution approved it in 1928. Nehru anticipated an Asian "federation" dependent on India and China. The Sino-Indian axis within an Asian federation did not in Nehru's thoughts exclude other Asian states as junior associates. Afghanistan, Burma, Ceylon, Iran, Malaya, Nepal and Siam were specially mentioned in late 1940. The association would be oriented either toward the United States, as he tended to say in the early 1930's, or toward the United States and the Soviet Union, as he thought in the subsequent years up to 1946. Thereafter, for reasons which will be discussed, Nehru preferred the Soviet Union over the United States within his increasingly diminishing attachment to Pan-Asianism.

Nehru's Asian outlook in the two decades preceding independence suggests that he viewed China and India as coequals, in effect, the only two major cultural and political entities in the continent. It was important to his shaping of India's foreign policy that the socialist Nehru found it possible to discover and welcome a nontheological, humanistic approach to life in Confucianist China, finding more to admire than in Brahmanical Hinduism, which he considered retrogressive in social and philosophical matters. Someone has said that Nehru had a Chinese soul in a Hindu body. Aphorisms aside, when he interpreted historic Sino-Indian relations in *The Discovery of India*, he wished that Chinese practicality might have influenced India to check extravagant notions. Still Nehru was not a cultural masochist. In his autobiographical *Toward Freedom*, he affirmed India's cultural gifts to the world, for "unlike Rome, Benares never dabbled in empire or thought of temporal power."[2] Whatever gaps existed in Nehru's research, he had convictions about India's nonexpansionist character that found their way into his stewardship. As to traditional China, Nehru was aware of its display of cultural superiority and expansionism in Asia. But he believed that the true China had emerged after the Manchus, partially cured of these imperfections. Once liberated from non-Chinese rulers and influences, he thought, China would naturally further a just peace in Asia and the world.

As early as 1927 Nehru indicated his objections to European penetration of China at the Brussels meeting of the Kuomintang-supported Congress of Oppressed Nationalities, where he spoke of British imperialism's misuse of Indian troops in China. Yet he recognized that China must be liberated from Asian as well as European masters. Before and after his dramatic, wartime visit to China in the summer of 1939, he praised Chiang Kai-shek's regime for its struggle against Japan. There was a Sino-Indian cultural lining to his views. When he welcomed Republic of China representatives in late 1940, he conceded that the Chinese and Indian societies had faults; but the virtues in them would emerge from a time of suffering for the benefit of all nations.

With the approaching certainty of independence, Nehru's outlook shifted from the notion of Sino-Indian leadership to focus on India as the center of several federations in Asia. In a revealing speech in Bombay on August 22, 1946, Nehru, then Vice President of the Interim Government, speculated about the new importance of Asia in world developments. He advocated an Asia forum which materialized in the 1947 Asian Relations Conference, sponsored by the Indian Council of World Affairs. Nehru spoke of one federation of India and Southeast Asia, a second of West Asia up to or including India and Southeast Asia, and another of "East Asia and India leaving out China," a less than clear idea. He maintained that all of the major regions of Asia "depend on India, economically, politically and for defense purposes."[3] Nehru did not, however, forget China, which he said had become more conscious of India because of the war with Japan. As to Chinese representation at a conference to discuss these ideas, he suggested that both the Kuomintang and the communists should be represented. Nehru's formula was not realized, for in the subsequent Asian Relations Conference, the Kuomintang alone represented China.

Nehru's observation in 1946 about India's military importance for other regions of Asia is of interest in the perspective of his later opposition to collective security in West and Southeast Asia. His defense thinking at the earlier time reflected the Second World War when conflicts in or near Asia enhanced India's strategic importance. The key to Nehru's viewpoint was the identification of real or potential opponents. With the defeat of the Germans to the west and the Japanese to the east and north, he believed that there was no subsequent need for India to defend itself within Asia through collective arrangements, because there were no longer any actual or likely foes. Pakistan became an exception, and against it, New Delhi secured friends in the Soviet Union and Afghanistan, as well as the neutrality of China until 1962. Yet, in large measure, free India's view of collective security pacts involving Asia has had much to do with this question of friend and foe. As a result, China and Russia have benefited from trustful attitudes at the highest policy levels in India.

Out of his political awakening that moved leftward following the Bolshevik Revolution, Nehru came to respect Soviet Russia as the champion of the national and social revolutions which aimed at the destruction of European imperialism and its capitalist source. Undoubtedly, he was saddened by the human costs of the Russian experiment and scornful of Indian communist opportunism. Still he did not consider imperialistic the Soviet Union's rule of inherited territories in Asia, for he accepted the Soviet government's promise to respect Asian minorities and to avoid Great Russian chauvinism, and he seldom questioned whether the pledge was implemented.

On relations between Russia and India, Nehru showed early in the two-decade period before the transfer of power a conviction, shared with colleagues, that has dominated the Indian government's outlook on the Soviet Union since independence. India has nothing to fear from Russia, and to believe otherwise is to fall victim to a British imperialist bogey, Nehru wrote in 1927 after his first Russian visit.[4] Russia and Britain are antagonistic owing to their pre-Bolshevik rivalry in world politics, and because after 1917 Britian—unique among the capitalist powers—tried to encircle the Soviet Union. National India and Russia should be the best of neighbors; both need to develop, and Russia has no desire or ability to acquire additional Asian territories. Nehru concluded that a liberated India should end British prejudices against Russia and usher in a new era of peaceful relations. These ideas were not overcome by later disappointments, among them, his experience in 1930 with the Russian-oriented League Against Imperialism of which he was an officer. As shown in Chattar Singh Samra's account of India and Anglo-Soviet relations, the League formed the All-India, Anti-Imperialist League in Bombay against Nehru's wishes and then expelled him, citing the Gandhi-Irwin Pact of 1930 as evidence of retrogressive anticolonialism. Later, the 1939 Soviet-German agreement disturbed him, but he explained it and the Finnish war as necessary Russian defenses against imperialism. When the Soviet Union had to resist German armies, Nehru warmly supported the embattled Russians while showing contempt for the Communist Party of India that had refused to join the Congress on the national question and instead aided the British war effort. Overall, Nehru's outlook before freedom interpreted the Soviet government as a benign force in world affairs. Consequently, it was not difficult for him to accept Russia as a legitimate power in Asia, to approve the invitation of Soviet Asian Republics to the 1947 Asian Relations Conference and to greet their delegates as sources from whom other Asians had much to learn.

China and Russia occupied a larger part in Nehru's pre-independence thinking about Asia than Japan, but he was fully aware of its relation to the other two states and to India's future. As a young man he was enthusiastic about Japan's defeat of Tsarist Russia, which he treated as a European power. Before the 1930's he joined other Indians to show respect for Japan's rapid modernization and challenge to the West, although they did not understand or approve its expansionist tendencies. The respect declined with Japan's move into Northeast Asia, the anti-Comintern Pact with Germany, and Japanese aggressions in China and Southeast Asia. These events disillusioned Indian nationalists, including Nehru, about the Asian power that had destroyed an opportunity to lead Asian continentalism against the West. Moreover, he made it clear in the second world conflict that he was not tempted to support the Indian National Army, sponsored by the Japanese to attract Indian dissidents to their cause. At the war's end however, he and Gandhi considered patriotic the motives of Subhas Chandra Bose, Nehru's rival in the Congress left wing a decade before, and other Indian National Army members. Entering freedom, the Nehru-led Indian government believed that Japan's case was a lapse from previous grace, a condition requiring restitution to those Asian nations which had suffered at its hands, but particularly to China.

II

From independence until 1949, India dealt with the Republic of China and then became the second noncommunist state, following Burma, to establish diplomatic relations with the People's Republic of China. Although Chiang Kai-shek had received Nehru's praise as an enemy of aggression in the prolonged struggle against Japan and had petitioned Roosevelt in July, 1942, to mediate with Britain in behalf of Indian nationalism, he and his regime lost legitimacy in the Indian government's view. The reasons for India's altered policy include Nehru's interpretation of Chinese communism as a radical fulfillment and purging of a Chinese nationalism which had become corrupt, and his conviction that in power terms the New China was bound to participate in Asia's reentry into world affairs. Although Nehru was concerned about the Mao regime's early move into Tibet, India became the leading noncommunist advocate of having it represent the Chinese state in the United Nations and of the claims that, based on the Cairo and Potsdam agreements, it should govern Taiwan. The Sino-Indian crises have deflated without reversing India's position on these questions of special interest to another power in Asia, the United States.

After the conclusion of the Korean armistice, the appearance of the Sino-Soviet acceptance of nonalignment and the ending of French power in Indo-China, Peking shifted from a "two camps" doctrine that had treated the Congress government as neocapitalist and turned to diplomatic methods to pursue its interests in Asia. These new conditions permitted People's China to acknowledge India's predisposition to establish friendly relations. The two countries proceeded in April, 1954, to sign the Sino-Indian Trade Agreement on Tibet, a document famous for *Panch Shila* or the Five Principles of Peaceful Coexistence. To the dismay or delight of later critics, Nehru's government gave no effective consideration to using the negotiations to secure China's recognition of the northeastern McMahon line and consented to the treaty's description of Tibet as a zone of China. Harold Vinacke has said that the Five Principles of Peaceful Coexistence are more indebted to 19th century international law than either China or India have conceded.

Panch Shila was not limited to Sino-Indian relations. In mid-1954 both nations jointly declared that the Five Principles would govern their relations with other Asian countries and with the balance of the world. Until 1959, when Tibet fell under extensive Chinese rule and Prime Minister Nehru ended his secret diplomacy in the first of many White Papers that revealed profound border difficulties with China, the Indian government considered these norms as insurance against Chinese expansion in Asia and influenced other Afro-Asian states to adopt a similar belief. Through the Five Principles, India found an expression for the notion of a Sino-Indian cultural axis, projected into moral principles rather than into a military alliance or a Pan-Asian organization. Applying the norms operationally, India's leader took the pledges of good conduct into the Asian-African Conference at Bandung in 1955, and into *Panch Shila* agreements with nonaligned and communist nations. Mindful of their immediate source and early history, no Western state has adhered to the Five Principles, a fact that India has considered as a defect of the West, not of their context or formulation.

It is now widely acknowledged among friends as well as critics of India that the *Panch Shila* era of Indian foreign policy rested on an optimistic estimate of China's intentions, leading to miscalculations about

Indian security and Chinese ambitions in Asia and Africa. Among the results of these miscalculations were the inadequate defense preparations in Kashmir and the Northeast Frontier Agency, contributing to the ease of covert and open Chinese expansion that led to border crises. The 1962 frontier reverses demonstrated India's military weakness and set into motion political and economic changes, including the release from the cabinet of Nehru's close associate and Defense Minister, V. K. Krishna Menon. Superficially beneficial to India's relations with the United States, Menon's departure hid something more basic—Nehru himself kept power after a setback which would have ousted most prime ministers. For a time a sense of unity overcame internal problems, but new defense spending jeopardized the Third Five Year Plan despite the revision of priorities and the receipt of new domestic and external funds. Although the Nehru government and affiliated segments of public opinion tried to prevent a change through deemphasis of Western military aid which India had requested and received, they could not prevent an increase in India's psychological affiliation with the West. The balance gained was diminished but not exhausted when Pakistan used American weapons against India in 1965.

Many Western observers, including Secretary of State Dean Rusk, thought that the 1962 crisis had raised serious doubts about the effectiveness of India's nonalignment. Yet leading Indians, such as President Radnakrishnan, found that nonalignment had been tested and found beneficial because the West and Russia had come to India's assistance. Some observers wondered about the low level of neutralist aid to New Delhi. Although the United Arab Republic lent some diplomatic help, India found less support on the frontier issue in the neutralist camp than it had anticipated. Later, when only Cyprus formally supported Prime Minister Shastri's call at the 1964 Cairo meeting of nonaligned states for a mission to visit Peking to urge a non-nuclear policy, India's semi-isolation in the community it had done much to build was clearly established. For this condition China's power or neutralist inconstancy was less responsible than the unorganized quality of the third world.

South Asian problems since 1962 include the drawing together of China and Pakistan at India's expense. The communist state and the CENTO-SEATO member have signed and implemented a pact on a common frontier in Kashmir that India denies has any existence. Because of the geography involved and India's caution since 1962, when its troops were adventuresome in the northeast, New Delhi is unlikely to try to unmake this Sino-Pakistani "boundary." Peking has endorsed self-determination for Kashmir and in early 1965 discussed its future with Sheikh Abdullah, a former Prime Minister of the state and periodic detainee of the Indian government whose friendship with Nehru became a victim of the Sheikh's doubtful loyalties. The crossing of the Chinese and Kashmiri issues became critical in the Indo-Pakistani struggle of 1965 when China echoed Pakistan's claim of Indian aggression, and India charged the two states with collusion with respect to arms and an unsuccessful Chinese ultimatum. Nonetheless, one does not apologize for Pakistan's misconduct in or before the 1965 hostilities by recalling that India was the first to accept the political support of a country outside of South Asia on the Kashmir issue during the 1955 Bulganin-Khruschev barnstorming of India. Not until several years later did China side with Pakistan, waiting until the Sino-Soviet dispute had developed. The contrary Indian view is that the Western military link with Pakistan in 1954, if not earlier Anglo-American diplomacy, had placed the main English-speaking powers behind Pakistan on the Kashmir question. India, however, welcomed Russia's support on the subcontinent's major territorial problem when it was still possible to resist this temptation. Later, China entered, not so much to aid Pakistan as to counter Russia in South Asia. Much of Peking's troublemaking on Indian frontiers, in Kashmir and among Indian radicals had as a target, not India, but the Soviet Union, which had gained influence in Indian domestic and foreign politics that China could not hope to acquire despite some progress in the 1954-1959 years of peaceful coexistence.

India's pre-1959 outlook on China had its impact on India's policies toward other Asian nations, especially Korea, Japan and the Indo-Chinese states. For Korea, India has endorsed self-determination, reunification and democratization, all to be realized through peaceful change. India has tended to merge the first two objectives and has not recognized either of the Korean regimes. Mindful of China and Russia, India has been discreet about expressing skepticism as to North Korea's ability to realize national unity and democracy. New Delhi's view of South Korea has aided this silence. Despite the Syngman Rhee government's establishment by elections supervised by the United Nations Temporary Commission on Korea, India held that regime unfit by India's nationalist and democratic standards. Criticism of the Syngman Rhee leadership began in the 1948-50 period of the Temporary Commission when the Indian members objected to the militancy of Korea's veteran nationalist. On abstract peaceful change, India seized an opportunity in the Korean conflict to apply the principle after voting hesitatingly in the United Nations to find North Korea the aggressor in mid-1950. Nehru's letters to Acheson and Stalin in July 1950, are instructive reminders of Indian diplomacy in this period. Proposing an end to the Korean conflict through additional Security Council action, they asked for the seating of Peking's representative there and the termination of Russia's boycott of the United Nations. Although K. M. Panikkar, Nehru's adviser and India's Ambassador to Peking whose memoirs suggest that he misunderstood the purpose of the government to which he was accredited, did not initially realize that the United States would automatically reject the proposal because of its stand on Peking and the United Nations, this was the predictable result that the communist powers used for their ends.

At the field level, the Nehru government sent a Gandhian ambulance corps to Korea instead of armed forces, much to Washington's disappointment. New Delhi explained that it did not have the resources to make an effective military contribution. In view of India's policies toward China and Russia, any other response from the Nehru government would have been out of character. The Indian effort to prevent the United Nations from citing People's China as an aggressor after its entry into the Korean War reflected concern to avoid offending China and Russia and a belief that only reconciliation could bring peace. The resistance also drew strength from India's previous role in warning the United States that China would enter the conflict if the United Nations forces crossed the 38th parallel. In all of this there was no Indian conviction that Asian states could resolve the Korean crisis. Nehru conceded that the war was chiefly a great power responsibility. India carried out the difficult task of heading the United Nations Neutral Repatriation Commission for Korea, sympathizing with its communist members on some issues but siding with its pro-Western members on other matters to leave an eclectic record. India's unofficial relations with the Republic of Korea improved after Rhee's exile and the development of Sino-Indian problems. Subsequently, New Delhi looked with disfavor on South Korea's dispatch of service and combat troops to South Vietnam as an unfortunate enlargement of the parties to a conflict in which Asians outside of the area should have no violent part.

In postwar Japan, Prime Minister Nehru became respected in academic, pacifist and socialist circles for his views on the human condition and the international order. Politically he received attention, not always favorable, from India's objections to the Japanese Peace Treaty of 1951. These points reflected his pre-1959 China policy, an earlier sympathy with emergent Japan, a fundamentalist understanding of national integrity, and his zone of peace idea. Nehru's dislike of John Foster Dulles should not be excluded. When the Indian government explained to the

United States in mid-1951 why it would not be one of the forty-eight
states to sign the Treaty in San Francisco, India complained that the
draft was faulty and there would be no opportunity to negotiate differences. Russia, China, and those Japanese opposed to the settlement welcomed the Indian objections, which represented an early and pronounced example of the gap between India and the United States in
Asian affairs. The distance was measurable in the Indian Note of August
23, 1951, to the United States.[5] It held that the Treaty did not concede to
Japan an honorable and equal place in the family of states nor provide
for the eventual participation of all countries interested in East Asian
peace, meaning Communist China and the Soviet Union. Moreover, New
Delhi objected to the Treaty's built-in defense provisions, alleged to in-
fringe on Japan's sovereignty, and to the territorial settlements making
the Ryukyus and Bonins trust areas of the United States. But India
wanted the Treaty to confirm Soviet Russia's absorption of the Kuriles
and Southern Sakhalin under the Yalta Agreement and to place Taiwan
in mainland China's control. A clearer explanation of why India went to
these lengths to advertise its differences with the United States may not
be available until the Nehru papers and relevant Indian and American
documents are made public. Meanwhile, the responsibility for the controversy should not be assigned solely to "Dulles diplomacy."

Consistent with its refusal to take part in the San Francisco meeting,
India concluded a generous, nonpunitive treaty of peace with Japan in
1952. Later, Japan joined the Aid-India Consortium, pledging 105 million dollars for India's Third Five Year Plan. Unlike several Asian states
which have experienced the aggressions of imperialist Japan, India
might be relatively undisturbed about a politically resurgent Japan in
Asia. The countries remain distant in cultural patterns and industrialization levels; moreover, they have competing economic interests in
Southeast Asia. The future of their political relations depends partly on
their economic dealings and partly on the outcome of their relations
with China, Russia and the United States.

On former Indo-China, India's policies have reflected its understanding of anticolonialism and nonalignment, and, even after its decline, the
Panch Shila approach to People's China. As V. P. Dutt and Vishal Singh
report in their Institute of Pacific Relations study, the Nehru government frequently viewed the struggle in the area as a popular revolt
against European imperialism or its vestiges. In the ascendent left-
nationalist circles in Indian public life, Ho Chi-Minh has been a respected Asian leader. Urging a ceasefire for Vietnam in early 1954, India
encouraged the convening of the Geneva Conference in April of that

year, originally called to discuss Korea. Displeased with Indian diplomacy on Korea, the United States kept India from becoming a formal participant. Washington, however, could not prevent its peripatetic critic, V. K. Krishna Menon, from gaining entry as Prime Minister Nehru's unofficial representative and self-appointed broker. Although the Geneva settlement revolved around a Soviet-French understanding about Europe, the result was that India probably had more influence than its formal role would have permitted. India became a vocal partisan of the Geneva Agreement's stipulation of nationwide elections in Vietnam for 1956—and a critic of those who said they could not be held.

Conscious of India's qualifications as a major nonaligned and Asian state, the powers chose India as chairman of the International Commission for Supervision and Control (ICC) for the three states. Despite its difficulties with China, India took a narrow interpretation of the ICC's restricted authority and power. Through diplomacy India aided the steps preparing the international guarantee of Laotian neutrality in 1962, subsequently giving support to Prince Souvanna Phouma's neutralists against rightists and the Pathet Lao. Unlike the United States, which from the start was unenthusiastic about the 1954 Indo-China settlement, New Delhi did not become disillusioned with it. There was a need to defer to Russia—the Geneva accord's co-chairman with Britain—a chance to benefit from the modest influence and prestige of ICC service, and an anticipation that the 1954 formula might help to produce a future settlement. Later India recognized its vulnerability as a neutral in view of the Sino-Indian dispute and the post-1964 changes in the military and political circumstances of Vietnam. India decided to remain with the ICC. To remain was not to actively seek restoration. Except for a mid-1966 proposal to use ICC patrols in Vietnam's demilitarized zone, an effort which failed because of Hanoi's resistance, India showed no strong interest in trying to revive what was beyond repair.[6]

In the 1960's India favored an additional Geneva Conference to deal with Vietnam. The support met diplomatic problems. In mid-1964, India agreed with Russia that a second meeting would be desirable, a position India repeated in the spring of 1965. Yet in mid-1966, when Mrs. Gandhi included in her ill-fated peace initiative essentially what Russia had wanted earlier, the Soviet Union refused to agree until the United States first ceased its bombings of North Vietnam, a condition she consented to on her subsequent Moscow visit to the disappointment of the United States. By the fall of 1967, when the Indian Prime Minister repeated this condition on her trip to Eastern Europe, Washington was no longer disconcerted about India's appeal, one of many in rising criticism at home and abroad.

In the second half of the decade New Delhi's preferred term for a peace meeting was "Geneva-style" conference, language that would permit inclusion of the National Liberation Front for South Vietnam. The NLF maintains an office in New Delhi with access to the higher levels of the Ministry of External Affairs. Specific Indian calls for the NLF's inclusion began in the joint communiqué of Tito and Shastri in July 1965. India did not ask that the NLF be given an exclusive voice for South Vietnam. To do so would have impaired India's *ad hoc* relations with Saigon, with which there is more trade and less tension than in Nehru's time, and also New Delhi's proud but dependent relations with the United States. India, long an advocate of one Vietnam, came to live with its division.

From their start in early 1965 until their ending in the spring of 1968, the bombings of North Vietnam troubled Indo-American diplomacy. Deploring them, India urged "political" over "military" policies for the ravaged country. Believing that the appeal of neutralists at Belgrade in the spring of 1965 for negotiations without conditions had influenced Washington, India welcomed the American shift soon thereafter, in President Johnson's Baltimore speech, to an unconditional approach to political talks. When subsequently the United States postponed Shastri's scheduled visit to Washington in June, India understandably interpreted the action as pique over its objections to the bombings. Shastri was not consoled by a simultaneous postponement of an Ayub Khan visit to America. Mrs. Gandhi's Washington visit in the spring of 1966 erased some of India's displeasure. Helpful were speedy American food aid to drought-stricken India, the President's mention of India's role in the ICC and the United States' full turn by this date of endorsement of the Geneva accords. In the American background, noticeable after Mrs. Gandhi's trip to Moscow, loomed disappointment over India's refusal to acknowledge its stakes in the Vietnamese military struggle despite the efforts of Ambassador Chester Bowles and visitors from Washington. Overall, India would prefer neutralization as in Laos for all or any part of the region with minimal Western and Chinese involvement. How to first stabilize the zone is left essentially to major powers. With some exceptions the typical Indian outlook in the 1960's was that the Vietnamese crisis was a typhoon, its beginning and end beyond India's control. The 1968 start of the Paris peace discussions seemed to New Delhi to be the emergence of rationalism after years of madness. India has warmed to the Nixon Administration's announced intention to disengage American forces from Vietnam.

Elsewhere in Southeast Asia, Nehru's usual international thought has shaped Indian policies, although special interests have moulded some. New Delhi has long opposed efforts for an anticommunist grouping in rimland Asia. India objected to the participation of Nationalist China and the Republic of Korea in the 1950 Baguio Conference, causing their elimination from that exploratory meeting which achieved none of the collective security measures the anticommunist participants had desired. United States policy contributed to the result because it was then unwilling to make security commitments involving the Asian continent. From an Asian viewpoint, Nehru's belief that communism did not pose a threat to Asian peace contributed to the outcome. This conviction later influenced India's strenuous opposition to the Southeast Asian Treaty Organization. Shortly before SEATO's creation in the Manila Treaty, a meeting in Colombo of Ceylon, Burma, India, Indonesia and Pakistan revealed Indian objections to declaring communism a vital issue in Asia. This position conflicted with the thoughts of the pro-Western Sir John Kotelawala of Ceylon, but also with the opinion of the neutralist and socialist U Nu of Burma. Apart from communism, the Indian leader expressed views then and after the creation of SEATO which reflected his dislike of overseas spheres of influence, a belief that military strength increases tensions, and a reaction against Pakistan's membership in the pact.

With contiguous Burma, India has been a major power dealing with a smaller nation whose nationalism and foreign policy owe much to Indian sources. Questions about official and public treatment of the entrepreneurial Indian minority in Burma have frequently troubled relations. Responsive to its neighbor's struggles with radical and tribal insurgents, India sent arms to aid Burma's internal security in 1949. Here is one of the few exceptions to India's policy of nonsupport of the military infrastructure of the new states, many of them on good terms with New Delhi. Subsequently, India signed a treaty of friendship with Burma and extended important economic assistance. From 1959 to 1966 Burma's capacity to reciprocate with diplomatic help for India's case against China was limited by the Sino-Burmese frontier treaty and nonaggression pact of 1960. Isolationist and nativist policies of the Ne Win regime further shielded Burma from Indian influence. Rangoon resented Indian purchases of non-Burmese rice, some of it from the United States, thereby causing a problem elsewhere. Until 1967 Indo-Burmese relations seemed determined by Burma's suspicion of all outsiders. Since then the deterioration in Sino-Burmese relations has given the Rangoon government a new perspective, making closer ties to India an unanticipated development. Peking's recent interest in Naga instability near the Burmese border provides New Delhi with a special reason to cooperate with its small neighbor.

The relations of India and Ceylon have had more than some evidence of paradox. Pro-West when India favored neutralism, Ceylon adopted the latter posture in 1958, while India moved toward the West and away from China, permitting the Bandaranaike government to mediate between the two greater powers until replaced in 1965. After the 1965 elections produced a government led by the United National Party, its leader, Dudley Senanayake, announced endorsement of India in the Sino-Indian frontier dispute, although he said that formally Ceylon would continue to adhere to the 1962 proposals of six nonaligned powers, later clarified. If implemented, the clarified proposals would substantially restore the frontier position before the major Chinese offense began that year, and would establish a demilitarized zone in the Western sector. India accepted the clarified proposals *in toto* as a basis for negotiation with China, if the latter did the same. China accepted the original proposals in principle, but it interprets them differently and treats the clarification as distinct from the proposals. In effect, India has gained moral help for its relations with China from the new regime in Ceylon, the Colombo points having fallen into limbo since 1965. This favorable development followed Indian concessions in an agreement with the Bandaranaike government on the status of Tamil-speaking Indians in Ceylon. In an important change from Nehru's foreign and domestic policies, the Shastri government reversed India's previous opposition to repatriation of Tamils from Ceylon and formally agreed in 1964 to accept the return over a fifteen year period of over half a million Tamils, with some 300,000 to receive citizenship rights in Ceylon and the status of about 150,000 to be decided later. Although the Swatantra party and other segments of Indian political life, together with Tamil elements in Ceylon, are dissatisfied with compulsory repatriation, the agreement promises considerable improvement in relations. Ceylon's 1970 election of a leftist regime may bring strains.

Toward Indonesia, India's foreign policy has changed twice since 1949 when it urged the country's freedom and sponsored the twenty-two nation Asian Conference on Indonesia in New Delhi. Cordial relations followed Indonesia's emergence into the third world. As one of the five sponsors with Indonesia of the Asian-African Conference at Bandung, India led the new states to demand just treatment in world politics. In keeping with his view of People's China at that time, Prime Minister Nehru made special efforts to invite the Peking regime to the meeting and to present its revolutionary government in a pacific light. After

Bandung, India aided Indonesian claims to West Iran, but, out of concern for London and Malayan nationalism, not later to British areas of Borneo that became Malaysian. Indian diplomacy was reasonably successful in keeping Muslim Indonesia from disturbing Indian-Pakistani relations. When Sukarno's diplomacy began to show histrionic qualities which India could not always approve, relations began to cool. There was change, too, on New Delhi's part. By the time of the Belgrade meeting of nonaligned states in 1961, India's anti-imperialism had mellowed while Indonesia's variety had grown unstable.

Relations between the two states deteriorated after anti-Indian riots in September 1962, during the Asian Games in Djakarta. A Games official, who was an Indian national, had wanted to change its name because Indonesia had barred Israel and Nationalist China. Nehru blamed Peking for inciting the riots. Subsequently, India's support of Malaysia's creation, which the Djakarta government vehemently opposed, and Indonesia's gravitation into Peking's orbit with the aid of the Indonesian communist party brought difficult relations between the two states. The gap between India and Indonesia was dramatized at the 1964 nonaligned meeting in Cairo when Prime Minister Shastri acclaimed peaceful coexistence and President Sukarno espoused a confrontation of the "new, emerging forces" with the capitalist-imperialist camp, a line of People's China. Unlike Indonesia, India did not urge a second Asian-African Conference.

Because of Indonesia's rapport with China and the Malaysian issue, in early 1965 Sukarno identified India with neocolonialist and imperialist forces. Later that year he exercised Indian opinion when he gave full support to Pakistan's case against India. Soon his nation was convulsed. After the failure of the pro-Peking plot came the isolation of Sukarno by General Suharto and his followers and a second change in Delhi-Djakarta relations. The fall 1966 visit to India of Indonesia's new foreign minister, Adam Malik, opened a new chapter which can be called a victory for the precepts of nonalignment and economic development. Without a common fear of China the improved relations between India and Indonesia could not have emerged.

With Malaya and Malaysia, India's diplomacy has reflected practical choices rather than conventional responses to Asian problems. Following freedom, Nehru recognized the threat of insurgency in Malaya, preferring to describe the problem as "terrorism" rather than Chinese or communist expansionism. Because of the instability and out of deference to the head of the Commonwealth, India did not press for Malaya's freedom as it did for Indonesia's. After Malayan independence in 1957,

India sought close ties, for the most part effectively. Indian interests included a need to have friendship with a Muslim state to counter Pakistan, the advantages of markets and resources, and an Indian minority. These considerations and the deterioration in Sino-Indian relations after 1958 influenced India to condone without approving Malaya's treaty of defense and mutual assistance with the United Kingdom. India quietly encouraged the formation of Malaysia against the wishes of China, Indonesia, the Philippines and Russia. India demonstrated its cordiality at the 1964 preparatory meeting in Djakarta for a second Asian-African Conference, leading an unsuccessful but not terminal effort to secure an invitation for Malaysia. Similar evidence appeared a year later in Singapore when the Afro-Asian Standing Committee agreed over Indonesian and Chinese protests to permit their foreign ministers to decide the issue before the full assembly was to have begun in Algiers. Despite professions of neutrality, the two countries have not seen the Vietnam war in the same light, as shown by Malaysia's reception of President Johnson to the country during his Asian trip in the fall of 1966. Whether Singapore's forced secession from Malaysia complicates India's future relations in the area is an open question. Although displeased, India cannot prevent the two states from relying on Anzac forces when Britain withdraws in 1971, unless the new Conservative government decides to stay.

As with Indonesia and Malaysia, India's search for amicable relations with Muslim countries to offset Pakistan's Pan-Islamic diplomacy and to reassure Indian Muslims has been influential on its policies in West Asia. Other important factors have been the ideology of neutralism, opposition to Western imperialism and military pacts, historical doubts about Zionism, a concern about Peking's bid in the Arab world, and Indian predisposition to follow Soviet thinking on Middle Eastern issues. The Arab countries, especially Egypt, Iraq and Syria, have been the main beneficiaries of Indian policies in the area. India's response to the 1956 crisis, when it threatened to leave the Commonwealth if the British did not withdraw from Egypt, impressed the revolutionary Arab states with India's sincerity and usefulness. India has avoided taking sides on questions among the Muslim states, except in so far as it has objected to CENTO and the Islamic pact mooted by Saudi Arabia, blocs which offend through Pakistan's actual or potential membership. India's Arab policy has been moderately effective in keeping the Arab states from aligning with Pakistan on Kashmir and related issues. Considering the intensity of these problems, India might be given high marks. Western-made arms came from West Asian states to help Pakistan in the South Asian conflict of 1965, but at least some were from non-Arab sources with which India has less influence. India has been successful in convincing Muslim countries that Muslim Indians, several of them serving as Indian ambassadors and one becoming President of India in 1967, have not been ill-treated by a Hindu society.

On Palestine and Israel, India's policy has been heterogeneous, although in the 1965-67 years it moved to help militant Arab nationalism. Before freedom the Congress party expressed solidarity with rising Arab demands for self-determination, giving Arab and Indian nationalism a bond that is more basic in Indian foreign relations than New Delhi's view of Zionism. In the interwar period Nehru raised questions about fair play for the Palestinian Arabs when he commented on the Balfour Declaration. Together with other nationalists in the British sphere, he had an aversion to London's policies affecting peoples who had not been consulted about them. For his part, Gandhi told Zionists or their intermediaries that his identification with Jewish sufferings in fascist Europe and his judgment that the effort to found a Jewish national home in Palestine was an injustice to Palestinian Arabs were not inconsistent positions. Near freedom, Nehru recognized the growing pluralism of Palestine, suggesting that an Arab delegation and Jewish representatives should attend the 1947 Asian Relations Conference. The latter came, the former did not, although the Arab League had observer status.

On Palestine's future, the Indian government supported a united federal state of two communities, a scheme opposed by Arabs and Zionists, rather than the partition into two states which the United Nations approved. India was mindful of the human costs of dividing British India and of its own federal compromise. Holding to its belief and responsive to Muslim sentiments, India voted against Israel's admission to the United Nations. Yet, despite contrary opinion at home and abroad, India recognized Israel in 1950, principally to align with the United States and the Soviet Union, Israel's prime sponsors. Because of New Delhi's unwillingness, the two states have not exchanged diplomatic agents, although negotiations to that end took place in 1952. Muslim Indian leadership and Indian concerns about Pakistan caused the Indian government to refrain from the logical sequence to recognition. Consuls have been exchanged, though Israel is displeased that the Israeli consulate is in Bombay rather than New Delhi.

Having recognized Israel, Nehru tried unsuccessfully to have it included in the Bandung Conference. Later, under Shastri, the Indian government moved closer to extremist Arab views of Israel, permitting an official visit by representatives of the Palestine Liberation Organization. Nonetheless, he and Mrs. Gandhi did not heed advice to break all contact with Israel. Later, her government found Israel the aggressor in the 1967 conflict in West Asia. Israeli bombing which killed Indians in a UNEF patrol fueled New Delhi's emotions. India's evaluation of the 1967 crisis, the persistence of underlying factors in Arab-Indian relations, and Zionist displeasure with Indian diplomacy in the United Nations make an improvement in Indian-Israeli relations unlikely in the near term.

What may change as an outcome of the 1967 West Asian crisis is India's uncritical outlook on the results for India of its recent Arab policy. During and after the crisis, parliamentary and press questioning of the Gandhi ministry revealed serious discontent with the rigid approach of recent years which has bound India to favoring the Arabs against Israel and "progressive" over other Arab states. The UAR's military setbacks contributed to the calls for reassessment. Some opinion segments have begun to see that militant Arab ideology about Arab socialism and positive neutralism are not effective forces in West Asian affairs. The positive image of Gamal Abdel Nasser, with whom Mrs. Gandhi and Tito reviewed world questions at the 1966 Tripartite meeting in New Delhi, is not likely to diminish as long as he maintains his national position. A surface change in India's West Asian policy may derive from a public expectancy that the government should rely less on Menonist interpretations of Near Eastern problems. Any basic shift in India's West Asian policies, however, will have to wait on alterations in India's longstanding sensitivity to Russian preferences.

III

India entered freedom with no fear of the Soviet Union in Asia. On the contrary, Russia had a positive role to play, according to Nehru's thought which shaped the Congress party's views on foreign relations. In practical affairs, Russia's criticism of the Congress and Nehru as non-revolutionary prevented cordial relations until 1954. Uncertain India did not invite Russia or its Asian Republics to the 1949 Conference on Indonesia in New Delhi, a meeting the Soviet Union interpreted unfavorably. Relations improved during the Korean conflict and bettered noticeably after Stalin's death in 1953. India welcomed the subsequent Russian thesis of "many roads to socialism" and support for its view of Kashmir and Goa. Since 1955 India and Russia have had few differences in Asia.

The appearance of the Sino-Indian and Sino-Russian disputes in the 1958-60 period complicated without impairing good relations between the two nations. The Nehru government expected that Russia might restrain China; but the legacy of basic ties between communist states and the Sino-Soviet quarrel did not make it desirable or possible for the Khruschev regime to moderate Chinese pressure on India. Nevertheless, Russia, after an initially pro-Peking stance in the Sino-Indian crisis of 1962, soon criticized the use of force in boundary disputes and supplied India with jet fighters, light tanks, transport planes and roadbuilding equipment. A critical point came in September 1964, when Defense Minister Y. B. Chavan signed an agreement in Moscow which began a process helping India to acquire directly or through Indian facilities several squadrons of advanced supersonic fighters, and also naval craft, including submarines. These weapons the West would not supply for fear of upsetting South Asian parity. Moscow and New Delhi intend this aid to redress India's shift to the West after the 1962 crisis, which brought United States military grants of about $30 million. China's developing atomic capacity has influenced Indian diplomacy to maximize Russian concern for India's security. Pakistan's use of American arms and Soviet continuation of military shipments during the South Asian hostilities of 1965, when the West halted aid, have helped New Delhi to consider Moscow as its best military supplier. Moreover, the United States' 1967 announcement that it would resume military aid to India and Pakistan solely on a replacement, cash basis has contributed to India's belief that it has no real choice except to rely on domestic and non-American sources for major arms.

Russian aid has also been economic, valued in excess of a billion dollars. Memorialized in the Bhilai steel plant, the assistance includes managerial and financial help for a new steel complex at Bokharo, America's second Aswan. Russia's entry into the public-sector Bokharo project came after a United States study had found that it lacked feasibility, influencing Congress to withhold support despite Executive Branch urging of participation. New Delhi has found that harmonious aid relations have survived post-Khrushchev uncertainties. On his first visit to a major power, in May 1965, Prime Minister Shastri spoke in Moscow of Russia's respect for India's nonalignment, a respect demonstrated by Russia's pledge to increase substantially aid for India's economic development and to enlarge their trade. By 1967 Russia had begun to meet these pledges. The rising trade between Russia and India is symbolized by the trade pact between the two nations signed before Prime Minister Kosygin's January 1968 visit to New Delhi.

In return for political and material help India has made political repayment to Soviet Russia, the latter securing the former's assistance on several issues. Among them are Mongolia's application to join the United Nations, India's reaction to the 1956 Hungarian crisis, and its toleration of the Russian segment of Indian communism. Against China's thesis that the U.S.S.R. is a European power, India worked on behalf of Russia's inclusion as a legitimate Asian state in the aborted, second Asian-African Conference. To some a cloud appeared in Soviet-Indian relations through the Tashkent meeting in early 1966, where Russia acted as the honest broker between India and Pakistan. The official Indian view is that Russia's Tashkent role served Indian interests by helping to establish Pakistan's firm commitment to the cease-fire for the 1965 hostilities. Slightly to the left of the Gandhi ministry, in the Krishna Menon circle there is a further argument that Tashkent symbolizes the end of Western intervention in Indian-Pakistani relations and the emergence of peace-keeping by Asians for Asians. A different view points to Russia's post-1967 military aid to Pakistan and to the interventionist broadcasts of Moscow's "Radio Peace and Progress" as signs of the meaning of Tashkent for India and Russia. Because of India's predispositions and its critical relations with China, New Delhi is likely to continue its favorable interpretations of Soviet power in Asian and world affairs.

India's acceptance of Russia as a positive Asian power contrasts with its view of the United States. From the New Delhi standpoint the United States is a North American state which happens to exercise power in the seas touching Asia and in various territorial areas of East, Southeast and Western Asia. But the United States is not an Asian state nor a rightful Asian power. When secured on Indian terms, India has welcomed diplomatic and material help from the United States. An instance is the favorable reception of Ambassador John Kenneth Galbraith's endorsement of the McMahon Line, partially erasing the memory of Secretary of State Christian Herter's comment in November 1959, that the United States had only the word of a friend that India's understanding of its Northeastern frontiers was correct. The value of United States assistance to India exceeded six billion dollars for the 1946-67 period, or about sixty percent of India's external support, historic transactions which India acknowledged within the limits of pride and nonalignment. Even with India's recently improved agricultural production and its determination to be self-sufficient in foodstuffs by the early 1970's, the nation is likely to need surplus American food sales in the short run.

Several problems have undercut the limited, favorable response of India to certain kinds of American activities in Asia. There are political and economic difficulties based on the large, blocked rupee funds accumulated under P.L. 480 food programs. Relations will improve if, the American Congress willing, the funds are phased out. Especially troublesome to India is the extension of United States military power into Asia. Until 1962 India criticized this power as provocative in Asian affairs, directly judging SEATO a threat to Asian security, a charge not balanced by a similar evaluation of the Sino-Russian military alliance. It is true that, except for relatively moderate statements on the Vietnam war and sharper criticism of Pakistan's American arms, objections have been muted since the 1962 crisis when India sought and obtained American and Commonwealth air cover and ground assistance. Yet New Delhi has not held that American forces in or near Asia protect its noncommunist states from China or supply a stabilizing factor. The Indian view is found in Indian statements on United States naval patrols in the Indian Ocean, a nuclear-free zone for that sea, and Anglo-American plans to use some of its islands as communications links. To credit American power would be to testify against nonalignment. It would also conflict with an underlying current that interprets neutralism in a particular way, discouraging the military power of the Western democracies, but permitting that of the Soviet Union as a valid presence in Asia.

Nuclear questions affect India's views of the United States and Russia in Asian affairs. In the Age of Nehru, India was a leader of nuclear pacifism, with Gandhians and communists joining to urge an end to the new weapons. India contributed to the climate, if not the conditions, which produced the 1963 limited test-ban agreement which New Delhi has signed. The outlook has changed since People's China attained a military atomic power capacity in October 1964. Although the Congress party has decided not to militarize the country's impressive development of atomic energy, a decision reaffirmed after subsequent Chinese tests, ideas of security and bargaining have gained strength in official circles. For a time under Shastri, India looked to external nuclear guarantees from the West, the Soviet Union, or both. The United States helped this speculation when President Johnson said after China's first atomic explosion that America would not permit China to blackmail non-nuclear states. It is bargaining from idealism and nuclear potentiality that has emerged most strongly. The Gandhi government has resisted any antiproliferation treaty that would limit the have-nots without requiring the nuclear states to begin to disarm. Soviet-American agreement in 1967 on a draft treaty which would deny potential nuclear states such as India from acquiring nuclear weapons through their own efforts or by transfer had the result of stimulating rather than answering Indian objections. American and Russian ratification of the final treaty in 1969 found India still skeptical despite attempts by the two nuclear powers to convince the Gandhi government. Complicating the picture is the appearance of limited anti-ballistic missile systems in the United States and the Soviet Union. By protecting themselves, these nations will be better able to shield India against China. It is premature to estimate the full impact of a developed American ABM on American-Indian relations. In the past India has tended to equate United States deterrent or resistant capacities on or near the continent with basic miscalculations of Asian needs. This viewpoint persists regardless of India's acceptance of American military support during and after the 1962 border crisis and its tacit agreement that the United States is a partner in the development of Asia. The Indian outlook and a contrary American view have kept the two states from building a common Asian policy, leaving open questions of means and perhaps a conflict about ends as to Asian security.

The norm and method of peaceful change have played an important part in India's evaluation of the United States in Asia. On this basis India has in principle considered the United Nations as a beneficial institution in Asian affairs. The record, however, is an uneven one. In several instances India has encouraged and participated in United Nations activities in Asia. This is true of the Economic Commission for Asia and the Far East, Asian projects of the World Health Organization and the International Labor Organization, and the United Nations Conference on Trade and Development. Critical political issues have been another matter. On Kashmir, India originally looked to the United Nations for a judgment that Pakistan had committed aggression and for remedial action. When the United Nations bypassed Indian charges and mediated, India was disillusioned. In contrast, the Shastri government applauded U Thant's finding in September 1965, that Pakistan had broken a sixteen-year truce in Kashmir. Partly because of the decline of high expectations about the United Nations produced by the experience with Kashmir and partly because of the collapse of *Panch Shila*, India has not brought the Sino-Indian dispute to the formal attention of the world body.

When the United Nations has discussed the use of force, India has had reservations about the theory of collective measures. In specific instances it has given its support. India's initial vote with the Security Council's majority to resist North Korea in 1951 was qualified by subsequent neutralism, yet it stands. New Delhi participated in the UNEF for the Middle East. The awkward and costly ending of that experience in 1967, as well as India's earlier withdrawal under leftist African pressure from the peacekeeping force in the Congo, raise the question whether India will participate in future stabilizing operations of the United Nations in Asia or elsewhere.

The Goa affair is instructive here. Indian public reaction to the United Nations' debate on the absorption of Goa by Indian troops in 1961 showed considerable fear that the United Nations or the West might employ force to defend Portugal. It is highly probable that New Delhi knew in advance that this would not result. Nonetheless, the Goa episode did much to instill in Indian opinion a suspicion, expressed by C. S. Jha in December 1961, in the Security Council, that the United Nations would protect Western versions of international law but not the corrections of it offered by former colonial nations. After Indian emotions had subsided, New Delhi realized that the use of force had not damaged its standing in the United Nations and may have gained unexpressed respect for India, especially among Western members. In Asia, India's action was well received by its friends but opposed by Pakistan and China. For the future, India's absorption of Goa supplies the Peking government with a useful precedent for similar treatment of Hong Kong and Macao. Overall, the Indian government's view of principles and interests to be applied in Asia has differed with some United Nations decisions. Although active in the United Nations and supportive of the Charter, India considers itself a major state fully capable of mapping its own course without depending on an extra-national organization.

This viewpoint has influenced India's view of an intra-Asian organization or bloc. Regardless of intellectual support by Nehru and other Indian leaders for an Asian federation, the Indian government has not taken diplomatic steps within Asia to establish an inter-governmental Asian organization. The result of Nehru's wishes at the Asian Relations Conference of 1947, the semiofficial Asian Relations Organization, was established that year. Regional and Asian divisions prevented development, and it ended in 1955. At the official Asian Conference on Indonesia in 1949, Nehru asked for a permanent organization of Asian states, but he had little backing in the meeting and opposition from the West. During the Hungarian and Middle Eastern crises of 1956, the Asian Colombo states discussed machinery for joint and cooperative political action, but Pakistan did not participate and the hopes were not realized. In any event, by this time India had come to prefer Afro-Asian and global orientations.

More recently, some Southeast Asian states, energized by the Vietnam crisis and the prospect of the West's military withdrawal from the region, have endorsed regional and neo-continental cooperation on economic or political lines. One version, urged by Malaysia's Abdul Rahman, is an Asian organization similar to the Organization for African Unity to be composed of non-communist nations and led by Japan. A second model is security conscious and has the support of Thailand, Malaysia, the Philippines and Singapore. In particular, Singapore's Prime Minister Lee Kuan Yew has looked to India to consider the implications of Britain's closing of bases in Singapore and Malaysia, a step he favors. Another form, appearing in August 1967, is the Association of Southeast Asian Nations (ASEAN), consisting of Indonesia, Malaysia, the Philippines, Singapore and Thailand, which seeks economic cooperation and growth for its members.

The Indian government has made a mixed response to these ideas. New Delhi has ruled out a free Asia bloc led by Japan, a favorite thought of the Swatantra party. Although economic aid will be granted Singapore, Prime Minister Gandhi and Foreign Minister Dinesh Singh have discouraged Lee's vacuum theory and security concerns. With qualifications, ASEAN has been viewed favorably. In August 1967, and again in early 1968, T. N. Kaul, a high-ranking Ministry of External Affairs official, said that India welcomed ASEAN and would like to join, provided it is intended to serve economic purposes and has no political or military undertones. Working with Indonesia, India, if it joins, might perpetuate the kind of neutralism in Southeast Asia that Malaysia, the Philippines, Singapore and Thailand have usually found wanting in security terms. Under present leadership, India is not likely to enter a Southeast Asian grouping unless New Delhi's neutralism is given official sanction. Whether the small Southeast Asian states are willing to pay this price to gain Indian participation is a crucial question for the region.

Clearly, India has been a firm participant in economic regionalism, but on the foundation of East-West internationalism, not Asianism or national self-sufficiency, despite the announced intention to feed itself by 1971. New Delhi has benefited from the Colombo Plan and contributed funds to it without gaining sufficient agreement among other Asian members to establish planning or institutions on the Western European model. The affiliation of non-Asian donors gives the Colombo Plan a hybrid, funded quality, a characteristic India wants to maintain. New Delhi has a similar view of the Asian Development Bank, which came into being after the Johnson Administration in the spring of 1965 reversed an earlier position and decided to contribute United States equity. In contrast, India has shown no interest in the Asian and Pacific Council

(ASPAC), a grouping of nine states dating from 1966, which aims at economic and political cooperation. ASPAC's inclusion of Taiwan, South Korea and South Vietnam make it politically controversial from India's viewpoint. India has modified its typical view of Asian blocs to join the Asian Economic Council, a 1968 offshoot of ECAFE.

India has organized one power zone in Asia, in the Himalayan area. The result is based on the principle of military security that several Southeast Asian nations want but India avoids encouraging; yet on this matter India is no different than other states which find reasons for establishing influence in small, contiguous nations. Traditionally, Bhutan, Sikkim and Nepal have felt the conflict between Greater India and Greater China. Despite the rise of nationalism and communism, these concepts are still operational. As to India, with freedom it relinquished British influence in Tibet. Yet it did not fully apply the logic of self-determination to the in-between lands. The 1949 Indo-Bhutan Treaty ratified India's guidance of the external relations of Bhutan, which in theory retains internal political integrity. Dealing with the least powerful of the three Himalayan countries, India confirmed a protectorate status for Sikkim in the India-Sikkim Peace Treaty of 1950. The Sino-Indian dispute has enhanced the importance of the two Himalayan entities for India. Consequently, since 1962 India has tended to support the power of the royal courts, placing its security interests before advancing modernity in these entities. In recent years Bhutan and Sikkim have looked for liberalization of their treaties, but India is unlikely to change them significantly.

Toward Nepal, Indian policies have been more complex than toward the other two entities. The 1950 Indo-Nepalese Friendship Treaty upholds mutual respect for sovereignty and territorial integrity and provides for consultation between the states in case of external threat to the independence or security of either nation. Free India helped to oust the autocratic Rana family that had dominated the country for more than a century, encouraged popular nationalism and brought Indian involvement in military, intelligence and economic spheres. Without ending its own hiring, India discontinued British recruitment from Indian territory of Nepal's Gurkha soldiers. From India's standpoint there have been complicating developments. These include anti-Indian reactions, King Mahendra's suspension of democratic experiments in 1960, his ties as the world's only Hindu king to Hindu parties in India, Nepal's own ambitions in the Himalayas, and the entrance of American, Soviet and Chinese diplomats and technicians. A Chinese-built road linking Katmandu with Tibet is especially disturbing to India. The

Indian government has proceeded with considerate tact in its diplomacy with Nepal. Indicative of its new power, Nepal has convinced India to agree to the withdrawal of Indian security teams from the country by the end of 1971. There is little chance for Nehru's successors to shift to a policy of multilateralism. For it is People's China which supported and thereby discredited a movement toward a Himalayan confederation of the three nations, a possibility New Delhi views as a threat to its stakes in the area. In sum, Nepal may become troublesome.

To organize borderlands for the protection of national interests has been within India's capacity. Several factors have kept it from trying to organize power on a regional or continental basis. Among them are the vagueness of Pan-Asianism, the strength of nationalism it has encountered, the internationalism of Nehru and his successors, and the divisive influence on South Asia of Indo-Pakistani tensions. In retrospect, free India's great experiment in intra-Asian relations was the Sino-Indian association in the 1954-58 period. About this relationship India's attitude has passed through stages of optimism, shock and fear to guarded concern. From 1962 to 1967 negotiations were a moot point. More recently, Prime Minister Gandhi has indicated a willingness to enter negotiations with Peking, "should proper conditions arise." Essentially, the Indian government and people have grown accustomed to living with the Sino-Indian dispute, even when compounded by China's nuclear capacity and the Sino-Pakistani rapprochement. In place of *Panch Shila* and its aftermath, an armed posture toward China has appeared, a stand dependent on political and material aid from Russia and the United States.

As to Russia, India believes that it has acquired a basis for a firm Indo-Soviet relationship. It is not clear that the Soviet government will strengthen its cooperative association to the degree that Prime Minister Gandhi's pro-Russian advisers would like. Her demotion of Dinesh Singh and denial of a Soviet orientation in mid-1970 were cracks in a wall built by her father. In any event the Soviet Union has responsibilities to the socialist community—and high priority dealings with China and the United States—which limit its willingness to favor India more than it has done already. Russia may become especially cautious, avoiding a partnership relation with India and pursuing a fluid Tashkent policy that takes into account Pakistan after Ayub Khan as well as the usually receptive Congress government. And India may become truly neutral.

With regard to the United States, the prospects for an Asian option for Indian foreign policy are negative in terms of mutual agreement about power and methods. For America's presence and behavior in Asian affairs are suspect in the ruling circles of Indian politics. Part of the suspicion is based on United States ties to Pakistan and its conduct in Vietnam. A more basic explanation rests with the conflict between the values of progressivist neutralism that have prevailed in Indian foreign policy since freedom and the convictions of the American Executive Branch since the Korean War about the legitimacy of pronounced United States influence on political and security questions in Asia. The conflict is likely to persist unless there is a contrary change in the thinking of one of the two governments. A paradox in other ways, the Nixon Administration may prove to be adaptive to India's premises about Asia.

The prospects are not bright for establishing an Asian option for India on its relations with the Southeast Asian states. The relations have reflected some evidence of national interest but no impressive ambition and strategic ability to attract and lead an unstable region. Mrs. Gandhi's good-will trip to the area and Australia and New Zealand in 1968 was a provisional sounding for new departures. In West Asia, New Delhi's usual policy has left few elements on which to build a reciprocal relationship. Although there has been a modest return for its competition with Pakistan from India's Arab policy, the influence of India's Russian policy has produced weak foundations on which Indian self-interest can be promoted. With Japan, there is no concrete evidence that India will help it to lead noncommunist Asia as urged by some. For India is not yet able to begin to approach Asian problems with even the tentative self-confidence shown by Japan in recent years.

If there is no considerable foundation for an Asian option for India's external relations, there is one underlying basis which might be useful. It is more akin to a social ideology than to a political policy. The true division of the world, Nehru told the Governors of the International Monetary Fund and the International Bank in October 1958, is between the developed and the underdeveloped countries. Moreover, he said that in the latter there are "vast millions who are no longer quiet and who ought not to be quiet. They have no reason to be quiet." Nehru's comments symbolize how his country projects a meaningful formulation about the emergence and demands of Asia in world affairs. It has roots in the peasant Asianism expressed by Gandhi. The indigenous formulation is now subordinated to the tenuous ideology of Afro-Asianism and the cross-pressures of globalism that still control India's foreign relations. Caught between aspiration and weakness, India would do well in the 1970s to revive this formulation to help protect its integrity and establish national and regional strength.

CHAPTER VI

ARAB-AMERICAN RELATIONS: AN INTERPRETIVE ESSAY

By Elie A. Salem*

I

Relations between nations and civilizations call for a return to the roots. It is important for the Arabs to know what the United States is, what it stands for, and what are the values that determine its policy. This is imporant for them in order that they may clearly and effectively communicate with the American mind. It is equally imperative that the Americans know who the Arabs are, what values determine their behavior, what outlook they have toward the world; in short what the Arab mind is and how to communicate with it. This is made the more urgent by the global responsibilities of the United States at present and by the haphazard policies it has followed with respect to the Arab World. The fact that the policy of the United States towards this region is often described by American writers and spokesmen as being of an *ad hoc* variety necessitates a sober stock-taking on the part of American policy-makers. Nor have the Arabs any clear and consistent policy towards the U.S.; they continue to respond to American positions either with gratitude or with disappointment, depending on the issue at hand. Basic linguistic, religious, political, and cultural differences impede proper communication. Very little is done in the Arab World to teach Arab youth about America. Not even the American institutions in the Middle East attempt to do so directly. The national universities give the subject of international affairs only scant recognition. Movies, televi-

---

*Professor at the American University of Beirut, Lebanon, and a former student of Dr. Vinacke.

sion, radio, the press, travel, and the daily happenings reported through the mass media do indeed provide the Arabs with some information on the New World. Such information, however, is too little and too warped to serve as guidepost for policy. The challenge the Arabs face is whether they have matured enough to transcend nationalist astigmatism and to care as much about others as they expect the others to care about them. America, too, faces the challenge of knowing enough about the Arabs to be capable of devising policies based on facts.

THE ARAB

The term "Arabs" as used in this paper refers to the people inhabiting the Middle East whose native language is Arabic and who share in the Arabic historical and cultural tradition. Although accurate statistics are not available for all Arab countries, it is safe to estimate the number of Arabs at about one hundred million. About ninety-three percent of these are Muslims, and of the Muslims about ninety percent are Sunni (i.e. Orthodox) Muslims.

The non-Muslim Arabs are primarily Christians living in Lebanon, Syria, Egypt and North Africa. Christian intellectuals serve as cultural links between Islam and Christendom. To the West they are interpreters of the Middle Eastern mind, and to the Middle East they are instruments of change and a transmission belt. Among the Muslim-Arabs the minorities are Shi'i sectarians in Iraq and Yemen, and Druze in Lebanon and Syria. A pagan minority lives in the Sudan. The Arabs live in fourteen independent states and several autonomous shaykhdoms and undefined tribal groupings. They occupy a territory stretching from Morocco on the Atlantic to Kuwait on the Persian Gulf, and from Iraq in the North to Hadramout on the Southern tip of the Arabian Peninsula.

The North African Arab States of Morocco, Tunisia, and Algeria have had special relations with France since the French occupation of Algeria in the 1830's. With the defeat of Fascist Italy in World War II, Libya was made a U.S. trusteeship and was soon granted independence. Libya has cordial official relations with the United States, whose oil companies and business firms hold extensive concessions in the booming Libyan economy. Sudan's politics have until recently been treated as part of Egyptian politics. While this is no longer the case, the Sudan continues nevertheless to follow Egyptian patterns in its foreign policies.

Egypt (the United Arab Republic), Palestine, Jordan, Iraq, Syria, and Lebanon occupy a focal place in Arab politics because of their strategic and cultural importance. It is this area, the Arab East, that constitutes the main focus of this paper.

The major oil-producing countries, namely Saudi Arabia and Kuwait, maintain special relations with the U.S. because American firms are largely responsible for the exploration of their oil resources and for the modernization of these basically traditional countries. Since Saudi Arabia and Kuwait depend almost exclusively on oil, they are bound by the iron laws of economics to maintain friendly relations with their benefactors. If oil production was to cease for one reason or another the politico-economic system in these countries would collapse. Similarly, Iraq and Bahrain depend on their oil resources and consequently on Great Britain, which has preponderant economic interests there. The remaining Arab political groupings on the Persian Gulf and Indian Ocean are still highly traditional tribal groupings in special treaty relations with Great Britain. Under the heat of nationalism and of modernism the tribal-traditional portion of the Arab World is being rapidly transformed. The United States, Russia, Britain, Egypt and Saudi Arabia are all deeply involved in this transformation. Which policy this Arab grouping will follow will depend on the resources to be exploited and on political trends in Egypt and in Saudi Arabia. The Yemen also is in a state of transformation after years of civil war between revolutionary republicans and tribal traditional monarchists. Future relations between the Yemen and the United States depend on two factors, the relations between Egypt and the United States, and the type of government that will emerge in the Yemen as a result of the efforts at compromise now being pursued by republicans and monarchists. A third and greatly unpredictable factor may be added, the future political and institutional developments in the Saudi Peninsula. A revolutionary regime in al-Riyadh might very well change the focus of power in the Arab World and determine the political orientations of the states and shaykhdoms of the Peninsula.

THE ARAB EAST

This paper is concerned primarily with the Arab East and with its relations with the United States. The establishment of the state of Israel in Palestine at the very point where Arab Asia and Arab Africa meet brought a new factor to this region, a factor which, though not Arab, has become the primary concern of Arab politics and of Arab-American relations. Let us examine the underlying forces that govern the attitude and the political behavior of the people of the Arab East. Three forces immediately suggest themselves. These are as follows:

A. *Islam*: Islam is the religion preached by the Prophet Muhammad between 610 and 632 A.D. It is a religion rooted in Judaism and in Christianity, although it is in many respects distinct. Islam preaches the One God, Allah, the Creator of heaven and hell, the ultimate governor of the universe. It recognizes the Biblical prophets as well as the prophecy of Jesus but considers Muhammad to be the last Prophet and his calling to be the most complete and the most perfect. Islam provided Muhammad with the ideology and the movement to unify the tribes of Arabia, to make a nation out of them and to impregnate them with the zeal that ultimately led them to defeat the empires of the Persians and of the Byzantines and to form under Muhammad's successors an empire stretching from Spain to the very heart of Asia. Islam as the religion of almighty and purposeful Allah is based on confidence, victory, power, and glory, not on stoic humility. For the Muslim victory is natural; it is destined by Allah. This belief in victory helps explain the psychological depth of the crisis now faced by a people who, despite such theological assurance, are in fact weak and humiliated. The dignity and the glory of Islam as a religion are involved in the heated political controversy in the Arab East over the state of Israel.

B. *The Arabic language*: Like Islam, the Arabic language is a force in determining the direction of the Arab mind. Arabic was given a transcendental place by Islam because the Quran was revealed in it. And insofar as the Quran represents the direct word of Allah revealed to Muhammad through the Angel Gabriel, Arabic became a holy language, the language of God and of the angels. To the Arab his language is not merely a means of communication but practically an object of worship in itself. While other cultures manifest their artistic expression in painting and music, the Arabs have manifested theirs primarily through linguistic eloquence, verse and rhyme. A noted Islamic ruler is reported to have said: "My son, only he who excels in the Arabic language can rule the Arabs." The crucial role of words, especially the spoken word, on the unfolding of political processes may be seen in the hold of charismatic leaders like Nasser or Bourguibah on the masses.

Arabic is undergoing a radical transformation to accommodate modern intellectual trends. It is called upon to shift its weight from the poetic and oratorical to the analytic and scientific. The test now is not whether the language can change, but whether the Arab mind can overcome the pull of traditional Arabic language and force new styles, concepts and usages into its structure. The Arab has, in Arabic, one advantage over the American as far as readiness for communication is involved. The Arabic language has practically no deposit of literature dealing with America; while English does have such a deposit—but a deposit that is distorted by religious, cultural and political prejudices. Arabic has the advantage of innocence in this regard, and Arab writers have a unique opportunity to flood Arabic, in freedom, with the content which they choose. The Arabic language draws the Arab to his glorious past, to his solid roots and provides him with satisfaction. Great efforts are needed to make Arabic a vehicle of communication between the two civilizations. First Arabic must be enriched by new content, second the American must free his own language from the preconceived notions about the Arabs, and third the Arabs and the Americans must in larger numbers master each other's language. Otherwise communication remains but a myth.

C. *The Arab Culture*: For the past half century the Arabs have been attempting to rediscover their cultural heritage and to interpret it afresh to meet the needs of modern times. In view of their humiliation at the hands of the West they have been primarily concerned in identifying the bright spots of old, if only to reassure themselves of their competence. Every nation resorts to myth to fashion its purpose and to justify its existence. Myth is not necessarily nonexistent reality, although it may be an exaggerated projection of reality. The myth of past glory exercises great influence on the Arabs and on their behavior towards others. The Arabs have reason for pride in the past, provided such pride does not lead to xenophobic attitudes and self-contentment. Between the eighth and the twelfth centuries the Arabs built a dynamic civilization. They had assimilated, in the wake of Islamic conquest, the learning of Greece, Egypt, Babylon, Persia and India, and they preserved the classical masterpieces of the ancients. Arabic civilization made magnificent contributions to literature, history, religious studies, linguistics and geography. In the very area in which it was presumed to be weak, science, the Arabic civilization made brilliant breakthroughs. Until the sixteenth century some of the basic European scientific

references were Arabic. By the twelfth and thirteenth centuries
Arab philosophic and scientific literature was being translated
into Latin and transmitted to Europe. These translations af-
fected the awakening of Europe. The Arab, grieved by his present, has become a "me too." If he is shown a scientific American
achievement, he will remind you that he "too" in the past attained
such heights. His cultural sensitivity is too serious a matter to be
ignored. To gain his confidence and his empathy one must recognize his past attainment. This factor, though seemingly un-
related to current political developments, is at the very roots of the
strained relations that exist between the Arabs and the West.

These three factors are then decisive elements in the behavior of the
Arabs and in their relations with the outside world. A brief evaluation of
the Arab mind will be attempted below.

THE ARAB MIND

Any characterization of the Arab mind is fraught with danger. Nevertheless it is essential in examining relations between civilizations to attempt generalizations on the types of mind involved. What follows is an
attempt to explain the Arab mind and the forces that have molded it—
the desert environment, the geographic location on the planet, and the
cultural forces of the region. It is essentially poetic, leaning on rhyme,
verse, and the great odes of the past. The Arab is gifted in this area, and
his language provides him with the facility to excel. The Arab mind,
though poetic, is also concrete. It relates itself to concrete objects—to
the sun, the moon, the camel, the sheep, the tree, the desert. Unlike
the Greek mind, the Arab mind is not essentially theoretical and universalistic. The Arab is more inclined towards the detail, the particular, the object, and the anecdote. This is clearly apparent in the Arabic
poem in which each line stands by itself as a vivid and short encounter
with one idea. Arab historical works consist of compilations of events on
a year-to-year or month-to-month basis with little interpretation and
no theory.

The Arab is concerned with himself, his legacy, his culture, his religion; he has exhibited little interest in the outside world. This, of
course, is not a characteristic unique to the Arabs, but it is mentioned
here to emphasize the Arab ignorance of what America is all about and
the reasons for that ignorance. The Arab is obsessed with his *karāmah*,
i.e., his dignity, his image, his appearance. It is extremely important for
him that he appears respected and of high status. Nothing is more dev-

astating to the Arab than loss of face or humilition in public. This accounts in part for the well-publicized affront that the Arabs now encounter as a result of a military defeat (the June, 1967, war with Israel). The Arab is also personal, that is, he is greatly influenced by personal contact. He gives general issues personal attributes and tends to individualize events and to personalize trends of history. The Arab mind weakens before flattery, deference and public recognition and expects to be treated in this rather traditional yet "polite" manner. This is as true in the realm of politics as it is in the market place where the exchange of niceties must precede a transaction. On the other hand, if publicly insulted, if the *karāmah* is injured, he reacts violently. If, as has been suggested, the nationalization of the Suez Canal was Nasser's response to Secretary Dulles' sudden withdrawal of the Aswan loan, then this example serves as a case in point.

CHALLENGES

The conviction that the Arabs as Muslims were destined to victory, glory and dignity was confirmed in their eyes by their victories. With the decline of the Arab 'Abbasid Empire, the Arab World like most of the Middle East fell under Mamluk, i.e., slave rulers who had been imported by the Arab rulers from the outer stretches of the empire, but who became Muslims and governed by the precepts of the *shari'ah* (Holy Law). The Ottoman Empire with its base in Istanbul succeeded in the sixteenth century in assimilating the Arab East within its political hegemony. From the sixteenth to the nineteenth centuries, the Arabs lived under Turkish rule. Arabic ceased to be the *lingua franca* of letters, not only because Turkish became the language of the ruling class but because of the general decline of letters in that period. Nevertheless the Arabs as Muslims, not yet moved by secular nationalism, felt spiritually, culturally and politically secure under the Ottoman umbrella and felt proud of the Ottoman conquests in Europe. At the end of the eighteenth century the Arab World experienced its first serious humiliation at the hands of the West since the Crusades, and the Arabs have not yet recovered from its impact. Napoleon, anxious for imperial power, organized an expedition and occupied Muslim Egypt in 1798 as a step towards crippling Great Britain by cutting its communication lines with India. The conquest of Egypt by Napoleon, though short-lived, was the beginning of the rapid retreat of the Muslims in the face of emerging Europe. As Ottoman power declined, the protective shield was removed, and within a century the colonial flood of Europe swept through the entire region. In 1830 France started colonizing Algeria.

From Algeria, French colonization expanded until it gained control over Tunisia and Morocco. In 1911 Italy occupied Libya. Egypt, although it was freed from French occupation by the quick return of Napoleon to Paris, fell under British occupation in 1882. Although the circular of the British Foreign Secretary to the powers stated that the occupation was temporary, it lasted, nevertheless, until the mid-1950's when Nasser's revolutionary government reached an agreement with Britain on withdrawal. World War I brought about the destruction of the Ottoman Empire and raised new problems for the successor states which were born with the aid of Britain and France. Lebanon and Syria fell under French mandate. Palestine, Iraq and Transjordan fell under British mandate. By the end of World War I, all the Muslim Arab World with the exception of the then "useless" Peninsula (oil had not been discovered) was under the control of Christian European powers —the "strange infidel" conquerors from the North. All the key strategic places and shaykhdoms around the periphery of the Peninsula from Aden to Kuwait were under one form or another of British "protection." It is important to comprehend the sequence of events between 1798 and 1920 in the Arab World and to grasp the image in its entirety, to fully understand the psychological condition of the Arab and his resentment to colonialism, imperialism, and Western influence.

The confident and religiously reassured Arab, all of a sudden, found himself defeated by the West. He was not only defeated on the battlefield, but his very culture was retreating before the massive Western corrosions. The immediate reaction of the Arab was to reassert the validity of Islam and its flexibility to accommodate all contingent situations, and to create new organizations and movements to withstand the onslaught.

Arab nationalism arose to combine the dignity of former glories and the hope of the future. Its first objectives were negative, the withdrawal of foreign troops from the Arab World, the dissolution of political ties in which the Arabs were clearly indicated as the inferiors, and the elimination of the traditional institutions that delayed rapid progress. Its positive aims were independence, economic progress, political and cultural unity and the institution of a modern and viable Arab society.

II

EARLY AMERICAN CONTACTS

It is clear from the preceding paragraphs that there was no major political confrontation between the Arab and the American in this critical and formative period. America, therefore, had the opportunity to start its relations with the Arabs in a positive, if not corrective, manner. America, unlike Europe, was not a colonial power. To the extent they knew anything about America, the Arabs knew that it was essentially noncolonial, and different from the "old world"; and for some, it was an exciting liberal experiment conducted by people who were, for one reason or another, dissatisfied in Europe. At a time when America was coming unto its own, unifying and organizing itself, the Arab World, under the influence of the Napoleonic invasion and under the literary influences of Europe throughout the nineteenth century, was undergoing profound ideological ferment.

The nineteenth century was the century of confrontation. Egypt under Muhammad 'Ali had a special house in Paris where Egyptian trainees lived and appropriated French culture. Turkey similarly sent students and military missions to the various capitals of Europe in an effort to acquire the "Western magic" of technological and organizational "know-how." In the nineteenth century France, Italy, Britain, Russia and Austria sponsored schools, mostly of confessional nature, throughout the Levant states. While America's political preoccupation did not permit it to be seriously involved in Arab politics in the nineteenth century, it became gradually interested because of growing missionary and commercial interests. In Arab-American relations, the nineteenth century may well be noted as the messianic age, the age in which idealistic well-meaning Americans left the safety of their shores and embarked for a strange and distant world to preach the truth of Jesus, to gain new recruits into the faith and to do good in His name.

In the 1830's the political situation in the Arab East was conducive to missionary activity. Ibrahim Pasha, the son of Muhammad 'Ali, the progressive governor of Egypt, had launched a campaign against his suzerain, the Ottoman Sultan in Istanbul. To gain Western support he introduced a liberal policy in the Levant states that made missionary activity possible. In that period American missionaries established themselves in the Levant region, opened schools and conducted missionary activities. America's commercial interests were then at a minimum, and the only major interest the United States had was the protection of these missionary and educational establishments in the Arab East. The American missionaries set high standards by opening good elementary and secondary schools and by offering a rather modern educational curriculum in an area where learning, when existent, was by rote, traditional and the privilege of the few. They introduced the printing press, translated scientific works into Arabic, and learned the Arabic language to better communicate to the natives the values in which they believed. Those who came in contact with them recognized them as good men, hard working, dedicated; and they were on the whole not merely tolerated, but respected. In 1866 American missionaries in Lebanon and Syria sponsored the establishment of the Syrian Protestant College, the first modern institution of higher learning in the region. Its very establishment constituted an American challenge to the French, who always conceived of the Levant area as their sphere of influence. Within a decade the French responded by establishing their own institution of higher learning, the St. Joseph University. The Syrian Protestant College became in 1920 the American University of Beirut. By the end of the nineteenth century the College became a center of scholarly activity. Great classical works of the Arabs were published; the Arabic language, long neglected under the Turks, was revived. College students, now acquainted with the rich and hitherto buried legacy of the Arabs and with the new ideas of the West, organized themselves secretly in the service of the Arab national and cultural transformation.

The American University of Beirut provided an informal channel of communication between the Arab mind and the American. It did so by attracting American professors to the region, by providing them with a base for research, and by accommodating American students specializing in Islamic or Middle Eastern studies. In preparing its graduates through the medium of the English language, the University opened up the American educational system to a new Arab elite. Part of this Arab elite has in the past few decades joined American universities, government bureaucracies, autonomous research institutes and business firms, thus providing vital services to the American system. Graduates of this University in the Arab World have become the interpreters of the American mind to the Arab World, and vice versa, and the proponents of cultural communion between the two civilizations. As their number is small and as the problems facing the Middle East are manifold and diverse, the influence of these graduates on the region as a whole is limited, but nevertheless clearly discernible.

AMERICA'S IMAGE AT THE END OF THE FIRST WORLD WAR

Until the 1920's the Arab people knew America through the missionary, the educator and the lone businessman. During the war a fourth element was introduced in the person of President Wilson, and these four fashioned directly or indirectly a highly positive image of America in the Arab mind. Wilson's Fourteen Points exercised a magical effect on the Arabs at the dawn of their national awakening. As the Arabs had no thorough knowledge of America and of its foreign policy, they culled from the Fourteen Points an idealistic and exaggerated image of America. President Wilson was viewed as a liberator and defender of the oppressed. This was at a time when Britain and France were considered by Arab leaders as aggressive, imperialist and unreliable. In the Paris Peace Conference Wilson was solicited by Arab representatives to support their cause for independence and to help them against the claims made by Britain and France over the Arab East. (It should be recalled that during the war Britain and France concluded a secret treaty known as the Sykes-Picot agreement which would divide the Arab East into British and French areas of influence). Wilson's sympathy with the Arab desire for independence led to the dispatch of the King-Crane Commission. This fact-finding committee visited the contested Arab East and interviewed the leaders of the region. The Commission's findings revealed that the Arabs had rejected any foreign mandate, but that if any such mandate was to be imposed on them, they would prefer an American mandate. This fact must be underlined in view of the present relations between the Arabs and the United States. The King-Crane report to the League was ignored, and its content was rendered impotent by the rapid political developments in the Arab East, where a *fait accompli* situation was created. With the weakening of President Wilson and with the opposition of the Congress to U.S. entry into the League of Nations, America drifted into an isolationist foreign policy. From the Arab point of view this was an unfortunate development.

The Arab East continued under Anglo-French control until the end of the Second World War. The rise of the United States and of the Soviet Union as the two Great Powers, together with the development of the United Nations Organization, accelerated the independence of the Arabs and the withdrawal of British and French armies from the region. The wave of Western military incursions into the Arab World has by now receded almost completely. One factor, however, was introduced during World War I which has since become a major force in Arab-American relations. This is the Zionist movement and the establishment of the state of Israel in Palestine.

ISRAEL AS A FACTOR IN ARAB-AMERICAN RELATIONS

The European Jewish problem had translated itself politically into a Zionist movement at the end of the nineteenth century and has, since the early 1920's, become a decisive factor affecting the broad relations between the Arab and American civilizations. The Zionist idea is too well known to the American reader to necessitate special treatment in this paper; it will, therefore, be mentioned only as an aspect of U.S.-Arab relations. The Zionist organization had been seeking, since the end of the nineteenth century, a territorial base which would be converted into a Jewish home. Although territorial tracts in Africa and America were considered, none of these had any attraction for the Zionist movement. Only Palestine, the land of the Bible, had enough pull to unify the Jews for the establishment of a state. During the course of World War I, the Zionist organization secured from the British government the Balfour Declaration favoring the establishment of a Jewish home in Palestine without prejudice to the rights of the Arab population there.

When Britain assumed mandatory power over Palestine, the Balfour Declaration was incorporated in the mandate covenant. The Zionist organization in Palestine under the British umbrella sought the transformation of the home into a state. In the United States the Zionist movement tried to solicit formal and informal support for a Jewish home or commonwealth in Palestine. In June, 1922, it succeeded in persuading Congress to pass a resolution embodying the Balfour Declaration. The resolution, however, was considered by the Department of State to be an embarrassment. Difference of views on Palestine between the President and Congress on the one hand and the Department of State on the other is far from unknown. The President and Congress, more than the professional bureaucracy, are bound to be more responsive to the political, humanitarian and emotional pressures of American society. America's popular sympathy for a Jewish home in Palestine was based on the following:

1. Almost complete ignorance of the Arab World, of Palestine and of the type of society that existed there.
2. Identification with the Jewish claim to Palestine based on the American understanding of the Bible—the common denominator between Christian (especially Protestant) and Jew.
3. Sympathy for the Jewish people as a result of persecution in Europe.
4. Compliance with Zionist views as a result of active Zionist propaganda in the United States.

The Republican Administrations that succeeded Wilson, however, maintained a sort of aloofness in Middle Eastern affairs, leaving them in the hands of the British. While Congress continued to pass resolutions in support of Jewish emigration to Palestine and in favor of "reconstituting" Palestine as a "Jewish Commonwealth," the Executive was more reticent and apparently less concerned with the Jewish-Palestinian problem.

In 1945, after a brief meeting with the King of Saudi Arabia, President Roosevelt wrote him on April 5 concerning Palestine that "I would take no action . . . which might prove hostile to the Arab people." Immediately after the war the Palestine issue became an integral part of American national politics. In the congressional elections of 1946, Truman and Dewey outbid each other in support of Jewish emigration to Palestine and the establishment of a Jewish state. While Truman sympathized with Zionist demands he had no definite policy towards Palestine. Between January and March, 1948, the U.S. first supported the partition resolution but later rescinded that support. The U.S. delegate then proposed a U.N. trusteeship and pleaded with Britain not to withdraw its forces. President Truman stated, however, that if all efforts failed and a state of Israel was established the United States would recognize it.

Since its establishment, Israel has developed such close relations with the United States as to make its cause an American cause; and rightly or wrongly the Arabs believe that the new state has become the major interest America has in the Middle East. A more sober evaluation shows that America has at least five major reasons to be interested in the Arab East.

U.S. INTERESTS

There is first the strategic interest of the United States in the Arab East region which connects the two continents. Such interest is natural in view of America's global defense responsibilities, particularly since World War II. The Truman Doctrine represents the first serious U.S. commitment to the defense of Eastern Mediterranian regions hitherto under British hegemony. In an effort to save Turkey and Greece from falling under Communist control, President Truman asked Congress on March 12, 1947, to authorize the expenditure of $400,000,000 in military and economic aid to these countries. Through its air base in Libya, through the Sixth Fleet in Mediterranean waters and through friendly governments in the Arab World, the U.S. attempts to maintain the nucleus of a presence to face immediate dangers as they arise.

Second, the growing American business investments in the Arab World have been calling for governmental protection. Of these investments the most important in Arab-American relations are the oil investments in Saudi Arabia, Kuwait, and Libya. To determine the impact of oil industry on politics it is enough to point out that in Saudi Arabia and in Kuwait the budget is over ninety percent dependent on the oil industry—an industry which is too extensive to be effectively operated or controlled by these quasi-traditional states. These companies exert pressure on the U.S. government to initiate friendly policy towards the Arabs because it is difficult for them to operate in a region which is opposed to the policy of their home country. American movies, journals and musical records are playing a decisive role in the Westernization of the Arab World. Many upper class Arabs are highly Americanized. Beirut has become an outpost for American business activities in the Middle East. While politics may alienate, neutral business activities may strengthen relations between nations and may provide points of contact for future dialogue.

In the third place, there are the many cultural and educational American interests in the Arab World. These are in the form of universities, colleges, programs, high and elementary schools, and missions. The American University of Beirut and the American University in Cairo are perhaps the top academic institutions of higher learning in the Arab East. American educational institutions in the Arab World are exposed to the fluctuation of politics and are therefore subjected to all the tensions now arising in Arab-American relations. While these institutions are private and they have become centers of Arab intellectual and nationalist activities, they are nevertheless associated in the minds of the people with the political image of America. At the same time, they continue to be the most enduring bridges between the two civilizations. Business interests whose primary concern is profit are less enduring than academic centers whose concern is primarily service. Only such academic centers, reflecting the best and the most fundamental aspects of the American cultural tradition can serve as a medium for the Arab-American dialogue at a level higher than the passing, the ephemeral and the contentious.

The fourth major American interest in the Arab World is to keep it free from Soviet control. Since World War II, Russia has been intensifying its efforts to understand the Arabs and to influence their politics. To this end, Russia has established research institutes to study Arab culture and behavior, financed cultural missions, and granted scholarships to Arab students to study in Soviet universities. The Soviets have been supporting the budding Communist movements in the Arab World and have, at every opportunity, aligned themselves with the revolutionary reform movements in Afro-Asia. It is this tactical move—to appear to be on the side of the new—that has been responsible for the growing influence of Russia in the East. The United States on the other hand finds itself aligned with tottering regimes and consequently gives the impression that it is against nationalist movements. In the past decade the Soviet Union has entrenched itself in Egypt, Syria, Iraq, Yemen and Algeria.

In every major confrontation with Israel since 1954 the Arabs have had the support of the Soviet Union. The fact that the Arabs are not yet under Communist government is not due to the success of U.S. policy in the Middle East, but to the determination of Arab leadership to preserve Arab independence and their politico-cultural identity. Soviet advances into the Arab East, specially into Egypt and Syria, since the crisis of June 5, 1967, are of such magnitude as to arouse serious concern in Washington. If there was ever a time when American policy in the Middle East was at the crossroads, this time is now; hence the emphasis in this paper on the major issues that hang in the balance between the two civilizations.

Fifth, the U.S. has a politico-cultural commitment to Israel—a refugee state for the Jewish people, of whom a significant number live in the United States and play prominent roles in culture, business and the mass media. Israel has received and continues to receive direct support from the United States government in the form of loans, weapons, technical assistance and cultural exchange. The American people under the influence of the Zionist movement in America and the many other philanthropic organizations have developed profound interest in Israel and admiration for its achievements. Israeli spokesmen have been effective in their expert handling of the American mind. They have developed a series of likenesses between Israel and America and fashioned a language in common. Israel, like America, is portrayed as "hard working," "peaceful," "new frontier," "inventive," "progressive," "democratic," and "messianic." In picturing Israel as a struggling peace-loving state in the midst of the "unjust" Arab World, they have aroused the latent American sympathy for the "underdog." The strong bonds that were fashioned between Israel and America have reduced the freedom of the latter in pursuing an Arab policy in tune with the aggrieved and affronted Arab mind. In becoming the focal point of America's politics in the Middle East, Israel has put the United States in a precarious position as far as the rest of the Middle East is concerned. It is not yet clear what the United States intends to do to accommodate all the parties concerned in the midst of the conflicting claims and counterclaims that are and will be rocking this region.

III

POLICY FORMULATION

To judge the competence of the officials dealing with foreign policy matters in America and in the Arab East, it would be necessary to examine the entire educational and recruitment systems of both civilizations. This task is too big to permit anything but cursory treatment in this paper. The United States has made great strides in broadening its educational system to include the history and culture of foreign nations. Centers for Middle East Studies, with concentration on Arab-Islamic civilization, have mushroomed over the past two decades. Universities such as Harvard, Princeton, Columbia, Johns Hopkins, Michigan, California, together with less well-known universities and colleges, now conduct Middle East Programs, support research on the Middle East and maintain close contacts with developments in the Middle Eastern region. A new generation of American intellectuals is learning Arabic as well as Arabic culture and is therefore intellectually equipped to understand the Arab mind. Many of these are joining the various offices and agencies of the United States government that deal with foreign affairs. Books, journals and research papers on the Arab World are now available in growing numbers to the American reader. As policy becomes more intellectualized, based more solidly on facts, figures, and rational calculations of national interest, these intellectuals are bound to play a larger role in the future. But the Arabs believe that U.S. Middle East policy is determined more by the man in the White House than by the bureaucracy of the Department of State and other governmental agencies, although the latter commands expert knowledge of the Middle East. This was definitely the case under President Truman, who confessed in his own memoirs that he did not always take too seriously the advice of the "striped-pants" officials of the Department of State.

The influence of American missionaries and educators who worked in the Middle East has declined sharply over the past decade. The influence of Arab embassies in Washington, while difficult to assess, does not appear to be significant. In fact it is dubious whether men of the training of Arab embassy personnel can be effective in communicating with the American mind. It is precisely in the area of communication with America that Israel has succeeded and the Arabs have failed. Arab spokesmen in the United States have consistently addressed the American mind as if it were the Arab mind and have therefore failed to inform and influence. The bureaucracy shares in the formulation of U.S. policy, and it often must take a stand on the basis of very little knowledge. The United States has embassies throughout the Arab capitals. Many of these embassies, particularly those in the Arab East, are adequately staffed. These embassies not only collect information on developments in the Arab World, but also conduct intensive research on those aspects of Arab character that determine political behavior and communicate it to Washington.

If policy formulation in America with respect to the Arab World is restricted by the scarcity of experts in the right places, the case is more serious with respect to Arab policy towards America. Bureaucracies in the Arab World are more traditional and less informed on international affairs than their American counterparts. Academic centers, research activity, and mass media in the Arab World are not sufficiently developed to interpret American political developments accurately.

AMERICAN POLICIES

With the establishment of Israel, the decline of British and French influence in the Arab East, and the emergence of Soviet Power in the Arab East, the United States as the heir (willing or not) of the Western European legacy was compelled to react quickly and on an *ad hoc* basis to the rapid developments in this area. It has not yet had the luxury of formulating policy based on calculated judgment. Its policies are still fashioned in the heat of the conflict and are therefore closer to tactics than to strategy. To preserve the *status quo*, the U.S. joined Britain and France in a tripartite declaration on May 25, 1950, opposing any attempt to modify by force the armistice boundaries between Israel and the Arab States, and regulating the sale of arms to these countries in order to preserve military balance. While this declaration was not accepted by the Arab States whose virulent nationalism intensifies their sensitivity to foreign pronouncements on their behalf, it served nevertheless as a temporary deterrent to military action. The declaration was violated in 1956 when Israel, in collaboration with Britain and France, attacked Egypt subsequent to the nationalization of the Suez Canal. President Eisenhower opposed this military action and exerted American influence in favor of early withdrawal of foreign troops from Egyptian territory. The declaration was violated again on June 5, 1967, when Israel attacked Egypt, Jordan and Syria subsequent to Egyptian mobilization and continued radio threats from Cairo and Damascus. President Johnson used the crisis of June, 1967, as an opportunity to attempt a settlement in the Middle East. He favored the withdrawal of Israeli troops as part of a package deal, including recognition of Israel and of its right to passage through the Suez Canal. The rest of the package was considered by the Arabs to be an imposition on them that went beyond the confines of the Tripartite Declaration.

In the early 1950's, during the Eisenhower administration, great efforts were made by Secretary of State Dulles to institute a regional treaty organization with the Arab East including Turkey, Iran, Pakistan and Britain. The United States did not officially join this organization, which was known as the Baghdad Pact. Of all the Arab East states, only Iraq joined. The others under the leadership of Egypt and the pressure of Arab nationalist ideology opposed the pact. Newly independent nations are extremely sensitive about joint defense treaties, especially treaties with those who only recently were their lords and suzerains. In the absence of mutual agreements between Arabs and Americans, the latter had to act within policies consistent with their own global interests. Thus when in 1958 civil disorder broke out in Lebanon, the Iraqi regime collapsed before a military coup, and communist power in the region seemed to be in the ascendant, the U.S. found through the Eisenhower Doctrine the appropriate authority to land troops in Lebanon in anticipation of further developments in the region. The Eisenhower Doctrine consists of a number of proposals submitted by the President and approved by Congress on March 9, 1957, to limit Soviet advances in the Middle East. The Doctrine promises American support, if requested, to Middle East countries threatened by any nation controlled by international Communism. The support can take any of the following forms:

a) direct American military intervention;
b) economic aid;
c) guarantee of independence.

The Doctrine was accepted by the pro-Western regimes of Lebanon and Iraq and was rejected by the rest of the Arab states, presumably because it did not address itself to the Palestine problem. With the fall of these two regimes in 1958, the Doctrine has lost its usefulness, although it has remained a reminder to the Soviets of America's readiness to interfere if its vital strategic interests are threatened.

Since 1955 the initiative in Arab politics has been assumed by President Nasser, who has practically controlled the major policy matters of the Arab League. In an effort to achieve greater independence from the West and to maintain military strength in the face of Israel, Nasser embarked on a policy of friendship with the Soviet Union. This friendship provided him with political support against Israel and with military and economic aid including the construction of the Aswan Dam, the symbol of Egypt's liberation. As the U.S. could not provide the Arabs with significant political support against Israel, it had to satisfy itself with economic aid to Egypt, military aid to Jordan, and technical assistance. Although some of these items were substantial, none of them had the appeal of the political support provided by Russia. The political problems of the Arab East constitute the thorny knot in Arab-U.S. relations, and for America, in the words of President Eisenhower, the political situation there is a "tangle of conflicting considerations, one with so few possibilities of being resolved that it had to be lived with rather than settled."[1]

CONCLUSION

It is clear from the preceding that Arab-American relations have gone through various stages: idealism, neutrality and involvement. In the first stage, the ideal attribute was a result of Arab romantic interest in a state supporting independence and freedom. Wilson's policy in this regard was propitious. While Wilson expressed sympathy for a Jewish commonwealth in Palestine, this expression was not well known in the Arab World, nor for that matter were the Arab masses at that time conscious of the Palestine problem which had just begun to develop.

The stage of neutrality was essentially a stage of increasing economic and cultural activity with few political interests and political confrontations.

The stage of involvement, which has followed World War II, is highly political. Arab nationalist interest, Israeli interest and American strategic interest cannot all be accommodated within a romantic framework. That this stage will continue into the distant future seems now to be a realistic prediction. The complexities that have been introduced into Arab-American relations necessitate greater efforts on the part of policy-makers of both civilizations. Only after understanding the Arab mind and the forces that activate it and only after communicating with it at the level which it understands, will America be able to evolve a policy towards the Arab World which the Arabs can accept. Similarly the Arabs, who are bound by the realities of international politics to deal with the U.S., even in matters pertaining to the Arab World proper, must make greater efforts through their academic centers, diplomatic channels and the like to learn objectively about the American mind and to learn how to deal with it at a level which the American understands and appreciates.

As this paper is addressed to the American reader, the emphasis has been on the Arab, underlining his concern, his problem and his recent exposure to American politics. It has been my purpose to show that understanding the Arab mind is the *sine qua non* of a successful American policy in the Arab World, as understanding of the American mind is the condition for a proper Arab policy towards America.

CHAPTER VII

THE BRITISH
LABOUR PARTY
IN THE
CONTEMPORARY WORLD[1]

By Henry R. Winkler*

I   AT HOME

During the past two decades, the Labour Party has been by far the most successful of all the major western European parties professing the ideology of democratic socialism. In Germany, the Social Democratic Party exists in name, but it has long since, for all practical purposes, abandoned even lip service to socialist ideas. In France and Italy, social democracy has been challenged by parties of the extreme Left— and has seemed unable to meet the challenge with cohesion, let alone success. In country after country, no viable political alternative has emerged to challenge the parties of modernized conservatism—Christian Democrats, Tories, Gaullists—parties that have been so prominent in the western world since 1945.

Yet in Great Britain, a Labour Party came into office for six years after a sweeping victory in 1945 and, after years in the wilderness during the fifties and early sixties, once again assumed control, with a House of Commons majority of almost a hundred seats. What has been the character of this party? What have been some of its problems? Why has it been successful? How do we explain its transformation from a narrow sectarian group into a national organization appealing—unevenly, to be sure—to more than a working-class constituency? How, in other

*Dean of the Faculty of Liberal Arts, and Vice Provost, Rutgers, The State University, New Jersey, and a former student of Dr. Vinacke.

words, do we assess the process by which the Labour Party became domesticated? How did it prepare for its contemporary exercise of power, however limited that power may have been in practice? Let me first concentrate on the home front, on internal issues, and then turn to foreign policy and international questions.

The contemporary Labour Party is almost exactly fifty years old. Its roots go back, of course, much further, to the political reforms of 1867 and 1884 which gave the franchise to manual workers but hardly provided guidance about how that franchise might be used. For decades, the defense of working-class interests had oscillated between industrial and political action, between trade union activity to improve the standards of labour and tentative efforts to collaborate with the dominant national parties in the hope that similar improvements might thus be fostered through conventional political channels.

By 1900 the trade union movement had come of age. Unskilled as well as highly-trained workers were organized in a series of societies more or less combined under the umbrella of a Trades Union Congress. And by that time, some at least of the leaders of Labour had become disillusioned with the effort to work through the existing political parties. For a time, the Liberal Party, a loose coalition with a radical wing of some strength, looked like a possible home for the working class. But by the end of the nineteenth century, for reasons almost all concerned with the special interests of particular groups in the Liberal Party, it seemed clear that middle-class Liberals at the local level were not ready to share office nor to formulate policies in cooperation with the increasingly impatient young leaders of the Labour movement.

But though the Labour Party was formed in 1900 (it was originally called the Labour Representation Committee and took the name Labour Party only in 1906), it was hardly an important force before the First World War. It had come into existence as a coalition of trade unionists and socialists. But some of the trade unions looked upon it with suspicion, and some of the moderate socialists, such as those in the Fabian Society, were not at all sure that independent political action was the answer to Labour's needs. Only the socialists of the small Independent Labour Party, founded in 1893 to send workingmen to Parliament, repeated some of the incantations of a nineteenth-century socialist dogma without making any considerable impact upon either their allies or the country as a whole.

From the beginning, then, the Labour Party was a coalition of elements quite as disparate as the constituent forces of an American political party. And the disparity was at least as sharp between those who called themselves socialists as it was between them and the supposedly less profoundly dedicated leadership of the trade union movement. Sometimes its prewar experience has been analyzed in terms of the conflict between socialist ideals and practical politics. But a number of careful scholars—among them Philip Poirier, Henry Pelling, Frank Bealey—have demonstrated in recent years how oversimplified such a formulation really is.[2]

Before the First World War the parliamentary position of the fledgling Labour Party was an exceedingly difficult one. Dependent upon the Liberals for most of its seats in the House of Commons and upon the trade unions for much else, limited by its leaders' commitment to parliamentary action and by their need to support piecemeal reform, the Labour Party remained a tail wagged by the massive Liberal bulldog of Prime Minister Herbert Henry Asquith and his chief lieutenant for domestic questions, David Lloyd George. Its parliamentary representatives hardly concerned themselves with any conflict between socialist ideals and practical politics. Rather they sought by compromise to make whatever gains were possible for the working class and above all to prevent their fragile party from being crushed in the Liberal embrace. For example, in order to gain Liberal support against a serious threat to Labour Party financing, the Party's secretary, a handsome, eloquent young Scot, James Ramsay MacDonald, felt compelled to strike a bargain in which he pledged his support for the contributory features of Lloyd George's new Insurance Bill, even though they were vehemently opposed by some members of his party. There was little question here of socialism, of course. The concern was with the survival of the parliamentary party and with the achievement of some fairly limited gains, mainly for the rank-and-file of trade unionists, whose leaders, but not necessarily themselves, supported the Labour Party.

Such ideological—as opposed to tactical—conflict as did exist came mostly within the ranks of the Fabian Society and especially of the Independent Labour Party. Philip Poirier, in a paper which so far as I know has not been published,[3] has shown how a growing minority became disillusioned with the policies pursued by MacDonald, flirted with continental schemes of direct action, became infatuated with alternatives to parliamentary action, and in some cases even wanted to sever their connection with the parliamentary party. From almost the beginning of its existence, then, the Labour Party did face the dissatisfaction of some of its constituent elements because its leaders' definition of the socialist future appeared to contain so little commitment to socialism in the intervening present. Yet I think it is clear that the socialist critics, however vehement their strictures, remained a vocal and even substantial, but not very effective minority throughout these early years. Those who wished to disaffiliate from the Labour Party or to jettison parliamentary politics in favor of direct action were at least logically consistent. But the rather ill-defined socialist touchstone of most of the disaffected hardly served as a serious criterion of action in the prewar state of democratic politics.

I have spent so much time on this early period because it seems to me that here we have the clue to the complex character of the Labour Party throughout its history—now as well as in 1900. Beyond this, I think that here we have the clue to its survival and its success. In contrast to the Labour Right, who have seen the millenial demands of the all-out activists—those who believed themselves alone to have imbibed the pure mother's milk of socialism—as a danger frightening away all moderate supporters of Labour; and in contrast to the Labour Left, who have seen "gradualism" as the main enemy threatening the soul of a future Socialist Commonwealth, I tend to see the tensions and the struggles within the Labour Party as contributing ultimately to its triumphs, rather than being responsible for the limited character of its accomplishments. How does one justify this paradox? Let me try, in the first place, by turning to the Party's history between the two World Wars.

Both the Labour Left and the Right can find arguments for their positions in that history. A tiny minority group before 1914—almost a coterie—the Labour Party became the official Opposition in the early twenties. Electoral progress was steady, and the Party even held office during two brief terms in 1924 and 1929-31. Ramsay MacDonald as Prime Minister in both these Labour Governments captured the imagination of many of his countrymen—and many foreigners—with his striking thatch of silver hair and his equally silver tongue. In the nineteen thirties, after MacDonald had broken with the Party over how to cope with the Great Depression, Labour slowly made a comeback. In that decade foreign affairs, after the advent of Hitlerism in Germany, became the touchstone of all policy. Although Labour suffered from a kind of schizophrenia on international questions in the era of appeasement, it nevertheless presented the only viable non-Conservative alternative to policies that even some Conservatives—Winston Churchill is of course the prime example—regarded as disastrous. And, once Churchill came to power in 1940, the leaders of the Labour Party became his chief lieutenants in the governance of England. Altogether an interesting, if somewhat puzzling, history. How has it been interpreted by those in the Labour Party to whom their history is, after all, part of the contemporary struggles within the Labour movement?

In the years before 1918, the conventional interpretation has gone, the Labour Party was, to be sure, a confederation of disparate groups. But once the war itself had opened up new possibilities, Sidney Webb and Ramsay MacDonald and Arthur Henderson—the so-called architects of the new party—had responded by working out an effective new constitution. No longer was the Party a mere coalition of pressure groups, but now it was able to forge ahead on a new basis, attracting members directly and finding a new cohesion and a new unity. Of course, there remained the cleavage—or at least the differences—as between the great trade union phalanx and the more socialist-minded brethren from the constituency parties. But such differences as appeared were minor and relatively unimportant, and in any event, usually reflected the instability of tiny splinter groups. The Party was clearly now committed to socialism, for did not Clause IV of the new constitution define the Party's aims as "the common ownership of the means of production, distribution and exchange"?

Richard Lyman[4] once used Francis Williams' book, *Fifty Years' March*,[5] to illustrate the orthodox interpretation. Williams, who was made a life peer in 1962 and died in 1970, had been a distinguished editor of Labour's *Daily Herald* between the wars and after 1945 served as Adviser on Public Relations to Prime Minister Clement Attlee. In his view:

> With the acceptance of the new constitution and the endorsement of the international policy contained in the Memorandum on War Aims and the domestic programme contained in *Labour and the New Social Order*, the Labour Party finally established itself. The formative years were ended. Now at last it was an adult party certain of its own purpose; aware also at last of what it must do to impress that purpose upon the nation.

Now to continue with Lyman's paraphrase of Williams, the adult party made a series of electoral gains in the twenties, even holding office for two brief periods in 1924 and 1929-31. Of course, the interwar Labour Governments were hardly impressive. But in each case, Labour was hampered by inexperience, by lack of a majority in the House of Commons, by the increasing weariness and conservatism of some of its leading figures, and (especially in 1930-31) by a world economic crisis beyond the control of any British Government. Even so, there were significant successes, like those of Arthur Henderson at the Foreign Office, and in any case Labour learned from its failures. After the General Strike of 1926 there were no more general strikes; after the two minority Labour Governments there were no more minority Labour Governments. More than that—we are still following Francis Williams—after the traumatic defeat and "betrayal" of 1931 (when Ramsay MacDonald became Prime Minister of a "National" Government) Labour set about defining its program and reinforcing its socialist determination, so as to be ready to take over at last when the British electorate should have come to its senses and overthrown the "National" Coalition. Finally in 1945, Labour swept to power—but let me defer 1945 until I have noted the sharply conflicting interpretation of the Labour Left and briefly commented on both these neat formulations.

The left-wing interpretation of the interwar years and what followed is, as I say, different from that presented by a Francis Williams. Argued in a volume of interesting essays called *Towards Socialism*[6] and sponsored by the New Left Review, outlined by Michael Foot in the first volume of his able biography of Aneurin Bevan,[7] put most cogently by Ralph Miliband in his book entitled *Parliamentary Socialism*,[8] this view emphasizes all that has been wrong in the earlier history of the Labour Party. Like the Socialist critics before World War I, these left-wing authors have been impatient with a leadership which accepted the necessity of compromise and of trimming, but which, above all, by operating as a mere political party, really rejected, in their view, the socialist aim of a fundamental reordering of society. By such lights, the interwar history of the Labour Party is almost disastrous, the tale of missed chances and opportunistic goals, one in which excessive devotion to parliamentary methods led to the effective rejection of most of what socialism stood for. Here is a quotation from Miliband, which will serve perhaps to indicate the flavor of this kind of argument.

> [The Labour Party's] accent, after the defeat of 1931 [he writes], had been on 'education and organization.' But it had deliberately refused to further that education by the organization, outside Parliament, of a militant movement in defence of working-class interests. To erase the stigma of the Labour Government's performance in 1931, it would have had to embark, after 1931, on something like a permanent crusade, in deed as well as in words, as a result of which it might have hoped, come an election, to do substantially better than ever before. But instead of the massive effort of which there had been so much talk after the catastrophe of 1931, there had only been the routine of speeches and of meetings, of eminently reasonable wage negotiations and of equally reasonable conciliation of employers and of the Government, of polite parliamentary debates and of equally polite representations to Ministers, with the occasional rally or demonstration, all suggesting that Labour had good intentions and even remedies—much less that it had an angry cause.[9]

In this view, the failures of the twenties and the thirties are emphasized and are attributed to an inevitable weakness of majority policy, its sin of gradualism, its commitment to parliamentary procedures, its mistake of "Labourism" in place of socialism.

Now it seems clear that the orthodox version is over-optimistic, that it papers over the cracks and the contradictions within the Party, and that it over-emphasizes accident and exceptional circumstances in explaining Labour's failures between the wars. Indeed, most official Labour Party histories, like most memoirs of participants in that history, read like campaign documents or anniversary brochures rather than like serious dissections of the problems and accomplishments of the past. Whether it is in Francis Williams' *Fifty Years' March* or in Clement Attlee's *As It Happened*[10]—the latter surely one of the most reticent memoirs in recent times—one gets little of the dilemmas, the uncertainties, the muddle of Labour Party policies and performance in the interwar years.

On the other hand, the left wing has been better at saying what was wrong than at providing alternatives. They have hardly suggested other paths that Labour might have followed, whether in international affairs —about which I shall want to comment later—or in the achievement of revolutionary change in a profoundly stable society. And, of course, their failure to suggest such alternatives in turn stems from their own commitment to democracy, which leaves them frustrated by its limitations, impatient of its slowness, but still unwilling to go all the way in rejecting its principles and even its procedures as they have developed in Britain. It follows, therefore, that their demonstration of what was wrong in the twenties and the thirties is rather more effective than their relatively vague suggestions as to what might have been done differently.

I would like to suggest that the very divisions implied in the two positions I have so sketchily summarized, far from being a detriment to the emerging Labour Party, were a positive advantage. Of course, splits occurred and constituent elements fell away. By 1932, for example, the Independent Labour Party had become so alienated from the mainstream of Labour thinking that it finally disaffiliated and found its own independent way to political oblivion. Yet when one considers the really massive breaks in party continuity in modern British politics—the Tories over the Corn Laws in 1846, the Liberals over Irish Home Rule in 1886 —one finds the Labour Party no more, and probably considerably less, subject to disruption than its competitors for public support in modern times.

Samuel H. Beer, whose *Modern British Politics: A Study of Parties and Pressure Groups*[11] is in my opinion the most brilliant American writing on British politics since the pioneer work of A. Lawrence Lowell, has argued persuasively—but not persuasively enough to persuade me —that what happened after 1918 was that the Labour Party, while it continued to be a coalition, became something more. He sees in the 1918 Constitution a genuine turn to ideology, a commitment to the establishment of a "Socialist Commonwealth." But I am struck by much of the evidence he adduces to support his conception of such a "socialist commitment." He notes the "huge mass party utterances"—conference debates, party programs, parliamentary speeches—that reflect not only responses to particular circumstances and special interests, but also a unified doctrine, even, as he puts it, "a system of thought."

Now I would argue that if this had really been the case, if this "system of thought" had been anything very much more than a rather vague series of changing plans fixed in a matrix of anticapitalist rhetoric and socialist aspiration, then the appeal of the Labour Party would have been considerably less effective than in actual fact it was. It is interesting that when Professor Beer seeks statements to epitomize the "socialist commitment" he turns to Bruce Glasier and to Robert Blatchford, both essentially pre-1919 propagandists, as often as he turns to the major leaders of the Labour Party, whose platform oratory hardly seems enough to pin down the precise character of the "socialist commitment." I am not really taking issue with Professor Beer. I am merely arguing that the idea of a "socialist commitment"—which could be generally accepted because it was so vague and tackled so few of the hard questions of definition—the idea of a "socialist commitment" does not tell us much about why the Labour Party—whatever its vicissitudes in the interwar years—managed to remain the second major party in Great Britain and to maintain the potential for power so dramatically exercised during the Second World War and after 1945.

The reason, let me repeat, seems quite clear. Rather than appealing only to that obvious minority of the electorate to whom socialism was an attractive doctrine, the Labour Party, like the American Democratic or Republican Parties, attracted a relatively wide spectrum of the population. For the intellectual Left, there were the theoretical formulations of a thoroughgoing socialist system of values and promises of "socialization" of essential services—which in practice meant nationalization of certain basic enterprises. For the organized working classes, there were promises of reforms to meet the demands of the trade unions— which in practice meant gradualist legislation within the framework of existing institutions. For the middle classes, most of whom would presumably have been frightened by a thoroughgoing socialism, as much as for the underprivileged groups in society, a somewhat rudimentary (rudimentary until the experience of World War II) vision of expanded social welfare services was held out. And, although I am not concerned with international questions for the moment, in a certain sense this eclecticism—inadequate though it may have been in practice—can be similarly seen in the tightrope balancing of Labour on questions such as that of rearmament. Weak though Labour's policy might have been in the Hitler era, it had the enormous advantage—I am not defending it—of avoiding the dangers of too one-sided a commitment either to the Left or the Right or even the Center, and thus the advantage of preserving the Party as a national rather than a sectarian group. In the United States, it has been argued, the very similarities of the two major parties—their substantial agreement on most fundamental questions—has preserved a modest choice within a framework of continuity. So in Great Britain—where the political terrain is so different—nevertheless the very all-things-to-all-men character of the Labour Party made it a possible alternative for many undoctrinaire voters, and so made it possible for the Party to grow and eventually to prosper. After all, the Liberal Party, which might have been expected to fill the role of a respectable alternative to Conservatism, had collapsed in the sequel to World War I. While the Labour Party did not become a second Liberal Party, it did in fact attract many who might have supported a unified Liberal Party as well as many socialists who found the Liberal version of politics inadequate.

The importance of this broad base to the fortunes of the Labour Party became quite apparent during the Second World War. When Winston Churchill became Prime Minister in the dark days of 1940, he set up a War Cabinet of five members. Two of them were Labour Party leaders, Clement Attlee and Arthur Greenwood. In addition, a considerable sprinkling of other Labour Party officials filled a series of crucial offices. In the course of time, Attlee, Ernest Bevin, and Hugh Dalton became the leading figures in the administration of home affairs, Attlee as Deputy Prime Minister, Bevin as Minister of Labour and National Service, Dalton as President of the Board of Trade. Churchill was immersed in the grand strategy of the war. As a result, the representatives of Labour had the opportunity to gain invaluable experience of government. Equally significant, they had the opportunity to commend themselves to the future electorate as men of good sense, good will, and genuine ability.

The sweeping Labour victory of 1945, won in an election held soon after V-E Day, came nevertheless as a dramatic shock. It was not a repudiation of Winston Churchill. It was an expression of hope that a fresh new group of men might attack the many problems of postwar Britain with greater imagination than the tired old team who seemed to dominate the Conservative Party. Whatever the reasons, the Labour Party, with a huge parliamentary majority of 146, took office pledged to implement a program of reform that had been outlined in its electoral manifesto, *Let Us Face the Future*. And, as Samuel Beer has noted, "to an extent unprecedented in British history," the actions of the Government reflected the promises of this party program.[12]

On the surface, the most radical legislation pushed through Parliament by the new government had to do with public ownership. Between 1946 and 1949, the Bank of England, the fuel and power industries, inland transport by road, rail, air, and canal, iron and steel were all nationalized. To Americans, looking at the British scene from a distance, this legislation appeared to herald a drastic policy, striking at the very heart of established relationships of ownership and power. In actual fact—and here I emphasize once more my central theme— "nationalization" in practice made relatively little change in the industries concerned. It was accompanied by generous compensations for the owners. It was confined, with one exception, to industries that could be regarded as public utilities rather than as primarily producers of manufactures for private profit. And it was implemented by the establishment of a series of national governing boards, mostly independent of serious parliamentary control and certainly a far cry from the "social ownership"—that is, "social management"—envisaged by the Labour Left. The hesitancy with which the Labour leaders approached the nationalization of iron and steel—the one industry slated for nationalization that could hardly be defined in conventional terms as a public utility—and the violent reaction to the proposal from a heterogeneous opposition merely emphasize how moderate, almost how uncontroversial, was the bulk of the nationalization scheme. Whether it was successful is not my point here. I simply want to emphasize that it reflected a fairly widespread consensus, and that it did not go far beyond that consensus. Indeed, the bulk of the services nationalized had already long been under substantial public control.

Even more widely acceptable to a general public were the social service measures of the Labour Government. Richard Titmuss, one of the architects of the famous Beveridge Report on social security, has indicated the main areas of public (or publicly supported) social and welfare services.[13] He lists them as:

1. Education from the primary school to the university.

2. Medical care, preventive and curative.
3. Housing and rent policies.
4. Income maintenance (including children's allowances, old age pensions, public assistance, and schemes for unemployment, sickness and industrial injuries benefits).
5. Special services in kind for dependent groups, the old, deprived children, unsupported mothers and various handicapped classes.

The Labour Government expanded sickness, unemployment and retirement benefits and provided maternity grants, widows' pensions, and death grants in the National Insurance Act of 1946. It passed an Industrial Injuries Act in the same year and also a National Assistance Act to cover the destitute not properly provided for by National Insurance. In education it proceeded to try to implement (though resources were desperately scarce) the provisions of R. A. Butler's Education Act of 1944. Its Rent Control Act of 1946, Housing Acts of 1946 and 1949, Children's Act of 1948 helped flesh out the skeleton of services listed by Professor Titmuss. And finally, its National Health Service Act of 1946—perhaps the single most important piece of legislation passed by the postwar Labour Government—nationalized almost all hospitals (nursing homes were excepted) and established a free and comprehensive medical service.

Like nationalization, the social welfare state appears on the surface to be extreme, radical, a full-fledged acceptance of the views of the Labour Left. Yet increasingly it was the Left that became frustrated by the administration of the social services and found them less than utopian. Why? For a clue, let me turn once again to Richard Titmuss. He has pointed out that "The principle of universality applied in 1948 to the main social welfare services in Britain was needed as a major objective favouring social integration; as a method of breaking down distinctions and discriminative tests between first-class and second-class citizens. But equal opportunity of access by right of citizenship to education, medical care and social insurance is not the same thing as equality of outcome. It is only a prerequisite—though a necessary one—to the objective of equalizing the outcome."[14]

And what tended to happen was this. The higher income groups made the better use of the National Health services; they received more special attention; occupied more of the beds in better equipped hospitals; had better maternity care; received more psychiatric help than members of the unskilled working classes.

In housing, state subsidies to owner-occupiers of many kinds of houses were on the average greater than the subsidies received by most tenants of public housing schemes.

In education, scarce resources allowed—even until today—only a relatively small proportion of young people access to good secondary and university programs. Immense sacrifices in earnings and labour foregone were called for from parents and children living in poor conditions, so that more often than not, despite the principle of universality, it was the middle-class youth who benefitted. There was a vast difference between universality in theory and in practice. Fundamentally, the advent of the "Welfare State" in Britain did not lead to any significant redistribution of wealth and income in favour of the poorer classes, although the services for all were improved. And this in turn helps explain both the frustration of the Labour Left and the overall success of the Labour Party.

That success was called seriously into question after 1949, of course. All that I have been noting—nationalization, social service schemes—took place against a backdrop of problems that have led a group of young writers to label the period from 1945 to 1951, the "age of austerity." Its symbols were the end of Lend-Lease and the negotiation of an American loan on particularly onerous terms, the terrifying fuel crisis of 1947 and the convertability crisis of the same year, the balance of payments crisis in 1949. Above all, its major symbol was Sir Stafford Cripps, courageous, ascetic, a bit bloodless, bringing in successive sacrificial budgets as Chancellor of the Exchequer, fostering the export drive at the expense of the domestic standard of living, swallowing the bitter pill of devaluation despite opposition from both Left and Right. And, as the difficulties of governing a country whose resources were simply stretched too thin became apparent, the Labour Party seemed to come apart at the seams.

When the Party, in the election of 1950, retained its majority in the House of Commons by a bare six seats, the stage seemed set for an all-out clash. The explosion was not long in coming. Hugh Gaitskell, the moderate ex-university teacher who succeeded Stafford Cripps as Chancellor of the Exchequer, had to cope with a mounting rearmament bill during the Korean War. Among other steps, he put charges on dentures and spectacles obtained under National Health. Aneurin Bevan, the stormy and able Welsh petrol of the Labour Left, not only protested; he resigned as Minister of Labour in April, 1951, and was soon followed by Harold Wilson, the President of the Board of Trade, and by John Freeman, Parliamentary Secretary to the Ministry of Supply. The occasion for the split was dentures and spectacles; the reasons were much more deeply rooted. The Left believed that the spirit had gone out of the drive to create a socialist Britain. They bitterly opposed the policy of consolidation pursued by Attlee and advocated by Herbert Morrison and increasingly by Hugh Gaitskell as the champion of the new right wing of the Labour Party. Morrison and Gaitskell, in turn, regarded the Bevan position (he was often supported by Harold Wilson, Richard Crossman, Tom Driberg, Ian Mikardo, and Barbara Castle—and it is interesting that not only Wilson, but also Crossman and Castle were influential in the recent Labour cabinet) as unsound and unrealistic. They were determined to smash it. There were other issues—a struggle for the succession to Attlee, first between Bevan and Morrison, then between Bevan and Gaitskell, and genuine difference of views on matters of rearmament and defense policy. Although Bevan and his friends made their peace with their colleagues, the Labour Party that fought the election of 1951 was out of heart and badly confused in the face of a well-mounted Tory revival. The Labour majority of six was transformed into a Conservative majority of seventeen, not a comfortable margin but a workable one.

Defeat opened the floodgates to further bitter and acrimonious conflict. The struggle for the succession eventually found Gaitskell triumphant, backed as he was by the leaders of the most powerful trade unions connected with the Labour Party. But during the course of the struggle the Bevanites coalesced as a strong faction, challenging the parliamentary leadership of the Labour Party on a host of issues. At first the issue was rearmament, the Bevanites convinced (rightly as it turned out) that Britain was overcommitting herself, the Gaitskellites insisting on a policy more closely attuned to that of the United States. As the years rolled on, controversy over general rearmament gave way to struggle over German rearmament and once again, in 1954, Bevan resigned, this time from the "shadow cabinet." Crisis followed crisis, each one more or less patched up, but each revealing what seemed to be irreparable cleavages within the Labour Party. When the Conservatives won a second election in 1955, this time by a majority of 59 seats in the Commons, there were predictions of a breakup of the Party—and even a little flutter of hope among Liberal supporters.

After the election, Hugh Gaitskell won the leadership of the Party in relatively easy fashion, and a reexamination of Labour policy was undertaken. Unofficially, in 1950 a group calling themselves Socialist Union published *Twentieth Century Socialism* and a year later C.A.R. Crosland continued the revisionist dissection of older ideas. Crosland in particular was much impressed by John Kenneth Galbraith's analysis of the "mixed economy." His essay on *The Future of Socialism*[15] raised serious questions about the effectiveness of nationalization as about many other traditions of British socialism. Arguing that the transformation of capitalism made it necessary for socialism to change its character, he wrote eloquently—but it must have sounded strangely to those brought up on the slogans of the past—of such things as liberty and gaiety in private life, of cultural and amenity planning, of the declining importance of economic problems. Clearly his revisionist dream, which Gaitskell shared, emphasized the reformist element in Labour Party policy, not its millenarial aspect.

All this came to a head in 1956, when Gaitskell, perhaps tactically less skilful than Attlee had been, tried to bring the Labour Party Constitution into line with the policies that had actually been pursued since 1949. He proposed to amend Clause IV by changing the phrase having to do with "the common ownership of the means of production, distribution, and exchange." After all, nationalization had been tried and the brave new world had not emerged. Surely, then, "socialism" meant something broader and more flexible and should be so defined. But Party tradition and the opposition of the Left were stronger than Gaitskell's logical inferences from Labour Party history. The revisionist attempt was given up. And the Party's principles were, as one observer has put it, if anything even more ambiguous after than before this abortive attempt at clarification.

Once again I have spent a considerable time in recapitulation because the Clause IV upheaval illustrates the point I have been emphasizing. Throughout the decade of the fifties, "With almost compulsive iteration, the same battles are fruitlessly fought out again and again through the same cycle of renewed confrontation, bitter strife, and temporary and indecisive compromise."[16] Two opposing conceptions of the meaning of socialism created at least two different factions. The Bevanites in some ways took over the role in the fifties that the Independent Labour Party had played in the twenties. There was, in other words, an essential continuity, if not on precise issues, then on the mode of division over matters of basic philosophy. The Bevanite struggle should have split the Labour Party wide open. Disheartened by unprecedented electoral defeats—1959 was soon added to 1951 and 1955—the Party by most continental standards, for example, should have been headed for oblivion. But it refused to collapse.

Part of the reason was personality. Gaitskell, learning to become an able tactician, solidified his position both among the trade unions and the constituency parties. Bevan and Harold Wilson both came into the "shadow cabinet." The former, in what turned out to be the last years of his life, deserted his own rebellious minority to support the Party leadership on virtually every issue. Part of the reason was accident. Anthony Eden's disastrous handling of the Suez affair in 1956 solidified the Labour Party behind Gaitskell and gave it a unifying issue. "Law not War" became the watchword of a revived leadership. For a moment the Labour Party became the spokesman for all those who were repelled by what they considered to be British aggression in the Middle East. Not that the country as a whole opposed the Suez operation. It did not. Popular jingoism, even in the Labour Party, was heated and widespread. But Labour was able to capitalize on the domestic effects of Suez— its evidence of the weakness of the British Government in the face of American pressure, its inability to hold down gasoline prices, the obvious collapse of the Conservative Prime Minister. And part of the reason, in the early sixties, came to be the ubiquitous economic difficulties suffered by the country. To be sure, Eden was replaced by a much more formidable opponent and for a time the euphoria of Harold Macmillan's early leadership tended to conceal the basic problems. "I'm all right, Jack" went hand in hand with "You never had it so good." But in the winter of 1962-63, unemployment rose alarmingly and the familiar routine of power cuts and electrical failure seemed to demonstrate that not a great deal had changed since Labour's "age of austerity."

In such circumstances, Gaitskellite moderation again began to seem an attractive alternative to the similar moderation of Macmillan or his successor, Sir Alec Douglas-Home. Revisionism was a coherent doctrine as developed by Anthony Crosland and Roy Jenkins. It was a doctrine that made sense to many in the middle classes who might have been Liberals if there had been the slightest chance of the Liberal Party's being effective. But at the same time, the continued existence of older "socialist" commitments, while it did not really satisfy many left-wing intellectuals such as R. H. Crossman or Ian Mikardo, nevertheless gave them a forum—and a hope—within the ranks of Labour. And, it goes without saying, both revisionists and fundamentalists elicited support from different groups within the working class itself. The precarious balance in the Labour Party somehow was maintained. I would argue that in some ways because of this, rather than in spite of it, Labour once again prospered.

This, then, has been the background of the most recent Labour Government. In 1963, Hugh Gaitskell, at the age of 56, suddenly succumbed to a rare disease. And his successor, not surprisingly if my analysis here has any validity, his successor was not the Gaitskellite George Brown nor the equally Gaitskellite James Callahan, but Harold Wilson, a man of the Left, the ally of Aneurin Bevan. An able speaker and an outstanding administrator, Wilson had been a bright young prodigy in Clement Attlee's cabinet. That he came from modest circumstances and had clawed his way to the top was an advantage among many Party members who rather resented the middle-class intellectuals in the Party's leadership. Though he had resigned office at the time of Bevan's first quarrel with Gaitskell, he had quickly found his way back to the fold. When the election of 1955 had revealed how inadequate was the Party's electoral machinery, Wilson headed the committee assigned to make inquiry and suggest remedies. His decisive election as Leader appeared to make possible the best of several worlds. He was a socialist of the Left, to be sure, but from the beginning he emphasized that change in leadership did not mean change in party politics. In a curious way, he took on the mantle of Gaitskell, emphasizing more vigorously the importance of science and education in the modern technological world, but clearly giving the impression that he was eclectic, open to new ideas, not particularly doctrinaire.

The mistakes of the Tories—and mishaps such as the sordid Profumo affair—combined with the reinvigoration of Labour to turn the electoral tide in 1964. Perhaps the Tories, like Labour in 1951, were simply too tired to give effective leadership any longer. The Labour Government of 1964 had only a four-seat margin in the House of Commons, a margin that made the conduct of legislative business, under constant harassment, a wearing and dispiriting experience. Finally, in 1966 a second election swept Labour again into real power, this time within a margin of about a hundred seats. I am told by a good friend in the Ministry of Labour that on election night the Prime Minister and his closest confidants were appalled by the margin of their victory. Wilson had hoped for a majority of thirty to thirty-five seats, big enough not to be threatened by the Tories, narrow enough so that all wings of Labour would feel compelled to maintain party discipline. With a margin of one hundred he had few sanctions with which to threaten recalcitrant followers, certainly not the possibility that Labour would be thrown out of office soon if they kicked up their heels too vigorously.

Yet the position was ticklish. I have dropped a number of names during the course of this paper—George Brown, James Callahan, Roy Jenkins, Anthony Crosland on the Right of the Party; Richard Crossman, Barbara Castle, Wilson himself on the Left. Every one of those names, in the early years of office, was on the list of the Labour cabinet, along with others representing virtually every shade of Labour opinion. Disagreements persisted, we can be sure, in the cabinet as they so clearly persisted among the rank-and-file in the House of Commons.

Indeed, once again there was evident what I suggested above—the kicking up of various heels within the Labour Party. The Vietnam war, commitments east of Suez, the German question, the pay freeze, devaluation—the issues read very much as they did at an earlier time. Even Harold Wilson, who had seemed to many as unflappable, calm, and unperturbed by problems as Harold Macmillan, occasionally lost himself and struck out at his Party critics like his predecessors. Indeed, in early 1967, he gave a public tongue lashing to his supporters which many felt would leave almost irremediable scars. And subsequent quarrels seemed to bring the party close to dissolution.

Perhaps. But I would suggest that the evidence is against such an interpretation. Throughout the years, the history of the Labour Party has been the history of tension among its various elements. The issues have changed somewhat, the alliances have often been modified, but the struggle over how far and how fast to move has been pretty much a constant. Consistently, these nagging and fundamental differences have arisen over the course of the years as the Labour Party gradually came to replace the Liberals as an alternative to the Tories in the governing of Great Britain. Increasingly, the Party's appeal had to be made, if it were to maintain its commitment to parliamentary democracy, to a broader sector of the country than to the working class alone. For many, this clearly indicated a refinement and a redefinition of the ideas and the ideals of the Party. For others, a smaller group, it made imperative an even more passionate dedication to the undiluted faith of the fathers of socialism. And at no time, not even in the halcyon years between 1945 and 1948 or at present, has this difference really been reconciled.

To many observers, this has seemed a handicap, a difficulty that will eventually break up the Labour Party. Again and again, in the public press—sometimes with considerable satisfaction—the pundits have predicted dire things for the Party. Yet those of us who have tried to apply the lessons of American political life to the admittedly different environment of Britain may be forgiven if we are not impressed by the doomsingers and prophets of disruption. For us, the multiparty, dedicated to a host of functions and serving a variety of constituencies, is no unfamiliar institution. For us, therefore, the very heterogeneity of the Labour Party, its ability to encompass such disparate views, seems an element of strength, not of weakness. And if this assessment is correct, then Labour's future does not depend, as so many correspondents write and as the historian Henry Pelling has recently implied,[17] on the ability of one man, Harold Wilson. Instead the Labour Party, like the Conservative, is likely to remain, *because of* its very character, one of the twin rocks upon which parliamentary democracy so firmly rests in the Great Britain of today.

II ABROAD

In the first part of this essay I tried to suggest that the very heterogeneity of the Labour Party, its conflicting interpretations of what constituted socialism and what to do about it, may well have been an explanation of the Party's growing strength rather than an indication of divisive weakness. I was concerned mainly with domestic issues and internal politics, leaving aside foreign policy until now. To a certain extent, I should like to use the Labour Party's attitudes on international questions further to illustrate the theme I emphasized above. I propose to try to see what happened to the foreign policy positions of the Labour Party as it gradually became transformed from a tiny propagandistic coterie into one of the major political parties in one of the major countries of the world. And perhaps a survey of what happened will help in understanding something about the international role of the Labour Party in the world of the present.

As in domestic affairs, the background out of which the Labour approach emerged is of some relevance. Before the First World War, working-class interest in foreign affairs was sporadic and slight. The workers newly enfranchised in 1867 and 1884 inevitably directed their political attention much more toward domestic issues than toward the obscure complications of external relations. Despite the enormous increase in British productivity over half a century, despite, indeed, the undoubted rise in the standard of life of the "average" worker, millions on the land or in the drab industrial slums continued to live in squalor and poverty. Of necessity working-class organization was primarily concerned with the "condition of England question." The new unionism, sweeping through the ranks of unskilled and semi-skilled labour toward the end of the century, dramatized the urgency of the struggle for economic and social advancement. But the very urgency of that struggle, in turn, made it certain that even when they turned to political action the unions would give but short shrift to questions of international import.

In similar fashion the socialist societies whose establishment paralleled that of the new unionism were largely occupied with a thoroughgoing criticism of the contemporary social and economic environment. Both the Social Democratic Federation, Marxist in its inspiration, and the Independent Labour Party, deeply rooted in a nonconformist tradition, worked to arouse the social conscience of their time to an awareness of the intolerable conditions hidden behind the superficial facade of industrial society. Until about the turn of the century, there is little evidence that either group paid more than lip service to an internationalism which, if genuinely embraced, might have led to a modest comprehension of foreign policy issues and their relation to domestic problems. Not even the Fabian Society, select, small, and exclusively intellectual, lifted its eyes far beyond the horizon off the British shores. Ambivalent on the issue of imperialism that came to a head during the Boer War, the Fabians tended to be silent on other international questions until the First World War made imperative some stand on the most crucial issues of the time.

In large measure, the prewar Labour Party inherited this indifference to the world of diplomacy and foreign policy. Understandably, the new party found virtually all of its energies absorbed in the struggle to defend workers' rights through the medium of Parliament. Occasional pronouncements by Party leaders on foreign affairs only served to emphasize how little attention they usually attracted. This is not to say that the Labour Party had no international outlook before 1914. Enough students have written about the "internationalism" of Labour's background to make it unnecessary to stress the point, but it is wise to keep this conception in proper perspective. The Labour Party and some of its constituent societies were indeed members of the Second International. On occasion it joined with its fellow-members in denouncing imperialism and colonial exploitation, branding militarism, and stressing the international solidarity of the working classes. But the legend of socialist solidarity, to be broken so irreparably when the European armies marched in 1914, even before 1914 represented an aspiration rather than a reality of international life. Certainly there is little evidence of any genuine temper of working-class internationalism among the rank-and-file of the Labour movement. Its presence among the leaders of the Labour Party can perhaps be more plausibly related to the myths of Labour solidarity than identified as a fundamental motivating force within the Party before 1914.

I am inclined to think that the heritage the Labour Party received from the Liberal tradition of the nineteenth century was much more important than the influence of socialist internationalism. The prewar internationalists of the Labour Party tended to be vague, imprecise, never really sure whether to support a policy of collaboration by sovereign states or to advocate the absorption of competing nationalisms in some broader world sovereignty. Their uncertain position almost exactly paralleled that of a minority of dissident Liberals who were moved in the years before 1914 to reject the imperial and diplomatic maneuvers of their own party as they had opposed those of the Tories. In both cases, the "liberal" protest—a kind of cry of conscience—stands out more clearly than any proposals for an alternative policy.

Perhaps the most instructive example of the essentially liberal character of much of the influence molding Labour's international attitudes is to be found among the currents of pacifism that ran so strongly in its ranks both before and after the First World War. Of course, there was an element of doctrinaire "socialist pacifism" in evidence before 1914. This element became more vocal and extended its sway in the first few years after the conflict. But "socialism" and opposition to "capitalist-inspired" struggles were not really the crucial determinants of the pacifism of the bulk of Labour's supporters. Labour pacifism was deeply rooted in the ethical soil of nineteenth-century English liberalism. Labour pacifists in the early twentieth century, like their Liberal fellows, came to their view of the evils of international conflict more frequently by way of Biblical injunctions and moral precepts than through a systematic socialist analysis of international society.

Taken together, these two elements in the prewar background of Labour—the indifference of the mass of its supporters to international questions and the essentially liberal attitudes that shaped whatever attitudes were in evidence—were of considerable influence in determining the course taken by the Party after the First World War. The very lack of interest in foreign affairs, which made the cataclysm of 1914 so totally unexpected to all but a tiny minority, bred compensating extremism once the war was over. Seen in retrospect, the international policies pursued by the British and other governments appeared mean and sordid, particularly to men who had paid so little attention to them in the past. As a result, when those who had opposed the war (and some who had not) hammered home the moral that no capitalist government could be trusted, that international cooperation was a chimera until most states became socialist, and that working-class solidarity across national boundaries was the only hope for a peaceful world, they found substantial support for their millenialism even among those in the ranks of Labour to whom socialism was hardly a crucial issue. At the same time, the more immediately optimistic idealism characteristic of the liberal strain in British society played its role in gradually persuading the Labour Party of the advantages of patiently strengthening international institutions by a program of "practical" cooperation among the nations. What I have called in one of my articles a "League of Nations policy" was in the long run negotiable because it offered an alternative to doctrines of class war with which the British socialist was uncomfortable, however much he may have been attracted to them in his period of temporary disillusionment. And that alternative in turn was based on more congenial conceptions of international morality, pacifism, and collaboration that represented a return to the liberal heritage upon which Labour's approach to foreign policy had in part originally been built.

In broad sweep, then, Labour's views on foreign policy can be described in terms of the rather variegated appeals I found in the formulation of domestic issues. But, for the moment, I am more concerned with the development of an official position on international questions, since I am myself convinced that what happened in the nineteen-twenties placed its imprint on all subsequent Labour positions. The 1914 war, as Carl F. Brand has commented, "ended whatever sense of detachment from world affairs existed in the Labour Party."[18] By the end of the war, the Party had become the leading British advocate of a generous peace of reconciliation. Although there were differences of emphasis within its ranks, the Party was able to reach something like a consensus on its rejection of any programs of conquest and annexation and on its support for a permanent international organization to ensure the durability of the peace. Actually, the consensus came about slowly. At the beginning of the war the Independent Labour Party remained consistent with Labour's prewar views, emphasizing the British Government's share in the responsibility for the convulsion and demanding from the very start the early negotiation of peace. The trade union majority of the Labour Party, on the other hand, joined with the Fabian Society in supporting the war and by implication, at least, the view that it must be fought to a finish. Nevertheless, these sections of the Labour movement eventually reached sufficient agreement to support a *Memorandum on War Aims* that may, without serious exaggeration, be labelled the first major pronouncement on foreign policy in the history of the Labour Party. The *Memorandum*, which preceded both Lloyd George's important statement of war aims in January, 1918, and President Wilson's Fourteen Points, became the platform upon which the Labour movement carried its case to the country in the last year of the war. By then, Labour's official leaders were unquestionably the foremost political force behind the drive for a moderate peace. In effect, they pleaded for a generous reconciliation with the enemy, whether as a result of negotiation or after he had been defeated. Since they were convinced that a League of Nations was fundamental to such a reconciliation, many of them came to believe that President Wilson's views were close to their own. When the Armistice was finally achieved, therefore, they looked forward with some hopefulness to the forthcoming conference called to discuss the "preliminaries" of peace.[19]

Needless to say, it is doubtful that this official position reflected the attitudes of Labour's rank-and-file. For a moment, at least, the Labour Party's leaders were out of step with most of their followers. To a country flushed with victory, warnings that peace must be built upon more than punishment hardly seemed worthy of attention. But by the time the Versailles Treaty was drawn up, the situation had begun to change. When the character of the proposed settlement became known, despair ran through almost every quarter of the Labour movement. The reaction was perhaps epitomized by Will Dyson after he had heard that Clemenceau, leading his fellow delegates down the Hall of Mirrors at Versailles, had stopped and said, "Curious! I seem to hear a child weeping." Dyson sketched the picture in a powerful cartoon. The weeping child, with the Peace Treaty at its feet, wore a band above its head entitled "1940."

As time wore on, words like "mockery," "barefaced swindle," "sheer and unadulterated brigandage" were used almost constantly to characterize the Treaty. Even when the Labour Party began to propose modifications of the peace settlement, its proposals were so extreme that they seemed designed to build a propaganda case rather than in the hope of any immediate success. Certainly, very few among the Labour leaders settled down to work within the system devised at Paris for the achievement of their ultimate aims. What is striking about the Labour response is not so much its dissatisfaction with many of the specific terms of the Versailles Treaty, but rather the air of hopelessness and rejection that permeated virtually all the movement's pronouncements in the immediate aftermath of 1919. Even in the case of the League of Nations, which it did not repudiate entirely, Labour insisted that until it was so revised as to be a different organization it could have no real value and merited little support.

And yet, despite the bitter spirit of repudiation that marked the immediate aftermath of the war, by the end of the twenties Labour had somehow managed to arrive at a responsible foreign policy, responsible in the sense that the Party came to accept the institutions of the international world in which it lived and sought to promote its hopes for European stability and security through those institutions. I have written about the twenties and thirties elsewhere, and this is not the place to repeat the details of my analysis.[20] For my purposes here it will be enough to note that what I have termed the "gradual development of a temperate, coherent, and even widely accepted foreign policy" was the resultant of a number of influences. Partly it reflected the simmering down of postwar emotions, the "second look" at policy after disillusionment burned itself out. Partly it was a response to the conscious and thoughtful efforts of a small group of able men, above all the dull and dedicated Arthur Henderson, to work out a policy based upon realistic international cooperation in place of what they held to be the anarchy of prewar international politics. And partly it was a reaction to two brief terms of office. In 1924, Ramsay MacDonald made a sparkling reputation as an international conciliator and earned the first great political triumph of any Labour minister. Between 1929 and 1931 Arthur Henderson demonstrated how patient goodwill might pay dividends in the relaxation of various tensions. Some years ago in an essay in *The Diplomats*, I wrote of Henderson as follows:

> . . . at a time when the British people felt themselves secure and most British leaders were unwilling to make any sizable commitments in Europe, he had some sense of the real difficulties faced by the beneficiaries of the Versailles system on the continent . . . he collaborated fully in trying to erect a genuine structure of international guarantees through the League of Nations in order to make disarmament possible. . . . His policy of appeasement, the development of the League, and then disarmament came closer to being one of effective collective security before 1930 than any within the realm of serious possibility. Seen in the light of the 1920's, it was a thoughtful, perceptive, and practicable line of approach. . . . By 1932, all the basic assumptions of the campaign which was supposedly to culminate in the progressive reduction of armaments had disappeared. It was now time for rigid resistance to the demands of an importunate German nationalism—and time also for equally firm support of France and the European order. . . . To change a way of thinking overnight, however, was difficult, and there were few who saw the issues clearly. If Henderson did not have the insight of a Winston Churchill after 1932, he had at least . . . opened up to Europe some of the avenues for a constructive approach to the problem of an enduring peace.[21]

In August, 1931, the second experiment in Labour Government was shattered by the Great Depression. Ramsay MacDonald, in one of the most astounding shifts in modern British politics, took over the Prime Ministership of a National Government whose Opposition was his own former party. For nine years, until well after the outbreak of the Second World War, that Government was in actual fact controlled by the Conservative Party whether the Prime Minister was Ramsay MacDonald or Stanley Baldwin or Neville Chamberlain.

Step by step, during the thirties, the hopes for a durable peace became more and more illusory. The economic crisis undoubtedly stimulated the determination of Italy, Japan, and Germany to rewrite the terms of Paris and redraw the frontiers of 1919—by arms if necessary. The Japanese invasion of Manchuria was the first major attempt to change the *status quo* by force. When the League of Nations was ineffective in dealing with the seizure of Chinese territory, the way seemed open for a wholesale attack on the established order. Soon the festering nationalism of German National Socialism became the chief touchstone of international relations. Faced with a Nazi threat to its own territory, the Soviet Union—for a brief period at least—shifted from its dogmatic isolationism and emerged as the advocate of "collective security" against aggression. Meanwhile, Fascist Italy moved toward an uneasy partnership with the Nazis in the Rome-Berlin Axis. When Hitler abandoned the League and openly announced a program of large-scale rearmament, the Western Powers should perhaps have acted. But France was ideologically divided and defensively minded, the United States aloof from European affairs. Leadership fell, almost by default, to Great Britain. But here too there were factors that blocked a firm stand against the Nazi menace. Fear of war, pacifism, mistrust of the Russians, the hope that "appeasement" of legitimate demands would satisfy Germany —all played their part. Particularly after 1935, the dictators won victory after victory. Italy's seizure of Abyssinia, the German reoccupation of the demilitarized Rhineland, Franco's triumph in the Spanish Civil War, the *Anschluss* with Austria, the seizure of the Sudetenland, the end of Czech independence, the turn upon Poland—the catalogue is familiar and depressing.

In Britain, from about 1933 to 1939, an impassioned debate was waged over the respective merits of appeasing the dictators or of uniting with other nations to resist their attacks upon the European order. The advocates of appeasement were, as we know, the formulators of British policy. Their policy was a failure. It did not prevent the use of force against Austria or Czechoslovakia or Poland. It was characterized, as a friendly critic, Professor W. N. Medlicott, has noted, by "a depressing lack of initiative, foresight, and quick thinking."[22] It made the mistake of ignoring the Russians almost completely, whatever may have been the purposes of the Soviet Union during those years before the war.

But was Labour's position any more realistic? Did Labour in the nineteen-thirties have a viable alternative to the policies of Simon and Hoare, Eden and Chamberlain? Many observers have felt the Labour Party did not, that the ambivalences and differences so manifest in conference resolutions and parliamentary statements reflected not only indecision but a basic unwillingness to face the possibility that collective security might—indeed almost certainly would—mean the need to use military force to bring the aggressors in Europe to heel.

Now much of this is true. Reginald Bassett has shown how little Labour really differed from the dominant Conservatives on Japan's Manchurian invasion at the level of proposals for effective policy.[23] Protests and calls for collective action appeared in large numbers, but at no time were they translated into more than emotional gestures. For a time after 1931, the leader of the battered Labour Party was George Lansbury, and Lansbury was a Christian pacifist. Labour was at one with Conservatives—as for that matter with American policymakers—in not even contemplating military sanctions. And as crisis followed crisis, Labour's foreign policy, certainly until 1935 and perhaps until 1937, was marked by confusion. It gave the clear impression that the Party was being torn apart by cross-purposes, perhaps like most groups in Great Britain during those difficult years. The nadir was undoubtedly reached in the Party's conference at Hastings in 1933. There a resolution supposedly committing the Party to resist war by a general strike marched along with a "League of Nations policy" including the use of collective sanctions. It is true that 1933 witnessed the high point of pacifist sentiment in the Labour Party and that subsequent conferences laid greater stress on the prevention of war by the positive organization of peace. But that a war resistance resolution could be accepted by the very conference that also supported the collective system illustrates the deep fissures in the Labour movement.

Even after 1935, Labour's uncertainties on international issues were clear. Let me cite just one example. While peace talks were going on at Paris in 1919, many within the British Labour movement came to support the view that German Austria should be permitted to unite with the new German Republic. The position, perhaps most cogently put by the distinguished journalist H. N. Brailsford, was in the circumstances of 1919 a liberating one. The people of Vienna and its environs, cut off from the markets and resources of the old Hapsburg monarchy, might well have been better off within the Weimar orbit. But such an *Anschluss* in 1938, when Germany was Nazi and Austria at least quasi-Fascist, held out doom and disaster for many hundreds of thousands, including the Austrian Socialists with whom British Labour had had close affiliations. Labour opposed the *Anschluss,* to be sure. But there was always the nagging feeling that it was after all proper for Germans to be united with Germans, that the *Anschluss* should somehow have been carried out years earlier, that it was at any rate too much to contemplate risking the danger of war to prevent it. The failures—at least the missed opportunities—of the twenties are reflected in the hesitations and rationalizations of the thirties.

Similarly, the issue of British rearmament after 1933 must be seen as it actually was and not as the myths of party polemics have made it seem. The authority of Winston Churchill, for example, is frequently cited to illustrate the irresponsibility of Labour's position. Here is Churchill on Labour in 1934: "The Opposition are very free-spoken, as most of us are in this country, on the conduct of the German Nazi Government. . . . But these criticisms are fiercely resented by the powerful men who have Germany in their hands. So that we are to disarm our friends, we are to have no allies, we are to affront powerful nations, and we are to neglect our own defenses entirely."[24] That is a caricature of Labour policy, but it has somehow come down as revealed truth, made plausible because down to 1937 Labour did in fact vote to amend the arms estimates proposed by the National Government. Senator Jacob Javits of New York once remarked, during the course of a television interview, that the only way to indicate Congressional disapproval of certain Administration policies might be in the vote on particular appropriations. He was not suggesting that all the appropriations were unnecessary or undesirable. He was reflecting on how certain kinds of criticism might most effectively be made. So it was with Labour in the thirties. The leaders of the Party were not pacifists, although when they voted against the arms budget they surely pleased the pacifists among their followers. But absolute pacifism, as the reality of the Nazi threat became more apparent, steadily diminished in importance. The Labour leaders did not trust the National Government, they did not believe that it was willing to pursue a policy of cooperative resistance to Fascist aggression through the League, they suspected that the Government was eager to make a deal with the Fascists—and consequently they voted against the armed services budgets. They knew that those budgets would be passed overwhelmingly, but they were using their votes to register disapproval of the Government's international policy. It was a technique, incidentally, that had a long and well-recognized history in Parliamentary tactics. But, of course, such a position cried loudly to be misinterpreted and misrepresented, so that eventually such Labour leaders as Walter Citrine, Ernest Bevin, and Hugh Dalton were able to demonstrate, as the German menace grew greater, the self-defeating character of the negative vote on the estimates.

I do not want to outline the history of Labour's approach to foreign policy in the thirties. I think I have written enough to indicate how badly divided that approach often was—and I have not even mentioned the tensions occasioned by Stafford Cripp's campaigns for the united front and the Popular Front. But in addition to disagreement and disunity there was also a developing unity and consistency. In many popular accounts, Ernest Bevin is the hero of this saga. Most undergraduate students of twentieth-century Britain can recite the story of the 1935 Labour Party Conference at Brighton. They can picture Bevin lumbering up to the platform, after George Lansbury's emotional soulsearching over force and collective security, ruthlessly to destroy the basis of Lansbury's position. Lansbury, with all his faults, and they were many, was beloved in the Labour movement. He had taken the leadership of the Party in the dark days after 1931 and had done his best to help pull it from the abyss. But his Christian pacifism seemed more and more irrelevant to the younger men who were becoming increasingly impatient with an appeasement policy that they regarded as acquiescence in evil. Bevin objected, as he inelegantly phrased it, to Lansbury's "hawking his conscience around from body to body," asking to be told what to do with it. The performance was brutal and there were protests, but the job was done. Soon Lansbury resigned the leadership. Clement Attlee succeeded him, and by 1937 Labour finally gave up its unrealistic posture on arms and on foreign policy and increasingly stood for effective action. The search for alternatives to force was seen to be an illusion. And in September, 1939, the Labour Party that entered the war was a united party, accepting the conflict in the certainty that it now had to be fought to a victorious end.

I would agree that most of this is accurate, though I think it overdramatizes the role of Ernest Bevin. Actually the policy finally accepted by the late thirties was pretty much the policy hammered out under the leadership of Arthur Henderson in the twenties. That, in turn, was why I spent so much time on the twenties. For in foreign affairs after 1931, it is my own feeling that Hugh Dalton, who had served as Henderson's Under-Secretary, was much more clear-minded and realistic much earlier and much more consistently than was Bevin. I think Dalton did more to educate the Labour Party to the facts of international life in this period than did Bevin. He wrote effectively, he spoke indefatigably, and he was convinced, from the beginning of the thirties, that to think of collective security without rearmament was wishful thinking. Much more than Bevin he emphasized that theme, until the concrete lessons of Abyssinia and the Rhineland and Spain began to convince others that the loud-voiced and blustering Dalton was right.

The war itself is almost a blank so far as Labour's international policies are concerned. To be sure, Labour issued pronouncements outlining its postwar aims in general and even in concrete detail. But once the Party's leaders entered into Winston Churchill's coalition government, they came to be more and more responsible for domestic affairs and tended, whatever their own views, to follow Churchill's lead on the many and involved issues of wartime diplomacy. Not that there were no problems. The Labour Party, for example, was almost torn apart on the issue of the Government's policy in Greece and in Italy. But in a sense, so long as the war went on in Europe, the Labour ministers could give no effective lead for an independent policy. The continuity of British policy was symbolized at the Potsdam Conference in July, 1945. By that time the Labour Party was in opposition, since an election had been set after the collapse of the German armies. When Labour won that election, Clement Attlee continued at Potsdam, merely changing his role from that of Leader of the Opposition to that of Prime Minister.

Continuity or not, for the first time after 1945 the Labour Party in theory had the opportunity to pursue an independent international policy. In 1924 and in 1929-31, the Labour Governments had been minority governments, dependent upon the Liberals and thus restricted in what they could undertake to do. Now, with a clear and substantial majority in Parliament, perhaps the situation might be different for Ernest Bevin, the new Foreign Secretary. Leonard Woolf, the veteran Fabian expert on foreign affairs, had already issued a call that Labour's foreign policy "must be founded uncompromisingly on Socialist principles." Bevin, to be sure, and his successor, Herbert Morrison, carried out an astonishingly widespread program in international affairs. Yet despite this, there was not much difference between Bevin, the conservative Laborite, and Anthony Eden, the liberal Conservative. Indeed, in a debate in the House of Commons on August 20, 1945, Bevin agreed that in the wartime coalition he and Eden had never differed on any important question of foreign policy.[25] Like Arthur Henderson, in other words, Bevin pursued a middle-of-the-road policy. And like Henderson, Bevin as a policymaker had elicited a very varied set of judgments.

The areas of choice for the new Labour Government were, of course, limited. It should be remembered that there is a vast difference between foreign policy statements when a party is out of office and foreign policy when it assumes the responsibility of government. In the case of Labour, foreign policy programs enunciated by the Party's National Executive before 1945 reflected the fact that Labour was an opposition party. After 1945, policies were developed by the Foreign Secretary in consultation with the Cabinet and the permanent officials of the Foreign Office. And, as Matthew Fitzsimons has pointed out, "This policy, in turn, required the support of the Parliamentary Labour Party, which could express its dissatisfaction and press for modifications but could not openly oppose Bevin's policy without overturning the Labour Government and jeopardizing Labour's domestic program as well." But even more important, Great Britain was "now a power with world interests, not a world power."[26] Year by year, the overwhelming strength of the United States and the growing might of the Soviet Union became increasingly evident. British policymakers were forced to recognize how narrow were the parameters of choice in their foreign policy.

My own feeling is that the most successful long-run international actions between 1945 and 1951 were in the field not of foreign policy, strictly speaking, but of colonial affairs. The freeing of India, made inevitable I think by the impact of the Second World War, was nevertheless a generous and imaginative policy that owed much to Clement Attlee's firmness and almost as much to Lord Mountbatten's tact. Partition was tragically accompanied by several hundred thousand communal murders, yet it is hard to escape the conclusion that no other solution could have avoided the bloodshed of the transition. India, Pakistan, and Ceylon entered a Commonwealth no longer restricted to governments largely made up of white British stock. In the Gold Coast, Sierra Leone, Gambia, Mauritius, Nigeria, liberal constitutions were granted, and in East Africa, despite complicated tensions among blacks, whites, Arabs, and Indians, constitutional progress was promoted. In most cases, the constitutions were first steps on the road to independence. I am not suggesting that these steps were evidences of Labour's generous spirit. Partly they were a response to the pressures for self-government felt in the colonial holdings of all the imperial states. Partly they simply reflected a necessary reduction of commitments by an overextended nation. Nor am I suggesting that success was invariable. Rhodesia, Cyprus, Guinea, Nigeria, even perhaps Ghana may be taken to illustrate the other side of the coin. Yet looking back to the late forties and comparing the British accomplishment with, say, that of Belgium in the Congo, one is tempted to give high praise for the strategy by which devolution was carried out in most cases.

These accomplishments may be most readily placed under the rubric of imperial policy. But it is on other gronds—always excepting India—that the postwar Labour Government's reputation as a great success in foreign affairs is usually based. I myself tend to demur somewhat from that judgment. A bit earlier I compared Ernest Bevin's middle-of-the-road policy with that of Arthur Henderson. Just as prewar Labour writers used to regard Henderson as the greatest Foreign Secretary of the twentieth century, so postwar spokesmen have transferred the mantle of greatest to Bevin. To be sure, on the surface Bevin's policy seems to stem naturally from the temperate, even cautious internationalism that Henderson persuaded the interwar Labour Party finally to accept. But it is increasingly my conviction, as I look back at the years between 1945 and 1951, that Bevin's tragic flaws of personality, his growing inability to accept criticism, the narrowness of his vision of international cooperation made much that appeared to be successful in the long run mistaken and self-defeating for Great Britain.

Most striking, of course, was his extraordinary mishandling of the Palestine mandate. One need not be a Zionist enthusiast nor a hundred and fifty percent American patriot to see that Bevin allowed his emotion to get the better of his judgment in a situation that was at best appallingly complex. James G. MacDonald's impression of Bevin in 1945 is revealing, however much one discounts MacDonald's own biases. "His bitterness against Truman was almost pathological," MacDonald wrote. "It found its match only in his blazing hatred for his other scapegoat—the Jews, the Israeli, the Israeli Government."[27] This was hardly a proper outlook from which to think through a balanced and coherent Palestine position. In a sense, it was Bevin's bumbling lack of sensitivity that impelled him to pursue what a delegate at the 1945 Labour Conference had already called "a traditional Conservative policy of power politics in Palestine."[28] The charge was, as a matter of fact, correct. And the irony of it was that the policy no longer worked. The British were, for all practical purposes, driven out, and the Israeli state that Bevin was certain could not come into being actually was forged in the fires of war. And yet—not surprisingly—no matter how incompetent was Bevin's policy, it was a popular one in Great Britain, popular at least until its failure became clearly manifest. It seems clear that if Bevin—let us say the Labour Government—had been more generous, more liberal, more patient even, in its response to terrorism and bloodshed, it would have faced much more popular opprobrium. The very fact that the "socialist" party did not act as socialists might, on the basis of countless propaganda statements, have been expected to act, ensured that even in failure the Palestine policy would not bring political disaster to the Party. But that it was a failure, there can be no doubt.

It is upon Bevin's European policy, however, that his reputation really rests. Faced with Britain's inability to keep the Soviet Union out of the Mediterranean, the assessment goes, he called in the Americans, whose Truman Doctrine protected British interests at the same time that it accomplished even broader purposes of western defense. He seized brilliantly upon the vague suggestions of George Marshall's Harvard speech to forge a Doctrine upon which to build the cooperative economic recovery of most of non-Communist Europe. As the cold war became increasingly threatening, he was a pioneer in shaping the defense of western Europe, by fostering the Brussels Treaty for western military union and then by promoting the more extensive North Atlantic Treaty Organization. Virtually all of these policies—perhaps the retreat from Greece is the exception—were in the mainstream of traditional British foreign policy. They were based on the view that security required military strength and that military strength required military allies. Although there was much lip service given to the United Nations, in actual fact it was the United States to which Bevin looked for both military and economic support. The very fact that Europe recovered spectacularly and that eventually the cold war relaxed into a kind of cold truce appears to be a testimony to Bevin's prescience and his skill.

Yet once again, I have nagging doubts. We have recently had a spate of books—written by responsible scholars, not hysterical crackpots— that have questioned whether in fact the so-called cold war was not the result of mistakes and miscalculations on both sides. For a change, not the motives but the judgments of western statesmen have been analyzed—and the possibility, at least, is raised that Bevin's inflexibility, along with that of both Truman and Stalin, may have made the conflict of interests—a conflict that of course existed—between the East and the West, more rather than less dangerous to the security and the healthy development of all the states of Europe. Clearly, much of this is conjectural and will remain so for a long time. But it is no longer as easy to swallow all the black-and-white certainties of the late forties and early fifties as it was for most of us at that time.

In any case, I suspect, the greatest single lost opportunity of the forties will increasingly come to seem to be the refusal of the Labour Government—and on this, as on most issues of foreign policy, it had the support of most Conservatives—to merge Britain, economically at least, in Western Europe. I know, of course, all the arguments that appeared valid to Labour then—and to many Conservatives—as they have appeared to many within the Labour Party to this day. Relations with the Commonwealth; tariff policy against areas outside the emerging Common Market; safeguards for British and Commonwealth agriculture; short-run effects on sterling; socialist planning versus the potentially restrictive policies of a European Union; all of these raised deep-seated and valid problems. But in the long run, it seems clear, Britain was going to have to pay a high price for the choice of a supposedly special relationship with the United States and with the Commonwealth, both of which were likely to become chimerical with the passing years. As the Common Market emerged, and as it later took on the stamp of Charles DeGaulle's limited vision of a united Europe, the unfortunate consequences of the Labour Government's decisions in the early stages of European Union were to become increasingly apparent.

However one may sum them up, Bevin's policies did not command universal support within the Labour movement. He was, to be sure, in the mainstream of a middle-of-the-road internationalism supposedly building upon the work of his Labour predecessors who had taught the Party the meaning of international responsibility. But to some within the Party, needless to say, moderate internationalism and Bevin's close collaboration with the United States appeared to be almost mutually exclusive. The issue of rearmament, in particular, created a crisis that was perhaps more real than the controversy over spectacles and false teeth I noted earlier. It appears to me that the supporters of Aneurin Bevan were correct, that Great Britain could not afford the scale of rearmament urged upon her by the United States—especially after the outbreak of the Korean War—and reluctantly accepted by Clement Attlee's Government. But whatever the merits of the argument, in foreign and defense policy, as on domestic issues, the Labour Party seemed to speak with many voices. And the differences persisted much more bitterly when Labour went into opposition after the election of 1951.

I commented at some length about the searing—and tedious—conflict that raged within the Labour Party throughout the fifties and into the sixties. In part, perhaps in large part, it was a struggle for the succession, a quarrel over the direction in which British socialism was headed. But it was also, as I noted, a quarrel over foreign policy, a quarrel that reminds one of the controversies that wracked the Party in the years following the First World War. First rearmament and the Korean War, then German rearmament, then British production of the hydrogen bomb, then the broader question of an "independent nuclear deterrent," as it was euphemistically called—each raised fundamental questions that, in characteristic fashion, threatened irreparable divisions and resulted in none. Soon after Hugh Gaitskell had succeeded to the leadership at the end of 1955, he opened the way for Aneurin Bevan to become reconciled with the Party. The result—it seemed to many Americans an odd one—was that Bevan, who had opposed on the international front much that Gaitskell had supported, became the shadow foreign minister on the Labour front bench.

In a way, it was Conservative blundering that made this possible. I have the feeling that the pros and cons of the Suez crisis of 1956 were much less clear-cut than either American journalists or Secretary of State Dulles considered them to be. But I am also certain that Anthony Eden, who by now was Tory Prime Minister, mismanaged the Suez affair appallingly. He gave Labour an opportunity to rally to the defense of a United Nations position, to denounce the Anglo-French ultimatum, to call for censure of the bombing of Egypt and the use of British troops. In actual fact, several studies have suggested that there was a substantial rank-and-file nationalist support of Eden's actions.[29] After a time, Labour's leaders thought it wise to soft-pedal the Suez issue. But my point is that Suez enabled the various factions of the Labour Party to act in concert and thus to begin again the never-ending process of reknitting the rather ravelled fabric of Labour politics, of maintaining the precarious balance so characteristic of the Party.

When Harold Wilson succeeded Hugh Gaitskell as leader of the Party, its official position on international affairs hardly changed at all. Indeed, though Wilson in his own way had been a Bevanite, an article that he wrote for the *Atlantic Monthly*[30] a few months after taking over in 1963 might well have been written by Gaitskell or, for that matter, by Ernest Bevin. He emphasized that the Labour Party's approach to overseas affairs was conditioned by its loyalty to three groupings: the Western alliance, the Commonwealth, and the United Nations.[31] And it seems to me significant—to go back now to the argument that I began to develop in the first part of this paper—that with respect to none of the three loyalties was Wilson categorical to the point of irreversibility. Opposed to neutralism as he was opposed to German nuclear weapons, he threaded a narrow path between too much dependence upon the Americans and a totally unrealistic pretension of total independence. By most Englishmen, beyond a doubt, his position was accepted as the practical one, just as after he came into office in 1964, his foreign policy was so regarded. Neither of his Foreign Secretaries, Michael Stewart and George Brown, showed himself to have the tough fiber of Ernest Bevin, but on the whole they pursued Ernest Bevinite not Aneurin Bevanite policies.

Wilson, himself, with singular lack of success tried, to a certain extent, to play the role of mediator in the attempt to bring the Vietnam war to an end. But, much to the fury of the Labour left, he made no bones about his Government's ultimate, if reluctant, acquiescence in American policy. Thus, a measure of continuity was again discernible, though once more there was restlessness and more than restlessness over Vietnam, over military commitments east of Suez, over Rhodesia, over a number of other questions.

I have very deliberately avoided writing about the recent years in any detail. It has seemed to me more useful, since I am a historian of the earlier twentieth century, to go back and to comment, even if only in general terms, about the background that may help place contemporary policies into focus. Labour's international stance has been, on the whole, what most observers would, I think, regard as temperate and responsible. It came into existence as the Labour Party reached maturity and the possibility of having to take office. As it emerged, it reflected the "taming" of some of the more extreme notions of earlier socialist pioneers. It was more frequently a broadly liberal foreign policy than it was a socialist foreign policy. Arthur Henderson, Ramsay MacDonald, Ernest Bevin, Clement Attlee, Hugh Gaitskell, Harold Wilson—on the whole this is a roster of middle-of-the-road practitioners whose international positions, with obvious differences of emphasis, might well have been those of Austen Chamberlain, or Anthony Eden, or Harold Macmillan. But of course, just as the positions of the more moderate Conservatives have been on occasion challenged by their "backwoodsmen"—the reactionaries who have pined for the good old days of empire and have wanted little nonsense about international cooperation—so has the position of the moderate Labour Party leadership by its dissidents on the left—internal critics whose disgust over the policies of the center have again and again caused some observers to believe that the existence of the Party itself was being threatened.

If what I have had to say in this analysis has any merit, however, the Party's internal controversy over foreign policy, like its quarrels over domestic issues, is paradoxically an element of strength rather than of weakness. Despite the seeming contradictions, despite a great deal of public mud slinging, despite even abstentions and withdrawals from Party discipline, British electors of various persuasions somehow have managed to find something for almost anyone in the foreign policy of the Labour Party. As a result—to conclude with what I have been arguing all along—the Labour Party, like an American political party in a totally different environment, manages to have a breadth of appeal that explains, I believe, its viability as an alternative to Conservatism in the politics of modern Britain. Whether in present circumstances viability can be equated with effectiveness on either the domestic or the international stage is, I think, still an open question.

CHAPTER VIII

THE RADICAL RIGHT
IN WEST GERMAN POLITICS
AND THE GERMAN QUESTION

By Dieter Dux*

The electoral successes of the radical rightist NPD in seven recent West-German state elections have received only moderate attention in the United States.[1]

On December 30, 1966, the American Council on Germany released a statement interpreting the meaning of two German elections at the state level. This statement was signed by thirty-one American experts on Germany, including two former Undersecretaries of State, two former members of President Eisenhower's Council of Economic Advisers, several University Professors, including H. Morgenthau, and other prominent Americans. A large proportion of the signers know Germany well, not only as students of German affairs but also from long residence in that country. Some of them were active in one form or another in opposition to the Nazi movement and government. Many of them helped in the American effort to build German democracy after the war. Taking account of widely expressed fears that the two state elections in Hesse and Bavaria had demonstrated the rebirth of Nazism, the statement concluded that these fears had no foundation in fact.

Though the National Democratic party managed to obtain seats in four additional state legislatures in 1967, informed observers in the U.S. continued to look upon this revival of radical rightist voting patterns as a passing phenomenon, somehow tied to the economic and political strains and frustrations of the middle 1960's.

The German Government's reaction to the NPD did nothing to dis-

*Head of the Department of Political Science at the University of Cincinnati, and former associate of Dr. Vinacke.

courage such interpretations. In a press conference held in Bonn in November, 1967, Chancellor Kiesinger was quoted as having said that "developments up to now have shown a decline of extremist parties in the Federal Republic at least of the Right wing NPD."[2]

Most recently, the German Government's Press and Information Office took notice of sincere concern expressed in parts of the free world about the reported growth of the "neo-Nazi" vote in Germany. In a statement issued February, 1968, such concern was described as exaggerated, particularly when the right-wing revival is interpreted in terms of the economic recession and the difficulty of resolving the German Question. Unlike Chancellor Kiesinger, the February analysis did not predict a declining trend in the right extremist vote. But it was suggested that environmental factors and built in buffers would not allow a revival of consequence of radical rightist forces in West Germany.[3]

Very much in contrast to the faith expressed by the Western World in German democracy's ability to keep political extremes within bounds, the Soviet Union, as early as January, 1967, attempted to establish a connection between the alleged growth of militarism and neo-Nazism and the newly installed Kiesinger Government.

In notes sent to the embassies of the United States, Great Britain, France and West Germany, the Soviet Union demanded that the Government of Chancellor Kiesinger take steps to cut short "the activity of neo-Nazi and militarist forces." Moscow declared that militarization of West Germany and a hostile attitude toward East Germany encouraged neo-Nazi activities and asserted, "All this provides a climate that is more than suitable for the national-chauvinist, racialist activities of pro-Fascist elements." The statement continued, "Who can guarantee, in these conditions, that some new Hitler will not appear in West Germany, and armed with nuclear weapons to boot?"[4]

In July, 1967, a second Soviet statement attacked the proposed West German emergency legislation, and on December 8, 1967, militarism and neo-Nazism were once more the subject of a Soviet declaration addressed to the three Western Allies and West Germany. The Soviet note charged that, by permitting the rise of right-wing extremism, the Bonn Government was violating a provision of the Potsdam agreement banning the rebirth of Nazism.

While the Federal Government of West Germany had not replied to the earlier Soviet notes, the December statement was categorically rejected "as interference in its internal affairs and as a distortion of its foreign policy."

"The German people and its constitutional organs will know how to defend their free and democratic basic order. The Federal Government hopes that the Soviet Union will play its part in helping the German people to re-establish its unity by peaceful means and to make its contribution to a European peace order."[5]

The Chief of the Soviet Foreign Ministry's Press Department at a news conference held in Moscow on February 24, 1968, charged the Kiesinger Government with openly encouraging the National Democratic Party which he called "militarist and revenge-seeking." The Soviet spokesman condemned the Western powers for having rejected Soviet allegations in December that Bonn was fostering a neo-Nazi movement.[6]

The increasingly violent attacks on the Kiesinger Government, and particularly on its role in the alleged growth of Fascism in West Germany, resulted in the publication of two East German decrees in March and April, 1968: the first banned "Neo-Nazis" from entering or crossing East Germany, and the second extended the ban to West German cabinet members.[7]

Since neither right-wing extremism nor neo-Nazi movement are well developed concepts, it may be best to begin with a catalogue of attitudes and beliefs that define, for the purpose of this paper, the Radical Right.

1. Unwillingness to compromise on ideological issues, in political discussions, and arrangements.
2. Dedication to elitism, idealization of ascetic and self-denying attitudes.
3. Denial of individualism.
4. Irrational explanation of political actions and events.
5. Fostering of a folkish ideology.
6. Idealization of the military tradition and the role of the soldier.
7. Idealization of social, cultural and political models of the past combined with a pessimistic conception of their possible reattainment "under present leadership."
8. Pronounced nationalism.
9. Hostility to foreign groups within Germany.
10. Covert anti-Semitism.
11. Character assassination of political opponents.
12. Inclination toward conspiratorial theories, centered on the parties in power, the media of mass communication; and particularly on the intellectuals that use these media as a forum to disseminate their views.

There is considerable evidence that most of the one and a half million Germans that voted for the NPD in the past eighteen months share those beliefs and attitudes.

One tends to forget that the NPD in an important sense is not a new party but stands in the tradition of a bewildering number of rightist groups and grouplets that developed in West Germany after 1949; that is after the allies gave up their right as occupiers to license political parties. It is difficult to keep track of all rightist groups, but the ministry of interior reported that between 1959 and 1965, 126 organizations were founded and that ninety-eight ceased to operate.[8]

It is not difficult to explain why the Radical Right had a limited political potential in the immediate postwar period in West Germany. For one, the right middle class parties of the Weimar republic because of their collaboration with Nazism had lost all claim to political support in the second republic. Further, rightist movements—and in post World War II Europe their political posture tended to be essentially defensive—have traditionally done best in a political milieu where there was a strong party of the Left in power or threatening to be in power in the proximate future. Again, radical right groups in general aim at a reversal of an achieved or about to be achieved high degree of consolidation of the democratic order in society. For many reasons, the Adenauer period had not set a pattern of progress toward a democratic order sufficient to rally the Radical Right into an effective opposition. Also most damaging to the political growth of rightist movements was a decision rendered by the Supreme constitutional tribunal in 1952 that banned the rightist Socialist Reichs Party as unconstitutional.[9]

Finally, the deliberate alteration of the electoral law by a succession of legislative measures made survival difficult for smaller parties without a broad national base.

In the period from 1949-1965 the German electorate preferred the political center, and only to a minor extent moved toward the political Left. The sizable influx of expellees from eastern Europe, of returning prisoners of war, kept some of the parties of the Right alive for a limited time. But for all practical purposes the two major parties managed to absorb and collect around themselves the vast majority of German voters.

In the last German national election of 1965, eighty-seven percent of the German electorate opted for the two large democratic parties. Except for a hard core of voters, estimated at about two percent, the Radical Right, it seemed, was about to disappear from the political scene. An informed observer attending the founding convention of the

NPD in November, 1964, would have estimated the party's chances of success as minimal. The new party joined together two parties of the Right, the DP of North Germany and the DRP. Acting as separate political parties they had never exceeded the one percent level of support in a national election. Combined as the NPD they managed for the first time in the postwar period to pull together a sizable group of antiliberal voters and to mobilize them for political action.

It will be argued that a basic change in the German political environment of the middle 1960's produced favorable conditions for the growth of this radical rightist, nationalist party. It is not necessary to analyze the total complex of factors, events and actions that produced a renewal of radicalism and nationalism in Germany at that time.

A brief enumeration of some elements of significance may suffice: the despair about the lack of progress toward German reunification, the gradual deterioration of NATO as a viable defensive alliance, the difficulties of the EEC to advance toward political integration, the increasingly complex task of maintaining close ties with both the U. S. and France. The revival of nationalist tendencies among members of the socialist bloc and among some of Germany's West European neighbors left their impact on German public opinion.

On the internal side the desire became dominant to get done with the past, the Third Reich and the war, the period of national atonement. The coming of an age of a new generation, the weak chancellorship of Erhard; the feeling that Germany had entered a phase of stagnation in politics and economics, that affairs had deteriorated into routine without hopeful prospects for the future, all these elements contributed toward a tendency to demand that a fresh start be made. Chancellor Erhard in 1965 officially proclaimed the end of the postwar period.

The nature of the 1965 electoral campaign gave clear evidence that all political parties had become aware of the new mood in the country. All parties played up nationalist themes. May 8, 1945, on its twentieth anniversary, was by some described as the blackest day in German history. A Federal Minister laid a wreath at the memorial erected in the 1930's for the Condor Legion Air Group of Guernica fame. And more than one politician of the governing parties advocated the termination of war crime trials. It is perhaps an oversimplification to suggest this, but in some measure the debates surrounding the extension of the statute of limitation applying to the prosecution of war criminals represented the last occasion when the democratic parties accepted fully the consequences of Nazism.

The drastic change in the attitudes and expectations of the voting public produced a political climate favorable to the separation of the rightist element from the democratic parties and eased the way for the consolidation of rightist sentiment around a new political party. The NPD exploited the opportunity with considerable skill. It managed to combine in its program an appeal—not very subtly disguised—to the old Nazis, with slogans sufficiently conservative and nationalistic to attract the politically homeless conservative element. Making good use of the general feeling of dissatisfaction with the governing parties (who, it was claimed, had not been effective stewards of the national interest) the party emerged as the collecting point of the opposition.

N.P.D. PROGRAM

The party has no program in the traditional sense. Quite clearly in order to increase tactical flexibility, precise political formulations have been avoided. A manifesto developed at the time of the founding of the party, the rules governing the internal affairs of the party, and a series of speeches by party leaders and chief ideologues offer some programmatic clues.[10] It is easier to state what the party rejects: it rejects pluralism in the political community, in morals and in art. It is hostile to the so-called licensed parties, interest groups of all kinds, but particularly to labor unions. The NPD has frequently suggested that the influence of the intellectuals that "dominate" T.V., radio, and the movie industry must be curbed. It is critical of the current structure and function of the state, because the state is too weak. The party finally opposes democracy in the liberal, western tradition.

The party desires a system based upon discipline and order, based upon the folkish community. It favors the preservation or restoration of traditional national, moral and social values. It proposes the establishment of a strong visible leadership, based "upon the natural authority structure required in a genuine democracy."[11]

In a much more detailed fashion the following constitutional changes or reforms were proposed during the 1966 party convention.

1. It was proposed that all important political questions and constitution-altering laws ought to be submitted to the people for a decision by plebiscite.
2. The five percent clause which has tended to restrict the development of minor political movements ought to be eliminated.
3. The constructive no-confidence vote which in the past has protected the executive against irresponsible pressure from tempo-

rary majorities (on the model of the fourth French Republic) ought to be stricken from the constitution.

4. The inefficiency of the Bundestag is severely criticized. Parliamentary procedures, it is proposed, ought to be streamlined to the point where membership in the legislative body would not prevent a deputy from holding a full-time outside job.

5. A new representative body to be chosen in an unspecified manner should assume responsibility for the formulation and development of so-called "normal legislation."

6. The presidency is to be much strengthened. The occupant of the office should be directly elected by the people. Among his new powers would be the constitutional right to rule in the name of the people, particularly if the parliament is unable to act effectively because of internal divisions.[12]

There can be no question that taken together these proposals would weaken representative democracy. A parliament stripped of most of its legislative power would be under the domination of a president on the de Gaullist model. It is conceivable that the elimination of the five percent clause would bring back a party system not unlike that of the Weimar republic which in its last years could not produce a stable majority behind the government. The spectre of a weak parliament, dominated by a de Gaulle-like president using his emergency powers to replace the ordinary legislative process, may not be the model that the NPD would consider desirable.

But whether ultimately Germany be governed à la Hindenburg of the 1930's or in the fashion of de Gaulle since 1958, in either case the drift toward the right extreme would proceed with increasing momentum.

Among other programmatic formulations the following deserve attention. With a high degree of constancy there are demands for an end to foreign aid, to reparations and to arms deliveries to foreign nations. The latter two proposals are undoubtedly aimed at Israel. Still in the area of foreign affairs, the party appears to advocate an end to NATO, largely because of U.S. dominance over the alliance. The party prefers a European security system, somewhat like the Europe of Fatherlands of General de Gaulle, permanently neutral and beyond the control of either the U.S. or the Soviet Union. The territorial limits of the new neutral Europe are never defined with any precision. One gets the impression, however, that particularly in eastern Europe the new Germany will not be satisfied with the boundaries of 1945, or even of 1937. There are frequent references to the German right to territories in whose organic growth Germans have participated for centuries. This implicit expansionism is camouflaged partly by the expressed desire to establish normal diplomatic relations with all the European satellites of the Soviet Union. A truer indication of foreign policy goals is the proposition that relations with the Soviet Union are to be normalized by an active policy of pressure.[13] It is hard to accept this as factually correct, but a recent defector from the party charged in an interview published in the *Spiegel* that the party planned to use an alliance with Communist China as a means of forcing the Soviet Union to assent to German reunification.[14]

INTERNAL ORGANIZATION OF THE N.P.D.

The development of the NPD into a party with wider national appeal brought to the party an element less radical in political attitudes. Their involvement in the management of party affairs might have exercised a moderating influence.

An observation of recent developments leads to the conclusion that the very opposite has taken place. That is, as voter support came to the party from less radical rightist groups, the internal operation of the party became less flexible and more authoritarian. In part, of course, the rapid growth of party membership in recent months (more than a thousand per month) produces growth problems that could be handled most efficiently by a central elite. Nevertheless, the centralized internal organization of the party offers the average party member little opportunity to influence the formulation and development of the party's program or to assist in its execution. Under current party rules, the lower party organizations are not permitted to make decisions in conflict with national policy guides. Further, the Presidium of the Executive Committee of the party can declare a state of emergency during which it is in effect the sole arbiter of the party's activities.[15]

The exclusion of the average party member from active participation in party affairs and the right of the higher party agencies to control the lower ones have enabled the party to survive a number of leadership crises with comparative ease. The current leader of the party, for example, managed to get to the chairmanship by having the original founder of the party ousted by his own constituency party for "damaging attitudes."[16]

While neither of these two most recent leaders has a Nazi past, the brownish coloration is heavy in the national party Executive Committee, where twelve out of thirty members have a significant Nazi record.[17]

Indeed the most active and influential leaders of party affairs, Schuetz —the publisher of the *Deutsche Nachrichten*—, Hess—the strategist of electoral campaigns—as well as Anrich—the chief ideologist of the party, have a definite Nazi past.

The Bonn ministry of interior estimated in 1968 that at least ten percent of the NPD membership belonged to the Nazi party or the outlawed SRP and that another thirty-five percent have in the past been active members of since-disintegrated rightist parties.[18]

The constant assertion by party leaders that the party is purging itself of anti-democratic forces and particularly of former Nazis is obviously not sustained by the evidence. Of course, most disturbing is the heavy concentration of former Nazis in the higher party echelons.[19]

ELECTORAL SUPPORT OF THE NPD

An examination of the sources of electoral support for the NPD, based on the series of seven recent state elections, suggests some tentative interpretations.

It appears that the party has above average appeal to the age groups between twenty-three and sixty, that the over sixty age group and the very young, from eighteen to twenty-three, have not found its program attractive.

Voting districts with a preponderance of Catholic voters have shown themselves most resistant. The Bavarian election gives striking evidence of this: in predominantly Protestant Ober and Mittel Franken the NPD received as much as twenty percent of the vote. In the rest of Bavaria the Catholic constituencies supported the party—subject to a very few exceptions—at below the seven percent state average. Conversely, in predominantly Protestant Hessen the relatively few Catholic electoral districts stayed well below the state NPD voting average.

Using all seven state elections as a source of reference, the conclusion is justified that the economically underprivileged as well as expellees are likely to vote NPD in an above average manner. It also appears that the skilled worker group has been resistant to the NPD. However, a recent study by the Allensbach Public Opinion Institute concluded that up to forty-one percent of this group might be receptive to the party.[20] Most surprising perhaps, the German farmer as a group has not voted for the NPD. Given the history of pro-Nazi leanings of this economic sector and the European peasant's traditional inclination toward conservatism, it may be assumed that sizable portions of this group will defect to the NPD in future elections.

It is certain, consequently, that in the last three years the NPD has managed successfully the transition from the status of a minor party with limited regional and ideological appeal to that of a mass-based party.

It must be emphasized also that the NPD is not just the party of former, unreformed Nazis, of the unteachables, of those permanently hostile to the democratic process. If this were so, the problem of dealing with the party would be infinitely simpler. Constititional procedures exist and have been applied in the past to eliminate anti-democratic parties from active participation in West-German politics. In 1952 the German Constititional Court declared the Socialist Reichs Party unconstitutional.[21] In 1956, federal suit was brought against the Communist Party. In its decision the court withdrew the protection of the Bill of Rights from the party and declared it dissolved.

On purely constitutional grounds, however, it may be difficult to argue the case against the legality of the NPD.

Article 21, para. 2, of the Bonn Constitituion is of central relevance here. It provides: "Parties which according to their aims and the behavior of their members, seek to impair or abolish the free and democratic basic order or to jeopardize the existence of the federal Republic of Germany, shall be unconstitutional. The Federal Constititional Court shall decide on the question of unconstitutionality."

Relying on this article the Bonn Government ordered the trial of the Socialistische Reichspartei in January, 1952. The SRP had been founded in 1949, at the time of the establishment of the Bonn Republic. The party participated in a number of state elections and managed to elect approximately eight percent of the deputies in the Bremen Senate and eleven percent in the state legislature of Lower Saxony. In special elections, to fill vacancies in the first Bundestag, it succeeded in capturing two seats in the lower House of the National Legislature.

Enjoined by a preliminary judgment of the Supreme Constitutional Court from further political activities, the party dissolved itself in September, 1952. Nevertheless, the Court proceeded with the trial and toward the end of October, 1952, published its decision. The brief presented on behalf of the SRP had suggested that the language of Article 21 of the Constitution was broad enough to cover the political goals and activities of its members.[22]

In answer to the SRP's brief the Court proceeded to give specific content to the broad formulations of Article 21. Among the principles of a free and democratic basic order it listed: respect for basic human rights, popular sovereignty, separation of powers, a government responsible to the people and their representatives, an administration operating within defined legal limits, independence of the courts, rule by majority, an equal opportunity for political parties to function, including the right to form an opposition within the limits imposed by the constitution and to exercise this right in a constitutional manner. A refusal to accept the basic principles of a free and democratic basic order, as defined above, would justify, in the Court's opinion, the exclusion of the party from the arena of politics.

The court also took it for granted that, in the modern state, parties hostile to the democratic order would not advocate overtly its abolition by the use of force. The assault on the constitutional order was more likely to take the form of internal undermining of the existing order. Only when parties of authoritarian tendencies get into power are they likely to use force to destroy the constitutional order. (Even Hitler took an oath to support the Weimar Constitution.) Hence programmatic declarations and statements of political goals should not be considered as conclusive evidence of the ultimate aims of a political party. Only a careful examination of the whole range of political activities and particularly the words and actions of the leadership group would lead to a correct assessment of the true character of a party and of the ultimate aims of its political program.

Of particular relevance in the assessment of the true goals of a party the Court found to be its inner organization. If the internal organization of a party is not based on democratic basic principles, in most instances it is possible to conclude that the party will apply the structural order which it employs for the management of its internal affairs to the state. The Court argued that any party whose internal operation showed lack of democratic procedures would not permit, once in power, the formulation of the will of the state as the result of the free interplay of political forces. An authoritarian system would be the consequence.

In 1952, the court assumed the responsibility for establishing the limits where the denial of basic democratic principles in the internal order of a party reaches a scope that can only be interpreted as an expression of basic anti-democratic attitudes. Such a finding confirmed by other circumstances would satisfy the requirements for a party's dissolution under Article 21.

The Court, however, was careful to point out that more than an "abstract" judicial determination of the adequacy of democratic procedures in the internal operations of a political party was required. Among the body of evidence that the Court found supportive of its decision to dissolve the SRP, four specific factors related to the operation of the party appear to have been most decisive.

1. The party displays a negative attitude toward human rights, especially evidenced by its reinvocation of anti-Semitic policies and slogans.
2. In the political competition with other parties, the SRP's ultimate goal if attained would mean the end of the multi-party state and a return to a single party dictatorship.
3. The internal organization of the party is based upon the leadership principle.
4. The SRP, in its program, its ideological conceptions, and its political style, shows definite affinities to the former NSDAP.

It is difficult to estimate to what extent evidence available to the Coalition Government would sustain a case for the dissolution of the SRP before the Supreme Constitituional Tribunal. Certainly in 1952, and in the successor case against the Communist party in 1956, the Court took a narrow view of the right of extreme political parties to participate in West German politics. While there may be considerable political temptation for the Kiesinger Government to solve the problem of the NPD by seeking its prohibition through constitutional procedures, the two cases, but particularly the latter, have produced some political embarrassment for the Government. The desire to pave the way for the ultimate solution of the German problem by increasing the face to face contacts between representatives of East and West Germany has been hindered by East German insistence that without a safe conduct East German communists could not travel safely to the Western Zone.

There is currently some agitation in West Germany, particularly from prominent members of the SPD, for the amendment of the Bonn Constitution to legalize all parties except those that openly advocate revolutionary action against the state.[23] Besides benefitting the West German Communist Party, this constitutional change would also serve to protect the NPD.

More helpful to the official attempts to curb the growing political power of the NPD would be a change in the electoral law.

Chancellor Kiesinger in his speech before the Bundestag, on December 13, 1966, outlining the new coalition government's policy stated at length the case for electoral reform.

"The Federal Government feels that during this period of co-operation a new electoral law should be incorporated into basic Law which will create clear majorities in future elections to the German Bundestag after 1969."[24]

When the subject of election reform was raised in a press conference in November, 1967, the Chancellor expressed his conviction that both coalition partners were still committed to reform during the current legislative period. The electoral successes of the NPD, in the Chancellor's opinion, added urgency to the need for reform.[25]

In his "State of the Nation Report" of March 11, 1968, Mr. Kiesinger announced once again that the government was firmly adhering to its intention to create ". . . a simple majority electoral system which is intended to give one party the possibility of taking over the responsibility for the Government."[26]

On March 28, Paul Luecke resigned as Minister of Interior, explaining he had taken the step, "because I must fear that one of the most important objectives for which the grand coalition came into power can no longer be realized: the creation of a majority-forming electoral law as a decisive condition for the permanent stabilization of our democracy."[27]

The Ministry of Interior had completed a draft of an electoral reform bill, but Mr. Luecke had become convinced "that an electoral reform complying with the Federal Chancellor's government declaration of December, 1966, can no longer be realized in this legislative period" (i.e. before September, 1969).[28]

While Mr. Kiesinger, in his published comments on Luecke's resignation, made it clear that he did not share the Interior Minister's pessimistic assessment of the chances for electoral reform, it is not likely that he will prevail over the SPD's objections.

Historically, during the 1948-49 debates in the West German Constitutional convention, the CDU/CSU delegations favored a single member district system on the British model. Five out of six of the smaller parties represented at the convention, out of understandable self-interest, supported an electoral system based on proportional representation.[29] The ultimate decision of the Convention in favor of a mixed system thus largely reflected the position of the SPD.

That their choice was politically correct becomes obvious when one examines the general trend of subsequent electoral results. Disregarding the 1949 election which for a number of reasons does not fit the general pattern, in the four elections between 1953 and 1965 the SPD received the bulk of its parliamentary seats through proportional representation. Proportional representation proved least helpful to the SPD's electoral success in the 1961 election, the land reserve lists (P.R.) producing ninety-nine out of 190 (i.e., fifty-two percent) of the social democratic parlamentarians. In the prior election of 1957, 123 out of 169 (i.e., seventy-three percent) members of the SPD fraction in the Bundestag were elected by the proportional feature of the electoral law. On the average, during the last four federal elections sixty-two percent of the SPD Bundestag delegation were indirectly elected. The understandable preference of the SPD for the retention of the present electoral system is shared by the third party in the Bundestag, the FDP. Its political survival is tied to proportional representation, since in the last two elections it failed to carry a single electoral district.

However sincerely motivated might be the plans of the Christian Democratic Union and its sister party, the Christian Social Union, for electoral reform, both would be the primary beneficiaries of any change in the direction of the single member district system. In the last four elections, on the average, but thirty-three percent of their representatives gained a seat in the Bonn Parliament as a result of indirect election.

The natural bias of the Anglo-Saxon electoral system to translate popular voting majorities into larger parliamentary majorities would tend to reinforce, other things being equal, the CDU/CSU's electoral advantage.

Short of a major shift of popular sentiment in favor of the SPD, the party is not likely to support reform plans that would almost certainly reduce its parliamentary representation. Since recent state elections indicate a lessened level of voter support for the SPD, the conclusion seems justified that a change in the West German electoral system is not likely during the current legislative period.

In the absence of change, the NPD may emerge as a political factor of consequence in the sixth Bundestag.

＊　＊　＊　＊　＊

It may be assumed that legislative and constitutional procedures available to the Bonn Coalition Government will not be employed to curb the growth of the NPD.

In any event, an enlightened rejection of the party at the polls would provide a more desirable answer. In the past this has been the ultimate regulator of rightist movements in the Bonn Republic. However, the large existing reservoir of pro-rightist voters makes it unlikely that a natural solution can be provided in this way.

Certainly, the NPD receptive groups, i.e., Protestants, expellees, members of the lower middle class and the lowest economic strata of the German political community, have not been fully reached. Nor can it safely be predicted that the resistant groups, that is Catholics, skilled workers, the economically well-off and better educated and the farmers, will not migrate in considerable numbers to the new right in the next Federal election.

It is idle to speculate about the outcome of the next federal election in West Germany. However, it should be noted that it is widely assumed in West Germany that a sufficient percentage of the national vote will be cast for the NPD in 1969 to give the party substantial representation in the lower House.[30]

While such estimates may prove to be unduly pessimistic, the presence of NPD deputies in the Bundestag is not likely to strengthen the foreign policy position of any future West German Government, certainly not vis-à-vis the Soviet Union and Eastern Europe.

To an increasing degree, in 1968, the Soviets showed a tendency to rebuff the Coalition Government's efforts at détente in Eastern Europe on the grounds of the alleged connection between the Kiesinger government and the growth of Rightist extremism. Nevertheless, the basically new element of Kiesinger's foreign policy, to put détente in Eastern Europe ahead of German unification, has produced some significant successes. Diplomatic relations have been established with Rumania and Yugoslavia. Relations with Czechoslovakia were improving during the early months of 1968. The all but formal abandonment of any legal claims to the territories east of the Oder-Neisse line by the Kiesinger Government removed a major obstacle to the normalization of German-Polish relations.

If West Germany's desire to turn cold war confrontation into a détente in Eastern Europe has fallen short of its goal, it is largely due to East German obstructionism, supported by Moscow.

In 1967, four conditions were set forth which West Germany was required to meet if the signatory powers of the Warsaw Pact were to resume normal relations with the Federal Republic: (1) Bonn would have to recognize the German Democratic Republic as a state; (2) Bonn would have to recognize the demarcation line between the two parts of Germany and the Oder-Neisse line as national borders. (3) Bonn would have to renounce its alleged ambitions to obtain nuclear weapons and (4) Bonn would have to acknowledge that West Berlin is an autonomous political entity in the territory of the GDR.[31] The present policy of the Kiesinger Government permits acceptance of all conditions except the formal recognition of the existence of a separate East German state.

It would appear that only de-Stalinization of the East German regime or a change in the current German policy of the Soviet Union would make further progress toward détente possible. Within the proximate future neither is likely to occur.

The gravitational pull of West Germany could probably not be resisted by an East German regime less authoritarian than Mr. Ull-bricht's. The trend toward decompression in Eastern Europe has already produced a harder line in Soviet foreign policy. Recent events in Czech-oslovakia will tend to reinforce it.

On the problem of German unification the Kiesinger government has followed a middle course between wishful thinking and resignation. It is the Coalition Government's expressed hope that reason and ob-jectivity will some day prevail and provide a solution to the German question.

It is not certain that West German voters have the necessary patience. A vote for the NPD would be an expression of dissatisfaction with the foreign policy of the Coalition Government. If a sizable number of German voters exercise this option, the policy of small steps toward détente in Eastern Europe might well be replaced by more active political pressures on the Soviet Union and East Germany.

CHAPTER IX

THE JOHNSON STAFF AND
NATIONAL SECURITY POLICY

By J. C. Heinlein *

> I am not sure that there really is such a thing as "power" or "decision"
> . . . For one thing, there is just a build-up of big and small events and they
> may not be brought to your notice until the issue has already been decided;
> and when you eventually have to decide, it may be in response to the
> smallest of them all. That is not "power" or "decision"; you are too much
> in the hands of events.[1]

It is probably true that Lyndon B. Johnson was to an extent "in the
hands of events," and may have responded to one of the smallest,[2]
that Wednesday afternoon in April, 1965, when he ordered the landing
of United States military forces in the Dominican Republic. But it is
equally true that he did act—and in the company of certain advisers.
All American Presidents have consulted with others in making security
decisions—the practice dates back at least to 1793 when George Washington discussed the issuance of a proclamation of neutrality with the
Secretaries of State, Treasury, War, and the Attorney General—but only
in the past three decades have the traditional advisers to the President
been augmented and the sum brought into organizational units to the
extent that "the institutionalized presidency" is an appropriate label.
Many persons have been interested in the development and adequacy
of the machinery created since 1937 to provide the chief executive with
staff services; some have examined how Presidents Truman, Eisenhower
and Kennedy used their advisers in specific security policy situations
during their administrations. It may be useful to carry the analysis forward into the Johnson administration, to observe how staff arrange-

---

*Professor of Political Science, University of Cincinnati, and an associate
of Dr. Vinacke.

ments have changed and to raise again the question whether formal staff machinery was importantly involved in a particular security policy episode—the landing of troops in the Dominican Republic.

DEVELOPMENT OF THE PRESIDENT'S STAFF

During the first century and a half of our constitutional history, Presidents managed fairly successfully to satisfy the constitutional admonition "to take care that the laws be faithfully executed"; and to reach security decisions in the bargain, with the uneven help provided by the heads of certain executive departments, personal secretaries and private advisers. Beyond these few individuals there appeared in this period three agencies upon which a President could call for staff aid, although not created solely to serve him: the Cabinet, the Civil Service Commission and the Bureau of the Budget.

The Historical Presidency

The Cabinet appeared during the first term of Washington as a consequence of need and convenience. Having failed to elicit the consultation he required from House, Senate or Supreme Court, the President fell back upon his own appointees: the heads of the three executive departments and the Attorney General. Over the years weak Presidents have found the Cabinet a useful sounding board, even a congenial forum for policy discussions. Strong Presidents have made little use of it. Recent Presidents, with the exception of Kennedy, have championed its value, but even its sturdy friend, Eisenhower, discovered its members deficient as general staff personnel. Johnson may have been reacting to the Kennedy experience, as perhaps Eisenhower had to Truman's, in wishing to revitalize the Cabinet as a dynamic and major instrument of government. After a year in office he declared to its members that the Cabinet should function regularly as a consultative body and quoted with approval Harold L. Ickes' confidence to his diary: "You go into Cabinet meetings tired and discouraged and out of sorts and the President puts new life into you."[3] Within a few months, however, and even though a special assistant had been delegated as secretary of the Cabinet, one observer saw Cabinet meetings once again as not the place where substantive discussion occurred.[4] A year later another saw the Cabinet as an old but weakened and seldom used institution of the Presidency.[5] It seems probable that Cabinet competence, as a creative and coordinating body, does not lie in those areas where vital problems occur today. Insistent need for specialized knowledge, particularly in the security area, has caused recent Presidents to turn to other persons and to utilize other procedures.

The Civil Service Commission is the only other pre-twentieth century body which might be considered an institutional aid to the President. Since 1883 the early concern for reform in government employment practices has given way to a positive emphasis on using personnel procedures in support of broad administrative objectives. The Commission has functioned most obviously as a presidential staff agency when the chairman, or another person, has occupied a personnel post in the White House Office. The Liaison Office for Personnel Management established in 1939 was one of the original divisions of the Executive Office of the President. Its functions were delegated to the Chairman of the Commission by executive order in 1953, and the following year President Eisenhower named an adviser on personnel management in the White House Office. The title became special assistant in 1958, but the place itself was not included in Kennedy's office. President Johnson has relied on the Chairman in specific recruitment assignments but has not reinstated a personnel division in the Executive Office nor appointed an assistant in the White House.

The Bureau of the Budget was the last major staff aid to the President to be added prior to the appearance of the "institutionalized presidency" in the second term of the second Roosevelt. Some central supervision of expenditures had been exercised by Presidents since Jefferson, but not until passage of the Budget and Accounting Act in 1921 was there acceptance of the concept of the executive budget as governmental policy. Though the Bureau was placed initially in the Treasury Department, it was made immediately responsible to the President and from its inception was the most effective general staff tool yet available to him.

The Institutionalized Presidency

There have been advisory bodies around the President at least since the Cabinet became formalized during the diplomatic crisis of 1793. Even so, the modern insitutionalized presidency may be said to stem from the 1937 report of The President's Committee on Administrative Management[6] and may be dated from Roosevelt's Executive Order No. 8248 of September 8, 1939, which identified and described the functions of the original six divisions of the newly-created Executive Office of the President.

On Inauguration day, March 4, 1933, Roosevelt had available a group of cabinet advisers drawn from the old line executive departments and could anticipate limited help from a congeries of independent and quasi-independent agencies. Further, there was a Civil Service Commission, not yet a true central personnel body; a Bureau of the Budget, after twelve years not much more than a center for correlation of expenditure estimates; and a few clerks and secretaries in the White House itself. Three years later, after frenzied attempts at supervision of new and numerous anti-depression agencies, he discovered and reported to Congress that "the administrative management of the Government needs overhauling."

The President's Committee, to whom the problem was given by Roosevelt, returned five recommendations: expand the White House staff; strengthen other managerial agencies of the government; extend the merit system under a single administrator; overhaul the one hundred or more boards and commissions and bring them within major executive departments; establish executive responsibility for financial transactions and accountability to Congress. Notwithstanding Roosevelt's overwhelming victory in 1936, the climate in Congress was not favorable to the administrative reorganization proposal submitted in January, 1937. Two years later, with the "court packing" bill no longer an obstacle, a very similar reorganization bill was passed with little opposition.

The Reorganization Act of 1939 did not give congressional approval to all five points of the Committee's proposal, but it did authorize six administrative assistants in the White House and permitted the President to bring three essential management aids—budget, personnel and planning—within the new Executive Office. Of the six original divisions of the office, two, The National Resources Planning Board and The Office of Government Reports, did not survive the war years; another, The Office for Emergency Management, has been an inactive framework since the latter Truman years; and a fourth, The Liaison Office for Personnel Management, was not continued into the Eisenhower administration. The White House Office and the Bureau of the Budget, the other original units, have provided presidential staff support continuously for nearly three decades.

The Contemporary Presidency

Before attempting to ascertain how President Johnson used his advisers in a specific national security situation, the landing of troops in the Dominican Republic in 1965, it may be useful to observe wherein the original Executive Office blueprint has changed in response to the needs of his three post World War II predecessors. In most cases it is not worthwhile to do more than note when divisions of the Office were added or abolished.[7] It is relevant, however, to consider more fully structural and functional modifications in the two components most involved in the making of national security decisions: The National Security Council and The White House Office.

The National Security Council was organized in the National Military Establishment by the National Security Act of 1947 and placed within the Executive Office by Truman's Reorganization Plan 4 of 1949.[8] Though it has gone through organizational changes, its statutory function from the beginning has been "to advise the President with respect to the integration of domestic, foreign and military policies relating to the National security."

During Truman's administration military representation was reduced by elimination of the secretaries of the military departments, the Vice-President was added, and some additional membership flexibility was made possible. The only formal membership change under Eisenhower was replacement of the Chairman of the National Security Resources Board by the Director, Office of Defense Mobilization. Of greater moment were changes within the Council secretariat: the Senior Staff became the Planning Board, and the earlier "reporting unit" was replaced by a considerably more imposing Operations Coordinating Board. And of most consequence, perhaps, was the appointment early in 1953 of a Special Assistant to the President for National Security Affairs. This meant downgrading the Executive Secretary of the Council but underscored the important advisory role Eisenhower saw for the Council. Certainly, the Council was more active in the nineteen-fifties. Meetings were frequent and regular; the President usually presided; and "major" policy decisions were approved in awesome number.[9]

Not much more than the statutory membership of the Eisenhower National Security Council survived the early Kennedy years. Demonstrating that the Council, nearly as much as the Cabinet, is the President's creature, Kennedy abolished both the Planning Board and the Operations Coordinating Board in the belief that plans and operations should be integrated and responsibility for policy and execution concentrated. Whereas Eisenhower met regularly with his Council, in part a reaction to Truman's less systematic reliance on it, Kennedy preferred to discuss security matters with individuals and small groups and seldom called the Council into session. By the end of his first year in office, after Berlin and the Bay of Pigs, Kennedy sought "more orderly" relations with the Council and subsequently met with the statutory body, or a special committee thereof, biweekly or more often in response to emergency crises.

The White House Office, as seen by the Brownlow Committee, consisted of existing presidential secretaries—appointments, press and correspondence—and was to be improved primarily by the addition of administrative assistants, one of whose qualities was to be a "passion for anonymity." Roosevelt's White House staff of twelve in 1943 at the height of the war emergency was double the number of his professional aides in 1939, even though in only one year did he appoint as many new administrative assistants as the Committee had suggested. Truman's office was quite similar in terminology with one exception. In addition to the customary secretaries, special assistants, administrative assistants, special counsels and special executive assistants to the President, he created in 1947 the post of "The Assistant to the President" and appointed John R. Steelman to it. Truman did not delegate formal decision-making to Steelman or any other staff member. What he needed from his advisers was information and ideas; after the data had been assembled and the views argued, he was willing to make the decision and move on to the next.

That Eisenhower's professional staff was triple the size of Truman's is not important in itself. The interesting question is whether its complexity and the unprecedented authority vested in its chief, The Assistant to the President, contributed to presidential inaccessibility and blurred responsibility for decisions. Sherman Adams saw to it that the President was faced only with the questions which he, Adams, could not dispose of at a lower level. Only irreducible policy conflicts survived, and the President ordinarily entered the decision process after questions had been filtered through echelons of assistants. Eisenhower's staff organization and operation may have failed to keep him fully informed and possibly insulated him from early contact with serious problems. The puzzle for any President is to establish procedure patterns which will divert minor matters from his desk but permit him to become involved at an early point in the major ones.

Kennedy believed with Woodrow Wilson that the President is "the vital place of action in the system."[10] While a candidate he had declared that a vigorous chief executive, not one "praised for what he did not do," would refuse to tolerate an assistant to the president astride the single narrow path leading to the President. While Kennedy's view of the Eisenhower White House may not have been correct in all details, he expected his own staff, both institutional and personal, to help him meet and master problems, not shield him from them. Seeing himself

as the hub of the executive wheel, he wanted to be available and involved. In view of campaign criticism, it was predictable that Kennedy
would abolish the position of The Assistant to the President and reduce
the number of personal aides in the White House Office. Abolition of
the position, of course, did not in practice prevent one assistant from
being more equal than others; but overall reduction in numbers to a
midpoint between Eisenhower's high of thirty-two and Truman's low of
seven did facilitate presidential contact with staff members. It is imperative that a President who desires to immerse himself in the details of
policy be surrounded by a staff organized to supply him with facts and
formulae along several communication lines. This can be accomplished
by a relatively informal arrangement emphasizing staff flexibility. But
with the machinery in place there remains the matter of competence
of advice. It was low in 1961 at the Bay of Pigs; it was higher a year
and a half later. Perhaps a larger role for the National Security Council
in the policy process and a minor reordering of the White House staff
had some effect on the quality of the 1962 Cuba decision.

THE JOHNSON PRESIDENCY

A study of American Vice-Presidents who succeeded to the Presidency on the death of the President is titled *Seven by Chance*.[11] Lyndon
Johnson, who became the thirty-sixth President of the United States on
the death of John Kennedy, also became the eighth Vice-President to
succeed to the higher office and the second within the period of the contemporary presidency.[12] The circumstances of his succession counseled
initial humility but soon, as many observers have recorded, "Lyndon
Johnson came on strong."[13]

Every new President is aware that he stands in the place of Washington and is bound by the dimensions and traditions of the presidential
office-in-being; yet every strong President consciously or unconsciously
goes about the task of reordering it in his own image. Franklin Roosevelt was Johnson's powerful mentor in Washington and "was," the latter has reported, "just like a daddy to me always." Even so, in 1945
Johnson was quick to declare his independence by pointing to his votes
as Representative against Roosevelt positions.[14] And as President he
has been pleased to call attention to the larger winning margin in 1964
than 1936.

Johnson suffered, as did Truman, from comparison with a beloved
predecessor and from abrupt responsibility for partially unfamiliar burdens as well. Unlike Truman, however, in his presidential role he could

draw upon long and responsible experience in Congress and a useful apprenticeship as Vice-President. In part because Roosevelt had failed to prepare him for succession to the presidency, Truman, as President, helped create a governmentally meaningful existence for Vice-Presidents—and Johnson was a subsequent beneficiary. During the eight years of the Eisenhower administration, Johnson, as floor leader in the Senate of the opposition party, was quite willing to accept the advantages of the President's rather typically Republican belief in legislative-executive cooperation. On becoming Vice-President, Johnson did not move out of the Senate nor into another branch of government, but he did discover that he no longer was viewed by his old colleagues as master of the processes and products of their House.[15] As President, three years later, he did not deny inter-branch cooperation, but he demonstrated by the extraordinary early success of his legislative proposals —fifty-seven percent approved in 1964 and sixty-eight percent in 1965 —that he was willing, when able, to move beyond cooperation to control.

Few future Presidents have thought as systematically or expounded as fully their views of the powers and responsibilities of the presidential office as Kennedy.[16] Johnson, on the other hand, seems more at ease in the practice of political power than in the expression of its concepts. Nonetheless, about five years before succeeding to the Presidency, he proceeded to expound a theory of politics which with but slight modification could be utilized by a candidate—all the while insisting that he resented being asked his political philosophy. This was the discussion which opened and closed with the declaration: "I am a free man, an American, a United States Senator, and a Democrat, in that order."[17]

The manner of exercise of the powers and duties of the Presidency seems to depend in part on the view the occupant has of himself and his conception of the office. A revealing expression of Johnson's attitudes as incumbent came in an address to the Congress, March 15, 1965, a few days after the Selma, Alabama, march and about a month before the military rising in the Dominican Republic. By his presence and his words the President urged passage of the voting rights bill, but his message, titled "The American Promise," seemed also to describe the Great Society as it disclosed his personal goals as President:

> I do not want to be the President who built empires, or sought grandeur, or extended dominion.
>
> I want to be the President who educated young children to the wonders of their world. I want to be the President who helped to feed the hungry. . . .
>
> I want to be the President who helped the poor to find their own way

and who protected the right of every citizen to vote in every election.

I want to be the President who helped to end hatred among his fellow men and who promoted love among the people of all races and all regions and all parties.

I want to be the President who helped to end war among the brothers of this earth.[18]

A tendency to use the first person singular is not unknown in the White House. Truman wrote of extra-constitutional powers there for the taking by a strong President. The placard on his desk read "The buck stops here." Kennedy saw himself as the "vital center of action," prepared to exercise the fullest powers of his office—all that were specified and some that were not. With the exception of Eisenhower, who saw himself as a "constitutional president," Johnson's predecessors provided him ample precedents for taking a strong role as President. Some observers are concerned that he may have been too greatly encouraged by them; one believes that "this administration is probably more of a one-man show than any in recent history."[19]

The Johnson Staff

It is understood that insofar as statutes permit each President will determine the personnel of the staff agencies of his administration in accordance with his own objectives. We anticipate almost complete turnover in the Cabinet and those institutions which have been gathered since 1939 within the Executive Office of the President. Even though all presidents are apt to believe that the presidential office is badly in need of redoing, their ability to proceed will be influenced by circumstances. Eisenhower and Kennedy were anxious and able to break sharply with the past; even Truman, though initially restrained by a sense of propriety, rather quickly reconstituted Roosevelt's Cabinet and office.

It is likely that Johnson's concern for the prestige of the Presidency and a personal need to gain the confidence of the country underscored his plea to Kennedy's assistants: "I need you more than he needed you." That the plea would eventually lose its persuasiveness and the need be less urgently felt by the new President should have been foreseen.

The Executive Office of the President today, and at the time of the 1965 crisis in the Dominican Republic, includes two of the original components: the White House Office and the Bureau of the Budget. Three of the seven agencies added in the Truman period—the Council of Economic Advisers, the National Security Council and the Office of Emergency Planning—survive, along with two responses to the space age, the National Aeronautics and Space Council and the Office of Science and Technology, dating from the Eisenhower and Kennedy administrations. The Office of the Special Representative for Trade Negotiations was placed within the Executive Office in January, 1963, to facilitate the trade agreements program. The Office of Economic Opportunity was established there to administer and coordinate the poverty programs in 1964. Of the present nine divisions only two, the White House Office and the National Security Council, are likely to be importantly involved in the making of national security decisions.

There have been no membership changes in the National Security Council since the first year of the Eisenhower administration, when the National Security Resources Board was abolished and its Chairman was replaced on the Council by the Director, Office of Defense Mobilization—subsequently redesignated the Office of Emergency Planning. Thus in April, 1965, at the time of the Dominican affair, the Council consisted of President Johnson, Vice President Humphrey, Secretary of State Rusk, Secretary of Defense McNamara and Director Ellington of the Office of Emergency Planning. At that time McGeorge Bundy was both adviser to Mr. Johnson as Special Assistant to the President for National Security Affairs and chief of the Council's staff. The staff has continued to prepare for meetings and to follow the execution of decisions,[20] but without a return to the elaborate planning and operations coordinating machinery of the Eisenhower period.

Titles and places around the Council table help pinpoint participants in Council sessions, but they tell little about that body's functioning in the policy making process. The Council was established in 1947 as an advisory body to the President and it has so remained. It meets only when the President directs, and its policy papers become public policy only when approved by him in his presidential, not councilor, capacity. Furthermore, it is not the only instrument of council utilized by him in dealing with problems of national security. When the statutory Council is not considered an appropriate forum for discussion, security business may be settled in other groups meeting with the President, by written communications or at a lower level in the executive structure.[21]

After an early inclination toward individual and small group consultations in lieu of Council discussions, within a year Kennedy had prescribed regular meetings and he responded to the 1962 Cuba crisis by expanding the formal Council into an *ad hoc* group of a dozen or more advisers known as the Executive Committee. In turn, the Security Council has reflected the working habits of Johnson and his preference for a smaller version of Kennedy's "Executive Committee." For some months prior to April, 1965, the most classified intra-executive security conversations brought together the President, Secretary Rusk, Secretary McNamara and Special Assistant Bundy. Avoidance of full Council meetings, not to mention the oversize Executive Committee, may stem both from Johnson's enthusiasm for secrecy and concern about even innocent news leaks from a larger group, plus a belief that policy planning is best accomplished by officials with operational responsibilities. A somewhat larger group spun off from the Council when Bundy was recalled to temporary duty at the White House to serve as executive secretary to a special subcommittee concerned with a lasting settlement in the Middle East.[22] Though the President stated he might sit in now and then, he was not a member and it was understood that subcommittee reports would be considered within his smaller advisory circle.

Johnson's White House Office does not differ greatly in terms of titles and numbers from Kennedy's. In view of his 1960 campaign oratory directed at the Eisenhower staff system, it was not surprising that Kennedy kept the total of his White House assistants about midway between Truman's average of nine and Eisenhower's twenty-six. About twenty assistants, by one or another name, have worked in the White House during the Kennedy-Johnson years. Large or small staff is of slight significance when attempting to discover the role of staff in the security policy process. More important than size, were competent people obtained and retained, and were their skills efficiently organized within the Office?

Eisenhower saw Truman's relations with his aides as informal, the organizational hierarchy of his office not firmly fixed and staff spheres of influence too flexible. Kennedy believed his predecessor's arrangements, in particular the position of Assistant to the President occupied so conspicuously by Sherman Adams and Wilton B. Persons, had contributed to presidential inaccessibility and blurred responsibility for decisions. Johnson, controlled as he was by the circumstances of his succession, moved slowly to place the imprint of his own long experience in government on a staff in being. Though much has been made of personnel movement through the White House doors, the interesting point may be how long Kennedy appointees remained under a new President.

Harry S. Truman succeeded to the presidency on April 12, 1945, on the death of Franklin D. Roosevelt. Within a year only two members of the Roosevelt White House staff remained, and eight of the ten executive department heads were Truman appointees. After two years, with one single exception in the White House, the entire staff and Cabinet had been named by Truman. The other succeeding Vice-President in the modern period, Johnson, was not so precipitous. A year and a half after entering the White House and six months after his own electoral victory in 1964, there were still seven Kennedy appointees in the White House Office, and the total was about evenly split between old and new. Four years after Dallas, one person from the Kennedy group, an administrative assistant, remained in the White House; five department heads had spent a full seven years in the Kennedy-Johnson Cabinets, and a sixth, Lawrence F. O'Brien, had moved from the President's personal staff to the Post Office Department. Apart from Johnson's success in persuading Kennedy staffers to stay, it may be instructive to calculate the yearly rate of change in the twenty senior positions in the White House. Ten of the group which joined the President in the transition period departed during the first year. This, of course, was the period when most of the individuals who felt great personal loyalty to Kennedy left government service. There followed a thirty-one percent turnover in 1965; forty-four percent in 1966; and twenty-four percent in 1967.

It is this "revolving door at 1600" aspect of the Johnson presidency which has stimulated both critical comment and presidential defensiveness. Resisting some contrary evidence from staff members, Washington observers have concluded that Johnson is an "immensely difficult man to work for"[23] and that his methods "chew up manpower at a rapid rate."[24] But turnover *per se* was a less serious concern than maintenance of staff quality. Following Bundy's resignation one analyst believed a tendency toward "blandness and compliance" in the upper reaches of the government was both cause and effect of Johnson's "inability to recruit men of the first rank" for an increasingly inbred administration.[25] Near the end of 1966, James Reston saw the administration as possessing "many good qualities. It works hard but it is a desperate grind, without much inspiring leadership or intellectual excitement . . . . the atmosphere of this administration simply does not attract as many brilliant volunteers as the pressures and the Johnson system devour."[26] The President's defense to such journalistic assessments was to de-emphasize the role the departed had played (the "little State Department" in the White House basement was downgraded after Bundy left) and to emphasize the abilities of his staff members of the moment. Early in 1964 Johnson referred to one of his staff assistants as a "valuable hunk of humanity"[27] and after a full year in the White House he was convinced that "this staff of special assistants is one of the ablest and most broadly experienced, and I hope most harmonious and most dedicated, serving the President."[28] Of these ten special assistants lauded by the President in 1965, only three remained in the White House Office fifteen months later.

There has been a tendency for writers to resort to hyperbole when recording the impact of Lyndon Johnson on the presidential office. One was convinced that Johnson was "unlike any United States President the world had ever known."[29] Another tells us "no other modern President has immersed himself so thoroughly in the minutiae of the government."[30] And another advises us that "for good or ill, President Johnson is the government of the United States today. Everyone else is a subordinate."[31] It is not surprising that a person for whom government has been both vocation and avocation for a third of a century should turn out to be an active occupant of the White House. Of course Johnson is unique, as is every President, but simultaneously he is not completely different from some of his predecessors in his utilization of staff in making national security decisions.

It is clear that Johnson is not insulated from developing problems by a protective staff as Eisenhower may have been. "President Johnson," we are told, "doesn't sit at the top of a staff pyramid. He sits in the middle of a circle."[32] But this would seem to be the familiar spot deliberately chosen by Kennedy after rejecting the location Eisenhower had occupied beyond his Assistant's office. And it may have been more politic than accurate for Moyers to deny the hierarchical aspect of the Johnson staff. Many members have had direct access to the President but not all have had *equal* access, and even senior people must obtain clearance from the appointments secretary. It is probably true that "Mr. Johnson leaves no room for secondary spheres of power under his roof";[33] but if Moyers was not a staff chief in the manner of Sherman Adams he was at least *primus inter pares.*[34]

Our interest is not so much in demonstrating the existence of levels of authority in the White House Office as in determining how these personal staff assistants as organized and directed by Lyndon Johnson contribute to presidential decision-making. Some years earlier Truman became aware that many people in his office "tried to find out what I wanted to hear and then gave it to me" but the ones he wanted around him "did not do that."[35] Does Johnson want argument or acclamation? This may be the clue to his view of staff role. All of his aides contend that they give him "frank, blunt advice," yet concede that "disagreement with the President needs careful handling."[36] Some insist that he "seeks dissenting views"; others remain unconvinced and avoid differing with the President.[37] In large measure Moyers' departure from the White House was deplored because he was believed to be one of a very few there who could disagree with and stand up against the strong-minded President.[38] The answer may be that Johnson, as every President, needs aides and advisers and that for him, less than with Kennedy, the two groups do not coincide in his staff. Members of the former should be "agile, able to jump into almost anything and come up with facts and a set of recommendations";[39] each "has several areas of specialty";[40] a staff assistant should be able, according to Mr. Johnson, to "play any position here . . . if he needs to play first, second or third base, I hope he can do it."[41] A man in motion is "meet to be sent on errands," and can do a great deal for the President in terms of supplying information and freeing his time; but he is not apt to be reflective. His focus must be on the immediate operation rather than the substance of policy. Consequently, when the President requires advice on policy goals he may have to reach into the administration beyond the White House or to take council with long trusted confidants outside the government.

In an effort to identify more specifically the role of the staff in presidential decision-making, let us look at one national security episode in the Johnson administration—the decision to send United States military forces to the Dominican Republic in April, 1965. Obviously the decision in every formal sense was the President's. But with whom did he consult; who supplied information, alternatives, ideas? Which executive institutions were called upon? In a word, how was the decision made?

Dominican Republic, 1965

The meeting in the President's White House office on April 28, 1965, was a Wednesday afternoon variation on the familiar Tuesday noon series of executive inner circle discussions. Present with the President were his frequently consulted advisers on national security matters: Secretary of State Rusk, Secretary of Defense McNamara and Mr. McGeorge Bundy; the topic: a logistics problem from Vietnam. Then came the first of three cables from the Dominican Republic. "Shortly after three o'clock," Mr. Johnson has reported, "I received a cable from our Ambassador and he said that things were in danger, he had been informed that the chief of police and the governmental authorities could no longer protect us."[42]

The subsequent decision of the President to send American forces into the Dominican Republic meant a third United States intervention in that disturbed land within half a century. The island, Hispaniola, shared by the Dominican Republic and Haiti, was discovered by Columbus in 1492 and has known few extended periods of political stability since. During the first three hundred years, control moved from Spain to France and back again until establishment of the first republic in 1809. Following a second, and short lived, republic set up in 1821, the present republic was proclaimed in 1844 marking a successful revolt against twenty-two years of Haitian occupation. In the pathetic story of rebellions, intrigues and plunder involving many nations and nationals, we can take some pride in the outcome, at least, of a strange episode involving the United States one hundred years ago. A treaty of annexation to the United States was signed in 1869 but was rejected in the Senate by an opposition led by the Chairman of the Foreign Relations Committee. We assumed a different posture when an executive agreement in 1905 authorized this country to act as customs receiver to avert threatened interventions from European states. Fiscal improvement did not bring political order, and for eight years, from 1916 to 1924, the country was occupied by United States Marines. The customs receivership was finally terminated in 1941 by a treaty in which this country relinquished any right to intervene on its own initiative. The final sequence of events, culminating in President Johnson's order, began with the assassination May 30, 1961, of Generalissimo Rafael Leonidas Trujillo. After the dictator's death, his figurehead President, Joaquin Balaguer, remained in office for a time with the support of Trujillo's son, Ramfis, who controlled the military forces. By January, 1962, departure of most of the old Trujillo gang made it possible for a seven-man council of state under the leadership of its President, Rafael Bonnelly, to take control and prepare for the first free election in thirty-eight years. Juan Bosch won an overwhelming victory but within seven months, on September 25, 1963, was deposed by the military on the grounds he was too lenient toward Communists—and a three-man civilian junta took over. Increasing factional unrest involving, among other factors, an attempt to restore Bosch to the Presidency which his followers considered his constitutional right, resulted in overthrow of the Triumvirate in civil war which erupted once again April 24, 1965.

The Dominican problem was not brand new to President Johnson when the first cable arrived that Wednesday afternoon. As Vice-President he had been the official United States representative at the inauguration of Bosch, February 27, 1963, and three weeks after becoming President he had recognized the Triumvirate government of Donald Reid Cabral which succeeded the overthrown Bosch.[43] By the preceding Friday, April 23, 1965, a confusion of conspiracies within the Republic persuaded our State Department to call Ambassador W. Tapley Bennett home for consultation. Chaos in Santo Domingo gave concern in Washington, and on Sunday, the day after the military rising, a naval task force was ordered to a position off shore to be available to evacuate American nationals. Soon after noon Monday, Secretary Dean Rusk, Under Secretary George Ball, Under Secretary Thomas C. Mann, Assistant Secretary Jack H. Vaughn and Ambassador W. Tapley Bennett met with President Johnson. The Ambassador was told to return to his post immediately and to keep the President informed; the Department people directed the Embassy to begin evacuation of civilians the following morning. On Tuesday a cable from Washington outlined United States policy objectives: a restoration of law and order, protection of American lives, prevention of a Communist takeover. In Santo Domingo evacuation began, Ambassador Bennett returned, and principal leaders of the Bosch group went into asylum. In New York the *Times* announced: "the military-civilian revolt collapsed today."[44]

The announcement was premature. By Wednesday our Embassy in Santo Domingo was aware of increasing Castro-Communist influence among the "rebels," a general deterioration of the "loyalist" military position and increasing bloodshed in the city. Ambassador Bennett reported, in the first of three cables that day, the belief of a newly-formed "loyalist" military junta, that United States lives could not be protected and passed along their oral request that Marines be landed. This information and the Ambassador's opinion that troops were not then required was given the President during his Vietnam meeting with Rusk and McNamara. Within an hour the second cable reported worsening conditions and recommended that Marines be landed. Almost immediately thereafter, in a third cable, the Ambassador reported that he had asked the naval commander to provide helicopter evacuation and a platoon of Marines to protect the Embassy. He also suggested the Government consider whether larger armed intervention might be required to prevent "another Cuba." By six o'clock the President had ordered a landing; about seven o'clock he met with congressional leaders and at eight-forty read a statement on a television broadcast. A final cable later that night, in response to a call from Under Secretary Mann, contained a written statement from the military junta leader explaining that in his earlier written request for United States military assistance he had neglected to state that in his opinion American lives were in danger and that he could not protect them.[45]

The original force of Marines from the off shore fleet was augmented

Thursday night by about two thousand airborne troops from the United States. There had been frequent telephone communication between Washington and the Embassy, but there is no evidence that formal meetings preceded this second landing nor that it represented anything more than a realization that continued uncertainty in Santo Domingo required a more substantial commitment of military forces if our two basic aims were to be achieved: protection of American lives and prevention of a procommunist government.

Our purpose does not require detailing subsequent events in the Dominican Republic other than to note that Mr. Johnson sent two special presidential missions to work toward a temporary government acceptable to all parties; the Organization of American States sent both a three-man peace mission and inter-American military forces to replace United States troops; and a provisional government was created August 13, 1965. On June 1, 1966, in the third presidential election of this century, ex-President Balaguer won over ex-President Bosch.

Three important questions concerning the United States' Dominican policy, not central to our inquiry, should be mentioned briefly: Was our policy position candidly set out from the beginning? Was the intervention justified under international law? And was the policy "right"? Doubt about credibility grew out of the fact that the President's statements of April 28, April 30, and May 1 declared that our forces were "engaged in protecting human life" and in "establishing a neutral zone of refuge." Only on May 2 was it made clear, as it had been clear to the government from the beginning, that our intervention had a second goal as well: "to help prevent another Communist state in this hemisphere."[46] The question under international law on which there were differing opinions cannot be adequately covered here;[47] nor can we go into the more involved and controversial matter of the "rightness," in a policy sense, of the government's handling of the entire episode.[48]

To return to our basic question—how was the decision made—it seems that a determination to send troops was made by the President Wednesday afternoon, April 28, in the company of his closest security advisers: Rusk, McNamara and Bundy. True, several State Department officials, Under Secretary Ball, Under Secretary Mann, Assistant Secretary Vaughn, plus Rusk and Ambassador Bennett joined the President on Monday before the decision, and a large group, including General Earle G. Wheeler, Chairman of the Joint Chiefs of Staff and Vice Admiral William F. Raborn, Director of the Central Intelligence Agency, met in the Cabinet Room on Friday after the decision, but the evidence available indicates that the decision process did not spread beyond the small group.

President Johnson has described the scene when the second, and highest priority, cable arrived: "On Wednesday afternoon there was no longer any choice for the man who is your President: I was sitting in my little office . . . with Secretary Rusk, Secretary McNamara and Mr. Bundy. . . . At 5:15 . . . we received a cable that was labeled 'critic' . . . The cable reported the situation was completely out of control and . . . that only an immediate landing of American forces could safeguard and protect the lives of thousands. . . . Ambassador Bennett urged your President to order an immediate landing. In this situation hesitation and vacillation could mean death for many of our people . . . I thought that we could not and we did not hesitate."[49]

How did the Dominican decision compare with Korea, Lebanon and Cuba, 1962? Did the President make use of his oldest staff group, the Cabinet; or the newer agencies within the Executive Office, the White House Office and the National Security Council in particular? The Cabinet did not meet during the crisis. With the exception of Bundy, White House assistants apparently were not consulted. The National Security Council did not function as a body. Granted that President, Secretary of State, Secretary of Defense and Presidential Assistant for National Security Affairs might be considered a subcommittee of the Council, two of the five statutory members, the Vice-President and the Director, Office of Emergency Planning, were not importantly involved, if at all. Truman had a part in creating the Council and believed it should play a policy role; under Eisenhower it enjoyed higher status and accelerated activity; Kennedy had less enthusiasm for formal bodies but made use of an expanded Council Group, the Executive Committee. Even so, in none of the four security episodes did the Council function *qua* council in the decision process, and two members, Vice-President and Director, were consistently conspicuous by their absence.

CONCLUSION

Not many years ago some students of the Presidency believed that its problems of organization and management were well on the way to solution. For example, creation of the Executive Office, in the eyes of one expert, had brought into being not merely a twentieth century institution but one suitable for all centuries to come.[50] Another was convinced that the sophistication of staff arrangements and operations under Eisenhower represented the fulfillment of administrative theory.[51] But alongside these expressions of satisfaction is the paradoxical thought that while the presidential office is from one view adequately ordered, from another it may be seen as irrelevant in terms of policy making. Our question has been whether staff machinery presently in place has figured importantly in the making of security decisions. A negative answer would lead to the more difficult query: is the notion of "policy machinery" outdated, or will further tinkering with staff arrangements suffice to protect the legitimate interest all have in the making of "correct" policy decisions?

Though practices in the utilization of staff have varied, all four of the modern Presidents have been convinced, as Kennedy expressed it, that "no matter how many advisers you have . . . the President must finally choose."[52] It is illustrative that Johnson, in the midst of two hundred or more people in the White House and nearly fifteen hundred in the Executive Office agencies, not only wishes to control the executive decision process but also insists upon being "in on" most individual decisions. The American system seems to call for control of decision-making by the President himself, but in view of the mounting strains of the office and the possibly catastrophic consequences of mistake, should and can he be helped? Certainly he does not require a larger personal staff nor more institutional assistants, as the Brownlow Report urged in 1936. What he needs beyond these, as every President since Washington has needed, is the counsel of wise and independent men. Of course ultimate power should not go to his assistants, but when necessary, "adverse advice should be presented to a President in the most forthright terms right up to the end."[53]

In the absence of public disaster it is idle to talk of fundamental change in the structure of government, whether taking the form of a legislative cabinet, a plural Presidency, or a parliamentary system. But within the limits of the possible could new life be given the National Security Council? It was organized in 1947 as the main organ at the summit of government to advise the President with respect to the integration of domestic, foreign and military policies relating to the national security. It has not functioned as then anticipated. No president, since and including Truman, has felt any compulsion to collaborate closely with the council in making security decisions. Each President has consulted with whom he wished. Up to a point this is as it should be and must be. But might it not be helpful to add two or three *public* members—perhaps drawn from the academic community—to the Council and regularize its meetings? Observing defects in the institutionalized Presidency of the past quarter century, the answer is not a retreat to an earlier personalized Presidency.

A study of presidential staff and national security policy may conclude that the present staff as measured by accepted principles of administration is adequate, though in terms of impact on policy rather unimportant. The tendency of modern Presidents to make pragmatic, *ad hoc* responses to exploding crises without great reliance on formal bodies or precedent has emphasized the accident of personality in the office. Without foregoing the strengths of flexibility and personality, the President needs—and the public safety requires—the help of persons who are known to the law, are competent on policy questions and to whom he must listen. Such advisers might become available in a slightly recast National Security Council.

CHAPTER X

NATIONAL POLICY MACHINERY AND FOREIGN POLICY-MAKING IN THE UNITED STATES

By Edward R. Padgett*

One of the most significant aspects of evaluation of American foreign policy since World War II is that of the increasing attention given to the making and conduct of policy as contrasted with the traditional emphasis upon the substance of policy. How policy is made has, at long last, been recognized as being as significant as policy itself. In an increasingly bureaucratized world, policy machinery, while it cannot assure good policy, may improve the chances that it will be effective.

The renewed emphasis upon the machinery of the policy process is due to several factors: 1) the scholarly works of McCamy, MacMahon, Plischke, and London, to name only a few, have produced over a period of years an awakened interest in the conduct of policy and responsible inquiry into the question of how foreign policy is made; 2) the significant work of the Jackson subcommittee of the Senate Committee on Government Operations; and 3) the efforts of Snyder, Robinson, Sapin, Argyris, and Westerfield to investigate the decision-making process as applied to the conduct of foreign policy.

Developments of the post-World War II era have been characterized by a sustained growth in foreign policy commitments of the United States and by an attendant increase in machinery required to support such obligations. This has meant not only growth in the Department of State and in the Department of Defense, but in related government

---

*Professor of Political Science, University of Cincinnati, and an associate of Professor Vinacke.

agencies which share the varied responsibilities of the foreign policy process.

With regard to the three factors mentioned above, it is mandatory that the fact be recognized that the United States has had to create, during a period in which it assumed world leadership, means of formulating and executing policies which simply did not exist before 1940. The intricacies of government have been characterized by a dramatic change from a simplified structure, which permitted leisurely decisional processes, to one in which decision-making must cope with the demands of complex and very sophisticated problems which necessitate rather elaborate mechanisms and techniques in order to produce viable policy decisions.

The efforts of McCamy, MacMahon, Plischke and others have compelled us to re-evaluate the institutional framework within which the bureaucracy of the foreign policy machinery weighs alternatives and makes hard choices in determining policy. In the United States, the executive and legislative branches of government have been content all too often to engage in tinkering and in *ad hoc* changes which may or may not have produced the anticipated results. A foreign policy mechanism, such as the Department of State, originating in a milieu of housekeeping functions and of the demands of nominal communication with overseas field representatives, has become a large, if not sprawling, organizational force in which vital questions of control, coordination, delegation, and implementation have become of paramount importance. New fields of emphasis, the intelligence community, forward planning, scientific measurement and analysis of decisional alternatives, and methods of control of programmatic responsibilities such as personnel and budgeting, have all compelled our government to attempt to create new or reorganized organizational responses to major challenges.

Since 1947, the National Security Council alone, serving the function of an interdepartmental coordinating committee, has given rise to very real questions with regard to means of organization for effective production of policy. The Jackson subcommittee, while by no means without faults and limitations, has for the first time in recent decades produced a detailed and relevant re-evaluation of the requirements of a viable policy machinery, in addition to an assessment of the state of present organizational structure.

Social scientists in academic life, in research organizations which are sponsored by government (so-called "think tanks") and in government itself, have begun to produce a body of literature and policy proposals which clearly delineate major propositions and problems with regard to means whereby foreign policy can better serve the national interest.

Such propositions and techniques as bipartisanship in foreign policy formulation, the nature of intelligence and its use by the intelligence community, the creation of a defense establishment, and the utilization of behavioralism and systems analysis as problem-solving devices, especially in the area of the budgetary process, have all aided immeasurably in the creation of our present policy machinery.

One of the purposes of this essay will be that of specifying the broad outlines of these developments in the following manner: 1) to suggest in the context of an overview the components of the growth of the policy machine since World War II; 2) to evaluate the role of the Jackson subcommittee and its impact upon systematic analysis of national policy machinery; 3) to deal with several attempts to subject the conduct of foreign policy and decision-making in foreign affairs to rigorous evaluation; and last, 4) to analyse the implications of these efforts in terms of organization theory and behavior as they relate to foreign policy.

I

Any overview of the recent postwar decades of American foreign policy and the resultant growth of national policy machinery must at the outset make the assertion that foreign and domestic policy are unalterably interrelated. In effect, the foreign policy apparatus has become the focal point of our bureaucracy.

The year 1947, which produced the National Security Council, a Central Intelligence Agency and the Department of Defense, is in fact the take-off point for the modern world. The simplistic designs of the past were replaced by the new world of interdepartmental committees, intra-agency committees, planning boards and/or councils, *ad hoc* study groups, and elaborate plans for reorganization of the policy machinery.

The presidency became, largely as a result of wartime experience, the vital center of our governmental system. Foreign policy and its conduct became a cooperative venture in which the executive branch and Congress were to play, at least until the end of the 1950's, under the guise of bipartisanship roles of mutual trust and cooperation.

Standard components of postwar policy were large-scale programs which were implemented by treaties and executive agreements, based upon those qualities which in the apt phrase of Dean Acheson were secreted in the qualities of men. Individual presidents, dependent upon their conception of presidential style, were to evolve patterns of accommodation to organizational necessities. The National Security Council could, at the option of the chief executive, run the gamut from the over-institutionalization of the Eisenhower period to the less formal task force approach of the Kennedy era. Planning Boards and Operations Coordinating Boards could be utilized in attempts to produce decisions which would serve the national interest, even though many would suggest that they represented a lowest common denominator effort.

The policy machine as it developed had one major characteristic, that of the introduction of the layering process as Dean Rusk has termed it. Organizational change has produced a tendency to add at all levels of the hierarchy new layers in the organizational structure. One of the most difficult tasks of the postwar years has been that of producing effective decision-making at all levels of the administrative structure.

This tendency has resulted in what Robert Lovett has called the "foul-up factor." This is essentially the so-called merry-go-round of concurrences which has permitted various agencies to stake out a claim to the right of participation in—or at least the exercise of the right of veto over—any foreign policy decisions which might affect the operational responsibilities of the agency involved.

A clear distinction as to which of those agencies are advisory and which are operational has really not been made. Examples of this would be the role of the intelligence community and the basic functions of the Department of State. The assertion may be made cautiously that most organizations in the policy machinery have fulfilled a dual advisory and operational function.

Our leading officials have been compelled to bear a level of responsibility beyond human capacity. The planning function, particularly that of long-range planning, has been submerged by the demands of day-to-day or *ad hoc* operational requirements. Much, perhaps too much, has been said about the need for officials to have the opportunity to think and to isolate themselves from day-to-day operations in order that they may acquire perspective and balance.

The decision-making process is basically that of choosing among viable alternatives to momentous questions. All of the relevant data, the dependent and independent variables, and last the politically real facets of the problem must be given due weight. Roger Hilsman has clearly demonstrated in his writings the impact of politics upon foreign policy decision-making.[1]

The process of making foreign policy has been multilateralized, and in actuality the counter claims of the executive and legislative branches must be given due consideration. Decision-making is situational in nature, and all decisions are comprised of lower-level actions taken in different parts of the policy machine. Public administration specialists have suggested that, in many instances, subordinates actually structure the alternatives of choice which face superiors. The position paper, originating normally at lower levels in the hierarchy, can condition the frame of reference within which major policy alternatives are discussed and refined.

The policy process has produced such outstanding successes as the formulation of the Marshall Plan, which can be contrasted with the relative failures of the magnitude of the Bay of Pigs and the European Defense Community. On balance, the growth of the policy machine since 1945 has been characterized by the many known aspects of the bureaucratization of government and of the social order.

Government has seen in most areas the growth of an overlapping, highly intricate system of agencies, boards, committees and other organizational forms which appear to inhibit as often as they further the production of effective policy. This condition is a fact of modern administrative life. Decision-making has been multilateralized, and responsibility has been shared and fragmented.

II

Without any doubt, the most significant achievement in the analysis of National Policy Machinery has been that of the work and functions of the Jackson subcommittee of the Senate Committee on Government Operations. The myriad details of its work have been recounted elsewhere.[2] However, the important work of the subcommittee deserves some detailed analysis and criticism at this point.

The Jackson subcommittee, which began its work in 1959, has produced extremely valuable hearings, studies, and staff reports and recommendations. It can be given a large part of the credit for the philosophy of the task force approach to policy machinery of the Kennedy administration. Fortunately, it viewed its work as transcending the emotions of partisan politics or the influence of any particular national administration. Through the successive changes in its title—from national policy machinery to national security staffing and operations, to the present national security and international operations nomenclature—it has preserved its ability to direct its attention to major issues of the policy process and the administration of foreign policy. Its printed materials are too widely known in the academic community and to the informed public to have to be recounted here.

Senator Jackson, an important and effective member of the U.S. Senate, has been able to maintain an effective staff and to conduct the business of the subcommittee in a manner which sets a standard of excellence unmatched by almost any other subcommittee of Congress.

Basically, the subcommittee has been able to hear testimony from some of the most significant practitioners of the art of government, leading figures in the academic world, military leaders, and responsible social scientists. Its own reports and recommendations have been relatively wellbalanced and have only occasionally taken positions that were less than fully objective. Recently, its hearings and reports on planning-programming-budgeting systems (PPBS) have begun with an almost preconceived bias; this has produced some comment questioning what the subcommittee actually hopes to achieve.

The Jackson subcommittee has, on balance, recommended that a clear concept of our national interests be formed and that this be coupled with a recognition that radical additions to our policy machinery are unnecessary and undesirable. Quite correctly, the group has directed its attention to major administrative issues, such as those of coordination and control at all levels of government, the role and function of the major agencies of government, and the need for effective staffing and fiscal planning of agencies which play a role in the foreign policy process. The problems of overstaffing and the failure to produce effective leadership were carefully detailed.

The National Security Council was viewed as an advisory body which could aid in the determination of the "great choices" of policy formulation and in the avoidance of extreme institutionalization. The Departments of State and of Defense were viewed as needing improvement in the nature of their contributions to policy-making, and the Bureau of the Budget was assessed in light of its fulfilling an effective role in the policy process subject to presidential control. The important suggestion was also made that Congress put its own house in order so that it might deal with national security problems as a whole and successfully respond to requirements presented to it by the chief executive.

The nature of control and coordination at the Embassy level and within the infrastructure of policy-making agencies was delineated. The Department of State was deemed to be a problem in coordination, and a need to clarify the role of the Secretary was recognized as existing on an agency, interagency and field office level. Essentially, the role of the Ambassador and of the Country Team was viewed as being equally crucial. It was conceded that administrative problems must be given high priority in any evaluation of the needs of policy machinery.

More recently, the Jackson subcommittee has directed its attention to the limits upon American power and influence in a complex and modern world, coupled with a careful analysis of our alliance policy. These efforts have concentrated upon a review of shared problems with the alliance systems to which we are committed and of the relationship of fiscal policy to overall policy-making.

Essentially, the subcommittee has obtained expressions of the views of noted and experienced public officials which produced a body of so-called administrative wisdom. As Professor James Robinson has pointed out, the subcommittee, along with other studies made of Congress by national commissions, has tended to accept such expressions of wisdom as the major source of valuable knowledge about the political process. The assertion may be made that the work of scholars in public administration and organization theory has been largely ignored.[3]

Here, in essence, the dilemma of the Jackson subcommittee is revealed: its work has received most favorable attention from various quarters, yet several basic questions remain. First, has the subcommittee produced a frame of reference, much less a means, whereby effective improvement of the policy machinery can occur? Second, what conceptualization of a level of analysis has been produced? Or put somewhat differently, what has been learned with regard to our knowledge of organizations?

What does the term national policy machinery really mean or imply? Are we concerned with units such as councils, committees, and departments or other agencies which share in the creation of policy? Has the subcommittee been able to make explicit a set of assumptions which permit systematic evaluation of phenomena?

In any political system such as ours, the question can be asked: where are decisions made, by whom, and under which conditions? Which common characteristics of bureaucracy, decision-making, procedures, and policy formulation are measurable? Hopefully, the recurrence of decisional activities and of administrative behavioral patterns could be subjected to rigorous analysis. If the still rather loosely defined national policy machinery is to be carefully analyzed, a control group must be determined.

Is it not a rather basic premise in the United States that a chief executive can organize the multiple units of policy machinery, within limits, as he sees fit? Therefore, are we concerning ourselves with a problem of organizational issues or a matter of executive choice, or both?

On balance, the problem of policy machinery and its relationship to the work of the Jackson subcommittee has, so far, produced a general and somewhat simplified re-emphasis of such standard aspects of administrative life as those of coordination, control, delegation of authority, and of the myriad phases of decision-making. The studies of the subcommittee have perhaps evaluated such problems without really offering a series of concepts which could enable government to reform or reorganize its structure in order to remedy certain deficiencies, or to achieve specified organizational goals.

One such problem would be that of an analysis of the committee as an organizational form or type. How could a definition and an evaluation of the utility of a committee be made systematically? Why do committees grow in number and in authority in organizations? Is it really worthwhile to have, as in a committee, a shared type of responsibility built in as a component of modern organization?

Committees occur in organizations in constant variation and with little real duplication of membership and of tasks. When a chief executive can and does enlarge or contract the size and scope of certain committees at will, those whose behavior is to be analyzed vary in number, and truly reproducible situations become quite rare.

Systematic evaluation of administrative machinery, furthermore, must be genuinely comparable among organizational units of similar authority and responsibility. In addition, hierarchical relationships would have to be evaluated in terms of lateral as well as vertical applicability.

The work of the Jackson subcommittee has been in actuality the beginning of a major task. What is needed is the commencement of efforts to produce rigorous, scientific evaluation of national policy machinery.

III

Recent efforts have produced some noteworthy attempts to begin the task of systematic evaluation of administrative phenomena. It would be most appropriate at this point to note that there are two rather basic underpinnings for any attempt to evaluate administration. One is the rationalist hypothesis, which suggests that mankind in an organizational framework can structure priorities—goals and sub-goals. Sub-goals can serve as a means of implementation and form a basis upon which a nation-state can realize its objectives. Charles Lindblom has suggested that incrementalism, or the art of muddling through, is a more tough-minded and realistic view of how problem-solving is executed.[4]

Incrementalism implies succinctly that organizations can add an increment to what has already been decided. *De novo* and/or zero base decisions are difficult within the framework of organizational reality. Therefore, the options of decision-makers are somewhat limited.

What is needed, of course, is the creation of analytical techniques which will permit an understanding of the methods whereby insights into administrative processes can be gained, and the direction of systematic interdisciplinary research towards a comprehension of the realities of administrative behavior could be begun.

Several examples of modern research can be noted as means toward the realization of these objectives.

Burton Sapin and James McCamy have given us a perspective with regard to basic issues. Sapin has recognized the development of reciprocal understanding of new relationships such as those of Department of State and Department of Defense interaction. There has been an awareness on "both sides of the river" of common problems. These new patterns may or may not survive the departure of those officials who have done so much to bring about this new attitude towards working habits and perspective.[5]

McCamy has recently made an effort to delineate several approaches which seem quite appropriate: 1) foreign relations, although they enter into every agency of government, will be the full-time concern of only a few; 2) while questions of foreign affairs have come to dominate our behavior and that of other advanced nations, nations still tend to emphasize internal concerns as though they existed alone; 3) in most developed nations the military will be managed separately from civilian agencies; 4) the chief executive or head of government will be held responsible for events, as far as any person is held responsible; 5) because of being held responsible, these individuals will wish to control personally the main decisions of government; 6) coordination in the conduct of foreign affairs has to come from these individuals; and 7) the president or head of government, because of obvious limitations, cannot handle his job alone.[6]

Such assumptions clearly spell out broad guidelines to the conduct of foreign policy. Recent examples of more particularistic research tend to amplify problems of national policy machinery.

In 1966, hearings held by the Committee on Foreign Relations of the U.S. Senate related the behavior of nation-states to assumptions of the discipline of psychology. Nations were viewed as reflecting the thoughts and behavior which are determined by beliefs and expectations. The "self-fulfilling prophecy" was defined as "psycho-logic" based upon a judgment of the motives of another nation. The international arms race was described as a classic example of this. Ideology was seen to be a part of the reality world of any group. The genuine issues of our time were viewed as problems of reducing antagonisms which could be ameliorated by mutual understanding.[7]

A similarly oriented psychological evaluation of a sample of foreign service and Department of State personnel by Professor Argyris has produced some rather fascinating conclusions, tentative as they may be, that the behavioral patterns of employees are those of extreme caution, not "making waves," and an almost overwhelming deference to the opinions of superiors. The "happy ship" is viewed as highly esteemed, while those who do not work towards a nebulous consensus are viewed with either suspicion or overt distrust. A life-style, so conceived, raises the almost inevitable question as to how these individuals can effectively cope with the exigencies of short-and long-run policy-making.[8]

Certainly a world of sustained tensions can almost be made an *a priori* assumption. Those who conduct foreign policy cannot be merely "happy ship" people. They must realize, as the late President Kennedy often suggested, that any organization in which all is serene is an organization which is headed for deep trouble.

Without doubt, one of the most significant innovations of modern times has been that of the introduction of planning-programming-budgeting systems in the Department of Defense. An outgrowth of the work of Charles Hitch at the Rand Corporation, this system became the central focus of the revitalization of the Department of Defense. Since 1965, in accordance with Bureau of the Budget Bulletin 66-3, as replaced by Bulletins 68-2, and 68-9, PPBS has become a government-wide effort to deal with decisional choices in the budgetary process.[9]

Planning-programming-budgeting systems were in effect the application of systems analysis to budgetary phenomena. Systematic budgeting in the United States has been a rather recent development, dating from the Budget and Accounting Act of 1921. Long ago, the late professor V. O. Key, perhaps the most renowned political scientist of our time, posited the question with regard to budgeting—"Why spend X\$ for A instead of B?" Professor Aaron Wildavsky, who has applied rigorous analytic methodology to the budgetary process in recent years, has said in effect that Key's question is impossible to answer. Wildavsky has demonstrated that budgeting is basically incremental.[10]

Systems analysis, as applied to budgeting, has permitted the Department of Defense—and since 1965, on a beginning basis the entire Federal government—to structure priorities, to weigh alternatives, and to analyse the cost-benefits of specific programs of government. Unfortunately, as is too often the case in the United States, serious assumptions become fads—PPBS is the new one at most levels of government. Without question, the critics of PPBS, including Professor Wildavsky, are quite correct when they suggest that PPBS is an intellectual endeavor which has "captured" the Department of Defense and other agencies.[11] What is feasible with regard to weapons systems may or may not be suited to the requirements of line departments, state agencies, and local government. Cost-benefit analysis has proved itself to be of great utility under certain circumstances, but it must be empirically tested before sweeping generalizations can be made about its universal applicability. Certainly the major contribution of Wildavsky has been that of stressing the political aspects of the budgetary process. PPBS or any other system of analysis exists and functions in a political context.

The relevance of politics to decision-making has been reaffirmed by Roger Hilsman, who views the political process from the vantage point of being both an operating official and an academic, as one in which power and politics are intertwined.[12] Hilsman concurs in the opinion of the Jackson subcommittee that reorganizing the government will not solve the problems of national security policy. Assigning power to certain line departments does not mean that such power will be used. He further sees effective foreign policy as depending upon a capacity to predict events—such predicting to be based upon weighing and identifying factors which make clear the options of different situations as they relate to choices amongst alternatives.[13]

Unhappily, the changes which have taken place in the structure of government do not give us empirical evidence of much other than *ad hoc* incremental change. In September, 1966, the Department of State introduced a management program which had high hopes of enabling the agency to utilize systems analysis as a means of returning responsibility to operating officials. What was done was, in part, an introduction of new layers in the department—The Senior Interdepartmental Group and The Interdepartmental Regional Group—which would assist the Secretary of State and the Assistant Secretaries, respectively, in the production of viable policy proposals.[14] Benjamin Welles of the *New York Times* has noted recently the difficulties encountered by Under Secretary of State Katzenbach in executing major changes in the bureaucracy of the department. Welles views the Senior Interdepartmental Group as being moribund because of a lack of clearance with

Secretary Rusk and the failure of the group to move into high gear. The Nixon administration appears to be attempting to address itself to rather similar problems—those of the role of the National Security Council, the primacy of the Secretary of State, restructuring of the Department of Defense, the functions of Henry A. Kissinger as a top presidential aide, and the ever-present alternatives of a high degree of institutionalization of administrative structure as opposed to the more informal task force approach.[15] Once again, it is made clear that organizational change alone cannot produce anticipated results without commitment by those involved to fundamental change in operational activities. The Department of State is only now commencing the kinds of changes which began in the Department of Defense in the early 1960's.

IV

On balance, the most important implications of the existence of national policy machinery, and its relationships to the policy process, are those of the necessity of joining the new areas of knowledge in organization theory with the practices of the bureaucracy.

The period since World War II has been one of an exciting growth of knowledge and theory in what is called behavioralism. Behavioralism has been based upon a desire to go beyond a purely normative approach to administrative phenomena to an empirically oriented evaluation of data. Two categories of analysis have been productive—those of decison-making and systems analysis.

Herbert Simon has contributed the classic concept of the relevance of rational decision-making as an hypothesis of administration, one which permeates administrative organization. His pioneering classifications of decisions as programmed and nonprogrammed have given us a means of dealing with recurring and nonrecurring issues. Administrative man does indeed behave in an atmosphere in which there is a Gresham's Law of decision-making as routine decisions tend to drive innovative decisions from the marketplace.[16] Human beings in organization tend to prefer short-run issues to long-run problems. The intricacies of the foreign policy process make mandatory the need to plan and to predict. Careful analysis must take account of significant variables, both dependent and independent. The national policy machinery of the United States is an extremely involved sequence of interrelated councils, boards, commissions and agencies. The function of coordination and control must emanate from the office of the president and the presidency. Over a long period of years, innumerable reports —those of the two Hoover Commissions, the Wriston Report, and the Herter Committee—have said again and again that our foreign affairs apparatus must attract the best qualified people and must be so designed that it may function with demonstrated competence.

While no one can dispute this, the essential question remains as to how it can be done. Social scientists and those concerned with the behavioral aspects of administrative life have given us possibilities of systematically solving such problems. As Professor Robinson and others have suggested, analysis of policy machinery must give due consideration to recent social science efforts.[17]

As organizational life becomes increasingly complex, those in positions of responsibility must bring within the governmental system such techniques as give reasonable promise of success and improvement. The two best examples of recent decades are planning-programming-budgeting systems and developmental personnel.

Many social scientists have borrowed from the discipline of economics the concepts of macro and micro organizational levels.[18] The efforts of small-group analysis, while extremely productive in their own right, have not really aided us in dealing with large-scale organization. We in the United States have entered an era of existence in large organizational entities. Productive analysis of human relationships in such organizations is basically group analysis, which must draw heavily upon psychology and sociology. Human beings exist and work in an organizational framework. Administrative rationality is based upon those forms of behavior which are sanctioned and tolerated in group situations.

Organizations tend to shy away from penetrating evaluation of group needs. Consensus and the lowest common denominator approach have often replaced innovative action. Decision-making is basically the act of deciding to pursue a course of action. The policy-maker is harried by multiple considerations—the pressures of time and situation which lead to *ad hoc* decisional responses.

Organization theory has produced or attempted to produce paradigms which at least offer a means of solving basic problems. It is perhaps trite but true to suggest that we require much additional research. Current efforts in the study of decision-making and in systems analysis must be increased. Present efforts in government, at all levels, must be fully analyzed and evaluated. Efforts to implement planning-programming-budgeting systems and developmental personnel must be scrutinized so as to attempt to isolate and study pertinent observable data.

The central issue is that of how people behave in organizations when they make decisions. How do systems really function? Can rational administrative man engage in problem-solving? How can the awful choices among viable alternatives be made? How can the conduct of foreign policy make allowances for innumerable variables and political realities?

In our time, several means or techniques have been developed which show promise and/or effectiveness. The most durable has been that of the case study. American public administration has made the case study a basic tool of research. Case studies must be addressed to important issues of administration. As Herbert Kaufman has suggested, cases could be arranged in clusters so that certain propositions of administration could be verified or rejected. The case study is a means of reproducing real life, and we must move on from the assumption that people do interact in administrative situations. How do they interact, under which circumstances, and why?

Case study could be directed towards the careful analysis of specified administrative situations and problems. In most case studies, role players make decisions within a situational framework. Such studies if replicable could lead us to the making of significant generalizations about administrative life.

Decision-making theory must be related to the realities of both formal and informal organization. We need to know much more about motivation, group behavior, the nature of group goals, and the many implications of politics upon bureaucratic activity.

The newer approaches to administrative analysis, such as developmental personnel and planning-programming-budgeting systems, must be evaluated in terms of their applicability to varied administrative phenomena. At the same time, it must never be forgotten that we are dealing with the actions of fallible human beings, who act not only in rational ways, but who also behave in non-rational ones. Administrative man, a creature who would respond to organizational stimuli in standard responses, is by no means a fully developed concept.

The basic problems would appear to be the following:

1) Scientific evaluation of administrative phenomena would be heavily dependent upon the analysis of replicable situations. In such agencies as the National Security Council, inter-and intra-departmental committees, the situational nature of such meetings is in a state of constant change or flux. Those who call such meetings may alter the attendance of those present at will. Relatively similar decisions will tend to be made by widely differing groups of people.

2) Variables, both dependent and independent, will be ex-

tremely difficult to control. Foreign policy and its problems are not merely internally controlled. Other nation-states will, of course, exert an external influence. Political power and the alternatives of policy resultant from it are extremely complicated.

3) Politics, internal and external, will significantly influence the activities of decision-makers. An individual human being can deal in one day only with a certain small number of problems. Much that he does will be of an *ad hoc* nature. However, comprehensive planning could help avoid too many *de novo* situations.

4) Planning must become an integral part of the administrative process. Systems analysis appears to offer workable means of forward planning. Many so-called planning devices, the Policy Planning Council of the Department of State for example, do not really fulfill a planning function. Both forward and contingency planning appear to be organizational necessities.

5) The efficacy of prediction would tend to become increasingly important. Scientific method would appear to have given us feasible means to resolve human problems.

6) Our efforts to resolve policy problems must be based upon a comprehension of both value and factual elements. No responsible social scientist is advocating an irresponsible dependence upon purely mechanistic assumptions. Methodology is a means to an end. The mass of factual data related to almost any conceivable problem requires systematic analysis.

7) Any analysis of policy machinery, no matter how rigorous, must produce tentative solutions which are clearly related to the basic determinants of policy. Policy machinery is also a means to an end. Its purpose is to create a basis upon which effective policy can be formulated.

8) A response to a need for the creation of a more viable policy machinery must endeavor to produce a means of establishing varied techniques which will innovate and reshape the old ways of conducting public affairs. We cannot afford tinkering and limited efforts to achieve coordination, control, and work flow. An affluent society must stop talking about the need for qualified people and put forth an atmosphere in which such individuals will seek out positions in the public service.

In the United States, the capabilities of our leaders will in large part determine the level of qualifications of those who staff the policy machinery. The issues of public policy call for an effort based upon utilization of our total resources. Those in government must seek out the expertise of academics, professionals, and technical experts. More reports such as that by Professor Argyris, with regard to the Department of State, are needed. Social science is a means of self-evaluation and not a destructive force.

In past centuries, the United States could afford leisurely and haphazard procedures, based upon trial and error. Modern technology has denied us such luxuries of time.

National policy machinery must be responsible to the popular will, but technical propositions can often be understood only by those who possess competence in special fields. Those who staff the policy apparatus deal in substantial part with secret or classified information. They have access to data, intelligence collation, and government position papers which define situations and applicable variables.

Administrative life is based upon the ebb and flow of crisis or near-crisis situations. Government has too often appeared to be at the mercy of issues to which so-called crash solutions are offered. Despite the involved work of the bureaucracy, great nations are found to lack specific data and seem to be unable to foresee even the general course of events.

While behavioralism is far from a perfected component of social science, it does offer striking possibilities for the future. No one would anticipate the creation of a perfect mechanism for the production of national policy. In fact, constant change would appear to be the order of the day. However, are we to be left entirely at the mercy of events with no ability to plan, to anticipate contingencies, and to utilize the means of quantitative analysis which exist today? We live in the age of the computer and the benefits of data processing. There are signs that new programs in government are beginning to effectively use such devices.

As the flow of paper and resultant paperwork increases, means must be found to permit operating officials to deal with the tasks which occupy them. We can either solve our problems or be overwhelmed by them.

The work of committees and subcommittees such as the Jackson subcommittee must, of course, continue and be expanded if possible. The utilization by such bodies of the tools of modern social science will greatly enhance the possibility of producing viable suggestions for organizational change. One must note, however, that the executive branch itself has a definite responsibility to further responsible self-evaluation.

Only the future course of events can determine what the effect of planning-programming-budgeting systems and developmental personnel will be. PPBS may produce new means of program effectiveness. New concepts such as that of the executive assignment system in the Civil Service Commission give us hope for the future.

Basically, the creation of a viable national policy machinery depends upon effective and forceful leadership by the president and by his subordinates at all levels. National policy machinery cannot assure effective foreign policy, but it can afford us as a nation the means of solving basic policy problems in a systematic manner. We can meet the challenges of the future by adequate responses, or continue to muddle through, or fail completely. The choice is ours and that of our leaders.

NOTES

CHAPTER I (Burks)

1. Djang, Chu, "The Manchu Empire of China," in Linebarger, ed., *Far Eastern Governments and Politics* (Princeton: 1956), p. 45.

2. Fritz Morstein Marx, ed., *Foreign Governments: The Dynamics of Politics Abroad* (New York: 1949), p. 13.

3. "Research in Comparative Politics," *American Political Science Review* [*APSR*], XLVII, 3 (September, 1953) and, in greater depth, Roy C. Macridis, *The Study of Comparative Government* (New York: 1955).

4. Harold M. Vinacke was quite clear on this point: "The modern period is dated from the time of the movements to bring China, and subsequently Japan and Korea, into an enlarged contact with the world. Thus 'modern' is defined in terms of the Far East [primarily China, Japan, and Korea] rather than of Europe. Institutional changes commenced after that time, . . ." *A History of The Far East in Modern Times* (New York: 4th ed., 1941), "Preface," p. v.

5. George McT. Kahin, Guy J. Pauker, and Lucien W. Pye, "Comparative Politics of Non-Western Countries," *APSR*, XLIX, 4 (December, 1955).

6. Edwin O. Reischauer, "Jū-ku-seiki no Chūgoku to Nihon no kindaika" ["Modernization in nineteenth century China and Japan"], repr. from *Nichibei Forum* (November, 1963).

7. The point was made by this author in another context in "The Politics of Japan's Modernization: The Autonomy of Choice," *Political Development in Modern Japan*, ed. by Robert E. Ward (Princeton: 1968).

8. The late V. O. Key, Jr., regarded by many as a founding father of behavioralism, once stated that "a considerable proportion of the literature commonly classified under the heading of 'political behavior' has no real bearing on politics, or at least that its relevance has not been made apparent." Cited in *Apolitical Politics: A Critique of Behavioralism*, ed. by Charles A. McCoy & John Playford (New York: 1967).

9. Some similarity is apparent throughout villages of South, Southeast, and East Asia with respect to arrangements for, and attitudes toward, the settlement of disputes. "In most cases these have little or nothing to do with a formal judiciary or system of courts." Robert E. Ward, "Village Government in Eastern and Southern Asia: A Symposium," *Far Eastern Quarterly*, XV, 2 (February, 1956), p. 182.

10. Fritz Morstein Marx, *op. cit.*, Chapter 2, "Alternatives of Ideology, 2, the Confucian Tradition," p. 22.

11. *Ibid.*, pp. 21-22.

12. T. R. Jernigan, *China in Law and Commerce* (New York: 1905), p. 33, cited by Harold M. Vinacke, *Modern Constitutional Development in China* (Princeton: 1920), pp. 8-9.

13. Vinacke, *Constitutional Development*, cited, pp. vii-viii.

14. *Ibid.*, pp. 10ff.

15. *American Foreign Relations*, 1908 (Incl. I in No. 1005), p. 192; the italics were added by Professor Vinacke, *Constitutional Development*, cited, pp. 75-76.

16. For a translation of the document, see *China Year Book*, 1916, pp. 437-443.

17. Vinacke, *Constitutional Development*, cited, p. 178. President Yüan turned to an American, Dr. F. J. Goodnow, for legal advice. The latter's memorandum warned that China should not attempt to establish a Republic before laying the foundations for a viable parliament. Later, in 1915, Goodnow wrote: "I have no doubt in saying that the monarchial system is better suited to China than the Republican system. For if China's independence is to be maintained, the government should be constitutional, and in consideration of China's conditions as well as her relations with other powers, it will be easier to form a constitutional government by adopting a monarchy than a Republic." (China) *National Review*, August 28, 1915.

18. Paul M. A. Linebarger, *Government in Republican China* (New York: 1938), p. 195.

19. Chinese texts of all outstanding Chinese constitutions through the Double Five Draft were conveniently contained in Wang Shih-chieh, *Pi-chiao Hsien-fa* (Shanghai: 1937), pp. 699-796.

20. Tso Tao-fen, "A Few Questions Regarding the Constitution," in Ch'uan'min K'ang-chan She [The United Front Club], *Hsien-cheng Yun-tung Lun-wen Hsuan-chi* [A Symposium on the Constitutional Movement] (Chungking: 1940), pp. 1 ff., cited in Paul M. A. Linebarger, *The China of Chiang K'ai-shek: A Political Study* (Boston: 1943), p. 37.

21. Statement of Col. Ch'in Po-k'u, Chungking Office of the 18th [Communist] Army Corps Headquarters, July 29, 1940, to Linebarger, *ibid.*, p. 38.

22. Harold S. Quigley, "Free China," *International Conciliation* No. 359 (April, 1940), Appendix, p. 177.

23. Linebarger, *China of Chiang*, cited, p. 39.

24. The document was early made available in English: *The Constitution of the Republic of China* (New York: Chinese News Service, 1947). In view of subsequent emergency conditions, including the impossibility of carrying out administration and conducting elections on the mainland, the Republic of China (on Taiwan since December 8, 1949) has interpreted the Constitution "broadly." For example, a quorum of the National Assembly (elected on the mainland in 1947) has been defined as a fraction of members able to attend instead of a fraction of the original membership.

25. Ch'ien Tuan-sheng, *The Government and Politics of China* (Cambridge: 1950), p. 329.

26. *Ibid.*, p. 396.

27. From the Common Program to the Constitution of 1954; see Harold M. Vinacke, *Far Eastern Politics in the Postwar Period* (New York: 1956), pp. 139-141.

28. Two of these documents (the Common Program and the Organic Law of the Government), with editor's commentaries, may be conveniently found in Theodore H. E. Chen, ed., *The Chinese Communist Regime: Documents & Commentary* (New York: 1967), D2, D3, pp. 34-51.

29. The thirty-three-man committee included: nine members of the CCP Politburo (Chairman Mao, Chu Teh, Chou En-lai, Lin Po-ch'u, Kao Kang, Ch'en Yun, P'eng Teh-huai, Tung Pi-wu, Liu Shao-ch'i [Kao Kang disappeared from public view before the first meeting]); eight other members of the Central Committee; and two leading CCP bureaucrats. See H. Arthur Steiner, "Constitutionalism in Communist China," *APSR* (March, 1955), repr. in George P. Jan, ed. *Government of Communist China* (San Francisco: 1966).

30. The best account of the adoption process was given in Steiner, *loc. cit.*

31. The text of the Constitution is to be found in Chen, ed., *op. cit.*, D9, pp. 75-92.

32. Liu Shao-ch'i, "On Draft Constitution of People's Republic of China," cited in Franklin W. Houn, "Communist China's New Constitution," *The Western Political Quarterly* (June, 1955), repr. in Jan. ed. *op. cit.*, p. 248.

33. "On Coalition Government," (April 24, 1945), *Selected Works of Mao Tsetung* (Peking: 1952-53), Vol. 3, p. 1061.

34. "On the People's Democratic Dictatorship" (July 1, 1949), repr. in Conrad Brandt, Benjamin Schwartz & John K. Fairbank, *A Documentary History of Chinese Communism* (Cambridge: 1952), p. 455.

35. Steiner, *loc. cit.*, p. 198.

36. The Party Constitution is contained in Chen, ed., *op. cit.*, D15, p. 127.

37. Text of the translated draft was carried in *The New York Times*, January 8, 1969.

38. The laws of Old Japan have been compiled in a volume of less than one thousand pages: Hagino Yoshiyuki, ed., *Nihon kodai hōten* [Legal records of old Japan] (Tokyo: 1892).

39. See Horie Yasuzō, *Meiji ishin to keizai kindaika* [The Meiji restoration and economic modernization] (Tokyo: 1963), p. 27.

40. A recent, brilliant account exhaustively mining original Japanese sources is that of George Akita, *Foundations of Constitutional Government in Modern Japan, 1868-1900* (Cambridge: 1967).

41. Takayanagi Kenzo (Chairman of the postwar Constitution Investigation Commission), "A Century of Innovation: The Development of Japanese Law, 1868-1961," in Arthur Taylor von Mehren, ed., *Law in Japan: The Legal Order in a Changing Society* (Cambridge: 1963), p. 6.

42. Cited by Akita, *op. cit.*, p. 167. A very recent addition to the literature is Dan Fenno Henderson, ed., *The Constitution of Japan: Its First Twenty Years, 1947-67* (Asian Law Series, School of Law, University of Washington, No. 1) (Seattle: University of Washington Press, 1968).

43. Robert E. Ward, "The Commission on the Constitution and Prospects for Constitutional Change in Japan," *The Journal of Asian Studies*, XXIV. 3 (May 1965), p. 402.

44. For various interpretations of the procedure, see: Theodore McNelly, "The Japanese Constitution: Child of the Cold War," *Political Science Quarterly*, LXXIV (June, 1959), pp. 176-195; Robert E. Ward, "The Origins of the Present Japanese Constitution," *The American Political Science Review*, L (Dec., 1956), pp. 980-1010; Justin Williams, "Making the Japanese Constitution: A Further Look," *APSR*, LIX (Sept., 1965), pp. 665-679; and Sato Tatsuo, "The Origin and Development of the Draft Constitution of Japan," *Contemporary Japan*, XXIV (1956), pp. 175-187; 371-387; and, for the official GHQ version, SCAP, Government Section, *The Political Reorientation of Japan* (Washington: 1949), Vol. I, pp. 82-118.

45. Yoshida, Shigeru, "Japan's Decisive Century," 1967 *Britannica Book of the Year* (Chicago: 1967), p. 33.

46. Such a comparison was first and most ably accomplished by Harold S. Quigley, "Japan's Constitutions: 1890- and 1947," *APSR*, XLI (October, 1947), pp. 865-874.

47. For original sources, see John M. Maki, "The Documents of Japan's Commission on the Constitution," *The Journal of Asian Studies*, XXIV, 3 (May, 1965).

48. Harold M. Vinacke, *Far Eastern Politics in the Postwar Period* (New York: 1956), p. 4.

49. See Glenn D. Paige, "Some Implications for Political Science of the Comparative Politics of Korea," in *Report: International Conference on the Problems of Modernization in Asia* (June 28-July 7, 1965) (Seoul: 1966), pp. 388-405.

50. Cited by Shannon McCune, *Korea; Land of the Broken Calm* (Princeton: 1966), p. 135.

CHAPTER II *(Maki)*

1. "United States Initial Postsurrender Policy for Japan" was first officially published in Department of State *Bulletin*, XIII, No. 326 (September 23, 1945), pp. 423-27. It has since been republished many times officially and unofficially. The best single source, brief as it is, on the origins of occupation policy is Hugh Borton, *American Presurrender Planning for Postwar Japan* (Occasional Papers of the East Asian Institute, Columbia University, 1967). Stimson's own account of the policy statement relating to the ending of the war through negotiation is to be found in his (with McGeorge Bundy) *On Active Service In Peace and War* (New York: 1947), pp. 617-27. The most dispassionate (but not cold) and analytical account of the decision to use the atomic bomb against Japan is Herbert Feis's *The Atomic Bomb and the End of World War II* (Princeton: 1966). The Department of State's official documents on both the 1931-41 period and the Potsdam Conference are to be found in *Foreign Relations of the United States: Japan 1931-1941* (2 vols., Washington: 1943) and *Foreign Relations of the United States: Conference of Berlin (Potsdam) 1945* (2 vols., Washington: 1960).

CHAPTER III *(Cady)*

1. George B. de Huszar, *Soviet Power and Policy* (New York: 1954), chapter 19.

2. Secretary Acheson told Premier Attlee by trans-Atlantic phone in mid-December, 1945, that Washington would repudiate the proposed British treaty with Siam unless its terms were softened.

3. Shirley Jenkins, *American Economic Policy Toward the Philippines* (Stanford: 1954), p. 95.

4. Russell H. Fifield, *Southeast Asia in United States Policy* (New York: 1963), pp. 115-119.

5. See Jenkins, *op. cit.*, chapter 12 on "The Bell Mission."

6. John F. Cady, *A History of Modern Burma* (Ithaca: 1958), pp. 541-542.

7. Louis Walinsky, *Economic Development in Burma* (New York: 1962), chapters 6 and 7.

8. See George Kahin, *Nationalism and Revolution in Indonesia* (Ithaca: 1952), pp. 404-406.

9. *The Truth About Vietnam, Report on U.S. Senate Hearings* (San Diego: 1966), p. 187.

10. Russell H. Fifield, *The Diplomacy of Southeast Asia* (New York: 1958), p. 317.

11. George McT. Kahin and John W. Lewis, *The United States in Vietnam* (New York: 1967), pp. 382-383.

12. Fifield, *The Diplomacy of Southeast Asia*, pp. 226-228. The rice deal included other items in addition.

13. Robert G. Scigliano, *South Vietnam: Nation Under Stress* (Boston: 1964), pp. 47-60.

14. Kahin and Lewis, *The United States and Vietnam* (New York: 1967), pp. 111-120.

15. *Ibid.*, Appendix VI, pp. 388-395.

16. See Milton Osborne, *Strategic Hamlets in South Vietnam*, Data Paper 55 (Cornell Southeast Asia Program, 1965).

17. Kahin and Lewis, *op. cit.*, p. 152.

18. J. M. Halpern, *The Lao Elite: A Study of Tradition and Innovation* (Santa Monica: 1960), pp. 85-89.

19. *New York Times*, Jan. 19 and 20, 1967; see also the *Far Eastern Review*, LXII (Oct. 17, 1968), p. 169.

20. Seth S. King, "Sihanouk—Prince Under Pressure," *New York Times Magazine*, Sept. 13, 1964.

CHAPTER IV (*Vandenbosch*)

1. This was the official name of the dependency, but it was generally known as the Dutch East Indies.

2. For a discussion of the continuing influences of the pre-Dutch history, see the interesting article by Harry J. Benda, "Decolonization in Indonesia: the Problem of Continuity and Change," *The American Historical Review*, Vol. LXX, No. 4, July, 1965.

3. For the sake of completeness, it should be noted that of the three major ethnic groups on Java—the Javanese, the Sundanese and the Madurese—the first named alone constituted two-thirds of all the population of the main island and forty-five percent of that of all Indonesia, according to the 1930 census. Sometimes the political problem is seen as that of Javanese domination rather than that of all the people of the island.

4. In an interesting essay Justus M. Van der Kroef suggests that in the course of Indonesian history there are two antithetical themes: the "universalistic," which "attempted to project in varying degrees an identity of interests between the Dutch and Indonesians and was fortified by a variety of ideological rationales, especially those of historic liberalism and later by Neo-Liberal, humanitarian and Marxist views," and the other a "particularistic" trend, which "tended to emphasize socio-economic differentiation and subordination within traditional social structure and economic practice in Indonesia, and sought sanction from religious or secular principles usually designated as conservative." He wisely warns against identifying the two themes merely as "Liberal" and "Conservative." *The Dialectic of Colonial Indonesian History* (Amsterdam, 1963).

5. *Colonial Policy and Practice: A Comparative Study of Burma and Netherlands India* (Cambridge [England]: 1948).

6. In fairness it should be noted that nearly all foreign visitors to the Netherlands Indies were impressed with the material achievements of the Dutch colonial administration. Compared with India the Indonesians enjoyed a high level of welfare. The Indonesians are industrious and had developed a remarkable

culture, but the prodigality of nature in most of Indonesia tends to conceal poverty, whereas the extremes of nature in India accentuated it.

7. Ben Anderson, "The Languages of Indonesian Politics," in *Indonesia* (Ithaca: April 1966), p. 90.

8. Examples of this kind of judgment are not hard to find. Note the following: "Certainly in neither the contemporary official or unofficial accounts of the proclamation of 1848 [claiming the whole of western New Guinea] is there the slightest or even the most indirect of implications that any concern for the welfare of the native populations involved had any bearing on the actions taken." Robert Bone, *The Dynamics of the Western New Guinea (Irian Barat) Problem* (Ithaca: 1958), p. 17. This is not surprising; there was little such sentiment anywhere. At the time—1848—and for some years thereafter, slavery was still legal in the United States.

9. See Harry J. Benda, *The Crescent and the Rising Sun: Indonesian Islam under the Japanese Occupation, 1942-1945* (The Hague and Bandung: 1958).

10. *A French View of the Netherlands Indies* (New York and London, 1940), pp. 105ff. This is the English edition of *La Politique Musulmane et Colonial des Pays Bas* (Paris, 1939).

11. Bousquet suggested to Dutch friends that "the colonial ideal of the Dutch is the transformation of the native into a contented cow, that of the French into a citizen, in other words, a discontented person," *Ibid.*, p. 112.

12. *Staatkundig beleid en bestuurszorg in Nederlandsch-Indie*, 3 vols., (The Hague, 1929-30). Abridged English edition, 2 vols. (The Hague and Chicago: 1931).

13. When an American in the mid-fifties referred to Sukarno as the George Washington of his country, an Indonesian administrator present, to the writer's surprise, took sharp issue with the statement. "No two men are more unlike," he asserted. "Washington was a man of endless, frenzied words, but utterly without interest in or the talent for constructive leadership." In fairness to Sukarno it may be observed that the problems of government in Washington's day were simple, while today they are complicated and difficult.

14. Clifford Geertz in *Ideology and Discontent*, David E. Apter, ed., (Glencoe: 1964), p. 707.

15. Jeanne S. Mintz, *Mohammed, Marx and Marhaen: The Roots of Indonesian Socialism* (New York: 1965), p. 225.

16. Donald E. Weatherbee, *Ideology in Indonesia: Sukarno's Indonesian Revolution* (New Haven, 1966). He holds that Sukarno's thoughts represent a "reasonably coherent body of related ideas," contain an "analysis of the ills of society, an extensive criticism of antecedent political order, an outline of a better future society, and an action-oriented program showing how to move to that better society," pretend to universality and present a "whole way of life." *Ibid.*, pp. 86-87.

17. In his compulsion for system-making Sukarno may have been influenced by the Dutch, who are strongly inclined to think in terms of complete life and world views.

18. *Op. cit.*, (*Colonial Policy and Practices: A Comparative Study of Burma and Netherlands India*), pp. 272-73.

19. Tarzie Vittachi, *The Fall of Sukarno* (New York: 1967), p. 39.

20. John Hughes, *Indonesian Upheaval* (New York, 1967), p. 89.

21. Ben Anderson, *op. cit.*

22. Leslie H. Palmier, *Indonesia and the Dutch* (London and New York: 1962), pp. 179ff.

CHAPTR V (*Power*)

1. Asian Relations Organization, *Asian Relations: Report of the Proceedings and Documentation of the First Asian Relations Conference* (New Delhi: 1948), pp. 242-245.
2. Jawaharlal Nehru, *Toward Freedom* (New York: 1942), p. 273.
3. Jawaharlal Nehru, "Inter-Asian Relations," *India Quarterly*, 2 (October-December 1946), pp. 323-327.
4. Jawaharlal Nehru, *Russia and India* (Bombay, 1929), pp. 126-132. "Russia—How to Check Her Advance Towards India," is a chapter subtitle in Sir William P. Andrew, *India and Her Neighbors* (London: 1878).
5. *Documents on International Affairs: 1951* (London: 1954), pp. 606-608.
6. Paul F. Power, "India and Vietnam," *Asian Survey*, 7 (October, 1967), pp. 740-751.

CHAPTER VI (*Salem*)

1. Dwight David Eisenhower, *Waging Peace, 1956-1961* (Garden City, New York: 1965), p. 28.

CHAPTER VII (*Winkler*)

1. This paper in slightly different form, was delivered on April 19 and 20, 1967, at the University of Cincinnati as the Taft Lectures in History. Harold Vinacke honored me by being present at both lectures, and it seemed appropriate therefore to offer this essay as my thanks for all that I learned from him about being a scholar—and much more.
2. Philip Poirier, *The Advent of the Labour Party* (London: 1958); Henry Pelling, *The Origins of the Labour Party, 1880-1900* (London: 1954); Frank Bealey and Henry Pelling, *Labour and Politics, 1900-1906. A History of the Labour Representation Committee* (London: 1958).
3. "The British Labour Party: The Conflict between Socialist Ideals and Practical Politics before 1918," American Historical Association Annual Meeting, December 28, 1963.
4. "The British Labour Party: The Conflict between Socialist Ideals and Practical Politics between the Wars," *Journal of British Studies*, V (November 1965), pp. 140-152.
5. London: 1949.
6. Perry Anderson and Robin Blackburn, eds., *Towards Socialism* (London: 1965).
7. Michael Foot, *Aneurin Bevan. A Biography. Volume One: 1897-1945* (London: 1963).
8. Ralph Miliband, *Parliamentary Socialism: A Study in the Politics of Labour* (London: 1961).
9. *Ibid.*, p. 230.
10. London: 1954.
11. London: 1965.
12. *Modern British Politics*, p. 179.
13. "Goals of Today's Welfare State," in *Towards Socialism*, pp. 355-356.
14. *Ibid.*, p. 357.
15. London: 1956.

16. Beer, p. 227.
17. *A Short History of the Labour Party* (2nd. ed., London: 1965), pp. 129-133.
18. Carl F. Brand, *The British Labour Party. A Short History* (Stanford, California: 1964), p. 59.
19. Henry R. Winkler, *The League of Nations Movement in Great Britain, 1914-1919* (New Brunswick, New Jersey: 1952); Arno J. Mayer, *Political Origins of the New Diplomacy, 1917-1918* (New Haven, Connecticut: 1959).
20. "The Emergence of a Labor Foreign Policy in Great Britain, 1918-1929," *Journal of Modern History*, XXVIII (September, 1956), pp. 247-258; "Arthur Henderson," in *The Diplomats, 1919-1939*, ed. by Gordon A. Craig and Felix Gilbert (Princeton, New Jersey: 1953), pp. 311-343.
21. *The Diplomats*, p. 343.
22. W. N. Medlicott, *British Foreign Policy since Versailles* (London: 1940), p. 249; F. S. Northedge, *The Troubled Giant: Britain Among the Great Powers, 1916-1939* (New York: 1966).
23. *Nineteen Thirty-One: Political Crisis* (London: 1958).
24. Winston S. Churchill, *The Gathering Storm* (London: 1948), p. 117.
25. Parliamentary Debates, House of Commons, 413 (August 20, 1945), col. 312.
26. M. A. Fitzsimons, *The Foreign Policy of the British Labour Government, 1945-1951* (Notre Dame, Indiana: 1953), pp. 25, 29.
27. David Leitch, "Explosion at the King David Hotel," in *Age of Austerity, 1945-51*, ed. by Michael Sissons and Philip French (Penquin Books ed., Harmondsworth, England: 1964), pp. 80-81.
28. *Ibid.*, p. 84.
29. For example, Leon D. Epstein, *British Politics in the Suez Crisis* (Urbana, Illinois: 1964), who makes clear, however, that the view that Labour's rank-and-file, unlike its leaders, would have supported military action is not born out by the evidence.
30. The Rt. Hon. Harold Wilson, "Britain's Policy of Labour Wins," *Atlantic*, CCXII (October 1963), pp. 61-65.

CHAPTER VIII (*Dux*)

1. Hessen 7.9% November, 1966; Bayern 7.4% November, 1966; Rheinland-Pfalz 6.9% April, 1967; Schleswig-Holstein 5.8% April, 1967; Neidersachsen 7.0% June, 1967; Bremen 8.8% November, 1967; Baden-Wuerttemberg 9.8% April, 1968.
2. "News From The German Embassy," Washington, D.C., Vol. XI, No. 10, November, 1967.
3. "Neo-Nazism and the Federal Republic of Germany," German Information Center (New York, New York: February, 1968).
4. *New York Times* (New York: January 29, 1967).
5. "The Bulletin," Issued by the Press and Information Office of the German Federal Government, January 9, 1968.
6. *New York Times* (New York: February 25, 1968).
7. "The Bulletin," *op. cit.*, March 19, 1968; *Ibid.* April 23, 1968.
8. "Erfahrungen aus der Beobachtung und Abwehr rechtsradikaler und antisemitischer Tendenzen," Annual Report of the Ministry of Interior (Bonn, 1966).
9. Entscheidungen Des Bundesverfassungsgerichts, vol. 2, 1953, pp. 1-79.
10. Among many primary sources, most important are: "Wahlaufruf 1965";

"Deutsche Nachrichten," Sonderdruck VI/1965; "Das Program der NPD," adopted at the 3rd National Convention, Nov., 1967; "Satzung der NPD," adopted November 10, 1967; speeches by Professor Anrich "Mensch-Volk-Staat-Demokratie" (1966) and V. Thadden; "Ueberwindung des nationalen Notstandes" (1967).

11. Hans Maier, *NPD, Struktur und Ideologie einer nationalen Rechtspartei* (1967), p. 38.

12. "Das Program der NPD," *op. cit.*, pp. 3-4.

13. *Ibid.*, p. 2.

14. Fred H. Richards, *Die NPD, Alternative oder Wiederkehr?*, (1967), p. 51.

15. "Satzung der NPD," *op. cit.*

16. "Rechtsradikalismus in der Bundesrepublik im Jahre 1967," Bundeszentrale fur politisch Bildung, (Bonn, 1968), p. 3; cf. also the decision of the 8. Zivilkammer des Landgerichts Bremen, 8-0 Nr. 247/67.

17. "Rechtsradikalismus in der Bundesrepublik im Jahre 1967," *op. cit.*, p. 12. This report indicates that 22 out of 30 members of the Executive Committee belonged to the NSDAP, SRP, or other radical rightist organizations.

18. *Ibid.*, p. 12.

19. Three-fourths of the managing group of the D.N. Verlag, the publicity and propaganda agency of the NDP, were formerly members of the NSDAP. Similarly six out of the eleven official speakers of the party have a Nazi past.

20. H. Maier, *op. cit.*, p. 13.

21. Cf. the decision of the Supreme Constitutional Tribunal cited in n. 9.

22. *Ibid.*, pp. 9ff.

23. Minister for All-German Affairs Wehner speaking at a Convention of the Friedrich Ebert Foundation in Bergneustadt on May 22, 1967 said: "As for legalistic objections to intra-German contacts and some still do exist, up to the level of the highest judicial decisions, they must be done away with." Foreign Minister Brandt told a press conference in Bonn on November 10, 1967 that he personally favored relicensing of a German Communist Party "if it pledged loyalty to the Basic Law."

24. "The Bulletin," *op. cit.*, December 20, 1966, Supplement p. 1.

25. "News from the German Embassy," *op. cit.*, p. 5.

26. "News from the German Embassy," Vol. xii, No. 3, March 1968, pp. 9-10.

27. "The Bulletin," *op. cit.*, April 2, 1968, p. 82.

28. *Ibid.*

29. H. Jaeckel and H. H. Raas; "Die Mehrheitswahl-und was dann?" *Der Monat*, September, 1965, p. 25.

30. "Neo-Nazism and the Federal Republic of Germany," issued November 1968 by the German Information Center, (New York, New York) p. 5. In the 1969 election, the NPD failed by 0.7 percent to obtain the 5 percent of the votes necessary for inclusion in the Bundestag.

31. W. Brandt, "German Policy Toward the East," *Foreign Affairs*, (April, 1968), pp. 483-485.

CHAPTER IX (Heinlein)

1. Statement by British Prime Minister Harold Macmillan quoted by Henry Fairlie, "Johnson and the Intellectuals," *Commentary*, October, 1965, pp. 52-53.

2. President Johnson recounted an event of that afternoon: "As we talked with Ambassador Bennett, he said to apparently one of the girls who had brought him a cable, 'Please get away from the window, that glass is going to cut your head,' because the glass was being shattered. And he said, 'Do you hear the bullets coming through the office?'—where he was sitting while talking to us." Remarks to Committee Members of Congress, May 4, 1965, *Public Papers of the Presidents of the United States, Lyndon B. Johnson* (Washington: Government Printing Office, 1966), Vol. 1965, p. 490.

3. Charles Mohr, *New York Times*, January 16, 1965, p. 10. Mr. Johnson wanted his cabinet members to be as enthused as Franklin Roosevelt's Secretary of the Interior had been.

4. Alan L. Otten, "Lyndon's Cabinet," *Wall Street Journal*, March 16, 1965, p. 1. Substance was lacking in large part because "the President has already obtained the views of people who matter."

5. James Reston, "Washington: A Vague Rustle of Doubt," *New York Times*, May 20, 1966, p. 30.

6. The committee, composed of Charles E. Merriam, Luther Gulick and Louis Brownlow, chairman, viewed their task as investigation of the organization and functioning of the President as administrative manager of the executive branch.

7. There are twelve divisions in the Office today: The White House Office; Office of Management and Budget; Council of Economic Advisers; National Security Council, National Aeronautics and Space Council; Office of Economic Opportunity; Office of Emergency Planning; Office of Science and Technology; Office of the Special Representative for Trade Negotiations; National Council on Marine Resources and Engineering Development; Council for Urban Affairs; and Office of Intergovernmental Relations.

8. At inception the Council consisted of the President, Secretary of State, Secretary of Defense, Secretary of the Army, Secretary of the Navy, Secretary of the Air Force, Chairman of the National Security Resources Board, and such Secretaries of the executive departments and chairmen of the Munitions Board and Research and Development Board as the President might designate.

9. During Eisenhower's first year the Council is supposed to have won presidential approval of 305 "major" policy decisions. Bernard K. Gordon, "The Top of Policy Hill," *Bulletin of the Atomic Scientists*, XVI (September, 1960), pp. 289-91.

10. Woodrow Wilson, *Constitutional Government in the United States* (New York: Columbia University Press, 1921), p. 73.

11. Peter R. Levin, *Seven by Chance* (New York: Farrar, 1948).

12. John Tyler, the first of the eight, required less than a day to convince himself that he had succeeded to the office, not merely the powers and duties thereof, on the death of William Henry Harrison. His misreading of the Constitution complicated the problem of presidential inability and succession for over a century.

13. Philip Geyelin, *Lyndon B. Johnson and the World* (New York: Frederick A. Praeger, Inc., 1966), p. 123.

14. Rowland Evans and Robert Novak, *Lyndon B. Johnson: The Exercise of Power* (New York: The New American Library, Inc., 1966), p. 21.

15. The story of the attempt to make Johnson, as Vice-President, chairman of the Senate Democratic caucus is told by Evans and Novak, *Ibid.*, pp. 305-308.

16. See speech before National Press Club, *New York Times*, January 15, 1960, p. 14.

17. The statement which appeared in the Winter, 1958 edition of the *Texas Quarterly* is reproduced in William S. White, *The Professional: Lyndon B. Johnson* (Boston: Houghton Mifflin Company, 1964), pp. 122-128.

18. *Public Papers of the Presidents of the United States, Lyndon B. Johnson, op. cit.*, p. 286.

19. *The Economist*, March 13, 1965, p. 1134.

20. See letter to Henry M. Jackson from McGeorge Bundy, January 28, 1965. U.S. Congress, Senate, Subcommittee on National Security and International Operations, *Conduct of National Security Policy*, Hearings, I (Washington: Government Printing Office, 1965), p. 43.

21. *Ibid.*

22. Members of the subcommittee were: Secretary of State Rusk, chairman; Secretary of Treasury Fowler; Chairman, Joint Chiefs of Staff Wheeler; Director, Central Intelligence Agency Helms; Clark Clifford; Walt W. Rostow. *New York Times*, June 8, 1967, p. 1.

23. Stewart Alsop, "Johnsonization of Washington," *Saturday Evening Post*, February 26, 1966, p. 20.

24. Alan L. Otten, "L.B.J.'s Inner Circle," *Wall Street Journal*, June 16, 1966, p. 1.

25. *The Economist*, March 12, 1966, p. 999.

26. *New York Times*, December 16, 1966, p. 46.

27. Tom Wicker, "Johnson's Men," *New York Times*, May 3, 1964, Sec. 6., p. 11.

28. *Ibid.*, January 17, 1965, p. 38.

29. Geyelin, *op. cit.*, pp. 123-124.

30. Evans and Novak, "Washington Report," *The Atlantic Monthly*, October, 1967, p. 13.

31. "Report on Washington," *Ibid.*, July, 1966, p. 12.

32. Statement by Bill D. Moyers quoted in Otten, "L.B.J.'s Inner Circle," *op. cit.*, p. 18.

33. Roy Reed, "Johnson's Traffic Cop: One of the Most Important Men in the Capitol," *New York Times*, September 17, 1967, p. 70.

34. An episode that tells something of Moyers' place in the hierarchy developed in January, 1966. It was learned that a few weeks earlier White House switchboard operators had been instructed to record the names of callers and that drivers were told to keep a log of whom they transported where. When questioned, Moyers explained: "I do like to know, and have asked the special assistants to let me know at the end of the day, to whom they have talked." John D. Pomfret, *Ibid.*, January 19, 1966, p. 20.

35. Harry S. Truman, *Mr. Citizen* (New York: Bernard Geis Associates, 1960), p. 264.

36. *New York Times*, June 13, 1965, p. 73.

37. Otten, "L.B.J.'s Inner Circle," *op. cit.*, p. 18.

38. S. R. Davis, *Christian Science Monitor*, December 15, 1966, p. 1.

39. *Christian Science Monitor*, December 3, 1966, p. 13.

40. *Ibid.*, December 15, 1966, p. 15.

41. *New York Times*, April 1, 1966, p. 19.

42. Lyndon B. Johnson, Radio and Television Report to the American People, *Public Papers of the Presidents, op. cit.*, p. 470.

43. The most complete and reliable account of the Dominican episode is found

in John Bartlow Martin, *Overtaken by Events* (Garden City: Doubleday and Company, Inc., 1966). Martin, who was Ambassador to the Dominican Republic, tells the story of the recognition: "About 11 A.M. a rumor of counter-*coup* against the regime had come up from San Juan, Puerto Rico, through a U.S. military channel, had swept through the U.S. government, had reached President Johnson, and at twelve-fifteen the President had called in five Senators, George Ball, and Ed Martin and said we would recognize. By this time Sowash had telephoned King and learned that the rumor was false." *Ibid.*, p. 631.

44. *New York Times*, April 28, 1965, p. 1.

45. Martin, *op. cit.*, p. 657. The interesting point is not that American lives were not in danger but that a formal request for military intervention on that ground was not received in Washington until early Thursday, April 29, 1965.

46. *Public Papers of the Presidents, op. cit.*, pp. 461, 465, 466, 469.

47. On the single question of right of self defense, Charles G. Fenwick was convinced that "the old law of self defense that is still law" fully justified the landings, *American Journal of International Law*, LX (January, 1966), 64; while R. T. Bohan believed there was no real threat to the United States and that it was "rather, a matter of the protection of nationals," *Ibid.*, LX (October, 1966), p. 809.

48. A strong critic of Administration action was Senator J. W. Fulbright who deplored "inadequate and inaccurate intelligence from the men in the field." See his speech in the Senate on September 15, 1965. *Congressional Record*, Vol. III, pp. 22998-23008.

49. Johnson, Radio and Television Report to the American People, *Public Papers of the Presidents, op. cit.*, p. 221.

50. Clinton Rossiter, "The Constitutional Significance of the Executive Office of the President," *American Political Science Review*, XLIII (December, 1949), pp. 1214-15.

51. Edward H. Hobbs, "The President and Administration—Eisenhower," *Public Administration Review*, XVIII (Fall, 1958), p. 309.

52. President Kennedy was interviewed December 16, 1962, by three network correspondents and a portion of the interview was broadcast on radio and television the following day.

53. Erwin D. Canham, "The White House Men," *Christian Science Monitor*, April 5, 1966, p. E-3.

CHAPTER X (*Padgett*)

1. Roger Hilsman, *To Move A Nation* (New York: Doubleday & Company, Inc., 1967).

2. E. R. Padgett, "A Nation Looks At Its Policy Machinery," *International Review of Administrative Sciences*, Vol. XXXI (1965), No. 3, pp. 233-238.

3. James A. Robinson, "The Social Scientist and Congress," in *International Conflict and Behavioral Science, The Craigville Papers*, ed. Roger Fisher (New York: Basic Books, Inc., 1964), p. 269.

4. Charles E. Lindblom, "The Science of 'Muddling Through'," *Public Administration Review* (Spring, 1959), p. 79-88.

5. Burton M. Sapin, *The Making of United States Foreign Policy* (New York: Frederick A. Praeger, 1966), Ch. 11.

6. James L. McCamy, *Conduct of The New Diplomacy* (New York: Harper & Row, 1964), pp. 77-79.

7. U.S. Senate, Committee on Foreign Relations, *Psychological Aspects of International Relations*, 89th Cong., 2nd sess. (Washington: Government Printing Office, 1966), pp. 9-16. Testimony of Dr. Jerome D. Frank, Professor of Psychiatry, Johns Hopkins University School of Medicine.

8. Chris Argyris, "Some Causes of Organizational Ineffectiveness Within The Department of State," U.S. Department of State, *Center For International Systems Research*, Occasional Papers, No. 2 (Washington: Government Printing Office, 1967), Department of State Publication 8180.

9. U.S. Senate, Committee on Government Operations, Subcommittee on National Security and International Operations, *Planning-Programming-Budgeting: Official Documents* (Washington: Government Printing Office, 1967), 90th Cong., 1st sess. The full text of Bulletin 68-2 is found here. Bulletin 68-9 was issued on April 12, 1968. See also Subcommittee on National Security and International Operations, *Planning-Programming-Budgeting Budget Bureau Guidelines of 1968* (Washington: Government Printing Office, 1968) 90th Cong. 2d Sess.

10. V. O. Key, "The Lack of A Budgetary Theory," *American Political Science Review* (December, 1940), pp. 1137-1144.
    Aaron Wildavsky, *The Politics of the Budgetary Process* (Boston: Little, Brown and Company, 1964).

11. "Planning-Programming-Budgeting System: A Symposium," *Public Adminstration Review* (December, 1966); "Symposium on PPBS Reexamined," *ibid.* (March-April, 1969).

12. Hilsman, *op. cit.*, pp. 541-543.

13. *Ibid.*, pp. 564-568.

14. Department of State, The Office of The Deputy Under Secretary for Administration, *A Management Program For The Department of State* (Washington: September, 1966). See also, John R. Probert, "Streamlining The Foreign Policy Machine," *Public Administration Review* (September, 1967), pp. 229-236.

15. *The New York Times*, November 12, 1967, p. 78. February 5 and 7, 1969, April 13 and May 7, 1969; *The Washington Post*, January 1 and May 15, 1969. Professors Schelling and F. Mosher have expressed some reservations as to the relationships of PPBS and Foreign Affairs, see Subcommittee on National Security and International Operations, *PPBS and Foreign Affairs* and *Program Budgeting in Foreign Affairs: Some Reflections*, Committee Prints 90th Cong., 1st and 2d sess.

16. Herbert Simon, *Administrative Behavior* (2d ed., New York: The MacMillan Co., 1957).

17. Robinson, *op. cit.*, p. 269.

18. Joseph W. Barr, *The Challenge of Macro-Leadership* (Greencastle, Indiana: 1966).